The World of Juliette Kinzie

 HISTORICAL STUDIES OF URBAN AMERICA

Edited by Lilia Fernández, Timothy J. Gilfoyle, Becky M. Nicolaides, and Amanda I. Seligman

James R. Grossman, Editor Emeritus

Recent titles in the series

Jeffrey S. Adler, *Murder in New Orleans: The Creation of Jim Crow Policing*

David A. Gamson, *The Importance of Being Urban: Designing the Progressive School District, 1890–1940*

Kara Schlichting, *New York Recentered: Building the Metropolis from the Shore*

Mark Wild, *Renewal: Liberal Protestants and the American City after World War II*

Meredith Oda, *The Gateway to the Pacific: Japanese Americans and the Remaking of San Francisco*

Sean Dinces, *Bulls Markets: Chicago's Basketball Business and the New Inequality*

Julia Guarneri, *Newsprint Metropolis: City Papers and the Making of Modern Americans*

Kyle B. Roberts, *Evangelical Gotham: Religion and the Making of New York City, 1783–1860*

Timothy B. Neary, *Crossing Parish Boundaries: Race, Sports, and Catholic Youth in Chicago, 1914–1954*

Julia Rabig, *The Fixers: Devolution, Development, and Civil Society in Newark, 1960–1990*

A complete list of series titles is available on the University of Chicago Press website.

The World of
Juliette Kinzie

Chicago before the Fire

Ann Durkin Keating

The University of Chicago Press

Chicago and London

The University of Chicago Press, Chicago 60637
The University of Chicago Press, Ltd., London
© 2019 by The University of Chicago
Published 2019
Printed in the United States of America

28 27 26 25 24 23 22 21 20 19   1 2 3 4 5

ISBN-13: 978-0-226-66452-1 (cloth)
ISBN-13: 978-0-226-66466-8 (e-book)
DOI: https://doi.org/10.7208/chicago/9780226664668.001.0001

Library of Congress Cataloging-in-Publication Data

Names: Keating, Ann Durkin, author.
Title: The world of Juliette Kinzie : Chicago before the fire/ Ann Durkin Keating.
Other titles: Historical studies of urban America.
Description: Chicago : The University of Chicago Press, 2019. | Series: Historical studies of urban America | Includes bibliographical references and index.
Identifiers: LCCN 2019009720 | ISBN 9780226664521 (cloth) | ISBN 9780226664668 (e-book)
Subjects: LCSH: Kinzie, John H., Mrs., 1806–1870. | Women pioneers—Illinois—Chicago—Biography. | Chicago (Ill.)—History—19th century.
Classification: LCC F548.4 .K43 2019 | DDC 977.5/03092 [B]—dc23
LC record available at https://lccn.loc.gov/2019009720

♾ This paper meets the requirements of ANSI/NISO Z39.48-1992 (Permanence of Paper).

Contents

Preface

Tracing Juliette

Wau-Bun: The "Early Day" in the North-West has been in print since 1856, far longer than any other book on Chicago history. Author Juliette Augusta Magill Kinzie related her own experiences and those of her extended family when the Chicago region was still part of Indian country; indeed, *wau-bun* is a Ho-Chunk word for dawn or early day.[1] In my previous project on Chicago's early history, I worked closely with *Wau-Bun*. While some historians have dismissed the work as romantic fiction, my research showed that much of it could be confirmed in historical records: Juliette was a credible source. After finishing my *Rising Up from Indian Country: The Battle of Fort Dearborn and the Birth of Chicago*, I decided to learn more about this Chicago historian.

I found that Juliette Kinzie led an interesting life going far beyond what she shared in *Wau-Bun*. Born in 1806 in Middletown, Connecticut, Juliette received an unusually strong education. In 1840 she married John H. Kinzie, a US Indian agent in Wisconsin; Juliette was part of a small but critical cohort of Yankees who migrated into the former Northwest Territory. Settling at Chicago in

1834, the couple raised a family as the city grew from a few hundred residents to over half a million. In the last decade of their lives, they endured the Civil War that split their family between North and South. I was intrigued by the idea of looking at early Chicago through the eyes of someone who witnessed Chicago's spectacular rise.[2]

I looked for more on Juliette and found a trove of correspondence, mostly between Juliette and her daughter Eleanor (Nellie) Kinzie Gordon, who lived in Savannah, Georgia, after her 1857 marriage. We have the letters because her daughter saved them, and also because her granddaughter, Juliette Gordon Low, founded the Girl Scouts of America. This serendipity meant that hundreds of these letters landed in archives rather than being destroyed or lost to mold in a musty basement or attic. So large a cache of nineteenth-century correspondence is rare. Few people had the interest and skill to craft such letters, and even then it is extraordinary that they have been saved.

It is particularly important that collections of letters by women survive, since their lives in nineteenth-century America remain largely undocumented. Kinzie's letters could provide insight into life in Chicago before the Great Chicago Fire of 1871 and perhaps serve as a western complement to the diaries of Juliette's contemporary, Southerner Mary Boykin Chesnut. Through Chesnut, we see Southern society during the Civil War as she offers striking personal reflections on the major political, social, and economic events of the day. Could Juliette Kinzie offer a counterpoint to Chesnut's world, exploring the experience of a Yankee migrant to the Old Northwest during this same period? Would she express herself differently in private letters than she did in *Wau-Bun* and other published writings?[3]

The first collection of correspondence I read was at the Chicago History Museum. The archive there holds microfilm copies of nearly five hundred letters written by Juliette Kinzie, most to her daughter Nellie. Beginning in spring 2013, I read the letters on two large reels of microfilm. The missives range from four to sixteen pages. Kinzie wrote with a strong and clear hand, filling the pages with humorous anecdotes about family members, servants, pets, and friends. Although she was loyal to those she cared about, Kinzie held strong opinions on current events and issues, and she was often sharply critical of leading figures of the day.

To me, Juliette Kinzie soon became just Juliette, someone with whom I was spending time snatched from work and family responsibilities. I was quickly drawn into her world and found myself retelling Juliette stories to my (usually) forgiving family, friends, colleagues, and students. I shared the way Juliette disparaged the handiwork of future Confederate president Jefferson Davis, who as a junior army officer had built the furniture she used as a young bride in Wisconsin. I related that she was not greatly impressed with a young prince of Wales when he visited Chicago, though she did find admirers of *Wau-Bun* among his entourage. Talking with Abraham Lincoln shortly after he was elected president, Juliette teasingly referred to him as the "father of the country," showing her ease in his company.

I began to look for more archival material on Juliette. In February 2015 I found another collection of her letters at the Georgia Historical Society in Savannah, as well as writings by Nellie. In the University of North Carolina archives, I viewed the originals of the microfilm letters along with more from Juliette and other family members that rounded out several story lines. Additional materials at the Middlesex Historical Society in Middletown, Connecticut, augmented letters in the Wolcott and Kinzie Collections at the Chicago History Museum. I also visited places associated with Juliette, including the Magill family's brick mansion in Middletown, Connecticut; the Indian Agency House in Portage, Wisconsin, built by Juliette and her husband early in their marriage; her daughter's house in Savannah, now maintained by the Girl Scouts; and her grave at Graceland Cemetery in Chicago.

As I read these additional letters and visited these sites, I began to reconstruct Juliette's life and world. She drew me into her family, household, and community. Though she was born 150 years before me, I saw that we shared experiences and qualities. We were both historians of Chicago and were fiercely chauvinistic about the city and its North Side. We both struggled to find time to write amid the demands of everyday life. I shared her strong sense of the "family claim" that kept her focus within her household. As I watched Juliette age past what she called the "meridian of life," I saw her thoughts and sentiments mirror my own.[4]

Perhaps because of these parallels, I was lulled into thinking her world was much like my own. But it was very different; she did not live in a modern world. During most of Juliette's lifetime, most Americans were not afforded unfettered freedom or equal rights. Only white men had full political rights and could control their own property and labor. In households across the country, those men also claimed the labor and property of their dependents, who included most women and more than four million enslaved people. Women, married and single, could not vote or hold office. Married women could not buy or sell property, and their husbands controlled any wealth they had.

Juliette lived on the cusp of modernity in a traditional world where inequality was the rule and households were the central unit of social, political, and economic organization. Every person in a household had a prescribed role determined by gender, race, and class. Juliette was not concerned much with individual rights; she focused on the responsibilities each person carried.[5] She did not rail against inequalities and restrictions but accepted them, as did her teacher, Emma Willard, who opined that "submission and obedience belong to every being in the universe."[6]

When her newlywed daughter complained, Juliette wrote forcefully that wives belonged to their husbands. She bluntly told her daughter that "as an individual you have ceased to exist."[7] But Juliette did not believe her daughter's spouse could act with impunity; he had to consider the needs of all those in his household. Indeed, Juliette believed that husbands should make decisions not as individuals but as heads of households. In her eyes, husbands did not have individual rights; they served as representatives of their households in the broader body politic. In the end, individual rights were not as critical as were family, religious, and civic obligations—the family claim.[8]

Today Juliette's perspectives appear misogynist as well as racist; in many ways they were and are. But it is unwise to dismiss her simply by the standards of our time. Before the Civil War, there was an emerging sense that individual rights extended beyond the propertied white men that Thomas Jefferson and the signers of the Declaration of Independence had in mind; but women and nonwhite men were still outside this expansion. Juliette accepted a subordinate (but privileged) role in American society, as she did for her daughter and most others around her.

This book is my quest to understand Juliette in her own time and place. She provides an opportunity to examine early Chicago through the life of one woman and her household, offering a counterpoint to the prevailing male perspective on these years. Juliette helped to create Chicago's earliest civic culture by following rules and conventions she had imbibed during a New England childhood. She did not lightly infringe societal norms. Despite what twenty-first-century readers might wish of a sympathetic and articulate woman of the nineteenth century, Juliette was not an advocate of women's rights; she was neither a vocal proponent of slavery nor an abolitionist. That she hewed to traditional notions and accepted the claim of family did not diminish her, nor does it negate the need to recognize and acknowledge her experiences. This book is an effort to understand the structural constraints she faced and to recognize how these factors determined her ability to feel, to act, and to imagine in a world so very unlike our own.

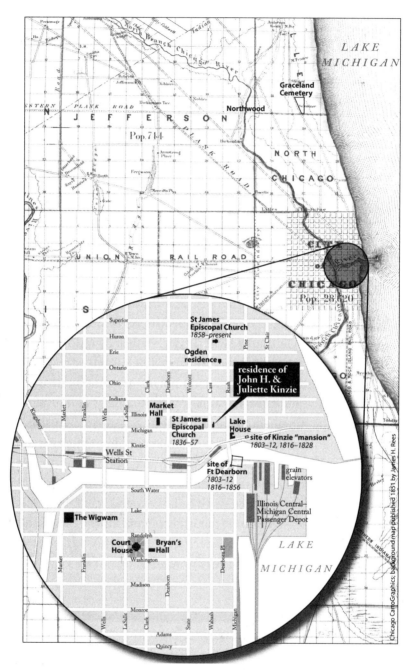

Fig. 1 Juliette Kinzie's Chicago, 1803–70. Dennis McClendon, Chicago Cartographics.

Introduction

The Michigan Street House

The northeast corner of Cass and Michigan Streets, just north of the Chicago River, was the center of Juliette Kinzie's life in Chicago. In 1835, just a little more than a year before Chicago became a city, she and her husband, John H. Kinzie, built a three-story brick house there on a half block of gardens and orchards. Initially among the wealthiest residents, they lived in the house for three decades and raised a family. Early neighbors built their own substantial houses on large lots, but over time railroads, factories, grain elevators, and docks came to dominate the area. Like many urban residents before and since, Juliette found there was no way to halt the inexorable change that is any city's lifeblood.

This house was the center of Juliette's life and of our story. I tell the story in three parts: how she came west from New England to build the Michigan Street house; the first twenty years in her house as she raised a family and shaped early civic culture; and the decade or so before her death in 1870 when her influence waned and she was forced to abandon her house and her city. Through Juliette's eyes, our understanding of early Chicago expands from boosters

Fig. 2 The Kinzie residence at 245 Michigan Street, the northeast corner of Cass and Michigan (now Wabash and Hubbard). Taken in the 1860s, it shows the mature trees and shrubbery in the gardens to the east and the tower of the original St. James Episcopal Church behind the house to the northwest. The buildings burned in October 1871 during the Great Chicago Fire. Chicago History Museum, ICHi-068395.

and speculators to include the world women created within and between households.

Focusing on households shifts the setting for early Chicago history away from rollicking local taverns and open-air real estate. The house itself embodies the tension between individual entrepreneurship and the creation of community in Chicago's early decades as an urban place. Juliette understood this tension. She supported her husband's speculation in Chicago real estate, even as she raised a family and helped build a community. The Michigan Street residence was at once her "beloved house" and also a valuable "business property."[1]

Before 1836 virtually no housing stock existed in Chicago. Needing roofs over their heads, squatters built shanties on land that did not belong to them. The more permanent structures were built of wood with balloon-frame construction. In contrast, the Kinzies' Michigan Street house was built on land they owned, with brick purchased for the project, and constructed by skilled labor with many architectural flourishes and amenities. The family paid for it with money gained from speculating in real estate.

The corner where the house sat was also new, a product of the grid recently imposed on Chicago land. The grid produced property owners and established a rigid order for the city's development, determining the dimensions of lots along streets laid out in the cardinal directions. The lots the grid created fueled speculation that made some people wildly wealthy while others were left behind. By building on a corner, Juliette and John were recognizing the power of the grid and endorsing the formal market economy.

Yet behind their front door and within the fence surrounding the property to the east and north, the couple produced much of what they ate, wore, and used as part of an informal economy. They raised a family there, welcomed friends and relatives, and worked to create a community filled with institutions, societies, and opportunities that reflected their vision of Chicago.

A visitor to Chicago today will find neither Cass Street nor Michigan Street, though the corner still exists. In the early twentieth century the street names were changed to Wabash Avenue and Hubbard Street. Since then the intersection has been elevated to accommodate a second level of traffic. The spot where Juliette's house once stood is now a ground-level parking lot dwarfed by office and residential towers. Still, this is the base of our story. We cannot stand in the same time and place as Juliette, but we can be in the same place at a different time. We can glimpse moments of the past at this one place, expanding our understanding of what has vanished from the landscape.

Getting to Chicago

It took the newlywed Juliette several weeks in 1830 to travel west from New York City through the Erie Canal and cross the Great

Lakes by steamer. She brought precious possessions that would eventually fill the Michigan Street house, as well as a vision of what American society should look like in the West. From an early age in Middletown, Connecticut, Juliette was imbued with a traditional notion of community responsibility. New England women were engaged not only within their houses but also in their communities. This view was reinforced by an Episcopalian upbringing that embraced a vision of a hierarchical society: everything—and everyone—had its place.

Juliette's Connecticut family also looked west to Chicago for business opportunities as the federal government expropriated Indian lands and sold them to settlers. Her uncle Dr. Alexander Wolcott had served as the US Indian agent at Chicago during the 1820s. He carefully gauged the best moment for family members to invest and move west. Juliette's traditional upbringing fused a New England communitarianism with Yankee business savvy.

When Juliette first visited Chicago in 1831, it had none of the trappings of an urban place. Aside from Fort Dearborn itself, there was little to distinguish the settlement except the Sauganash Hotel, which Juliette described as "a pretentious white two-story building, with bright blue shutters."[2] She saw no streets, no sidewalks, no bridges, no churches, no schools. The two hundred or so people— more than half of them soldiers and officers—lived at an isolated outpost of the US government in Indian country. The American, French, and métis residents were for the most part engaged in the fur trade or employed by the federal government. Around Chicago, the Potawatomi lived in villages and farmed their fields.

Chicago was part of Indian country; the Potawatomi and their allies controlled all but a narrow corridor of land in the region. The early years of Juliette's tenure in the West were punctuated by war against those Indians and expropriation of their lands. Juliette's uncle, her husband, and her father-in-law were all directly involved. As part of the 1833 Treaty of Chicago, Juliette's family was among the non-Indian claimants who received substantial payouts from the federal government as the Potawatomi were forced to cede their lands. Indeed, the Michigan Street house stood on former Potawatomi land that had been surveyed by the government, then claimed by her family.[3]

Juliette was well aware of the magnitude of the transformation precipitated by the forced relocation of Potawatomi from around Chicago and many Ho-Chunk (Winnebago) and Sauk (Sac) from Wisconsin. While she decried the expropriation of Indian lands and the tribes' forced removal, her family enriched itself on this dramatic transfer of valuable resources. Juliette knew that westward expansion entailed a conquest of people and land executed by the very visible hand of the federal government that benefited white American settlers to the detriment of Indians. But unlike many of her contemporaries who saw this expansion as an unadulterated good, she wrote sympathetically about the Ho-Chunk and Potawatomi families she got to know during her time in Indian country.[4]

Juliette's Chicago

When Juliette settled permanently in Chicago in 1834, she regarded the town as an extension of her own household, responsible for promoting a common good largely through private efforts. So it is not surprising that she was a community builder, supporting churches, schools, hospitals, musical groups, and a range of societies. Much of this supportive work took place in her parlor. Juliette was intent on establishing a Yankee culture in the West and building a foundation for a future Chicago. The large role of private spaces and organizations was particularly evident in new western cities like Chicago where there was no existing social infrastructure to rely on.[5]

Juliette's letters and writings point to the broad participation of women in this informal public sphere. It was not possible to sharply segregate work from home in early Chicago because there often were no distinct physical boundaries between public and private spaces.[6] Business and institutional meetings were held in homes, so women like Juliette were integrally involved in public activities not as "an alternative to domesticity," but as part of a household world.[7]

Juliette's role in early civic culture rested largely on networks of kin and friends that are difficult to document. Her letters and novels, however, take us inside the private world of her household, offering rare insight into the gatherings for conversation, reading, storytelling, painting, drawing, and other pursuits that formed the basis for Chicago's early public sphere. Ironically, while chroniclers and historians created narratives based on Juliette's history *Wau-Bun* and her other writings, they disregarded her seminal role in early Chicago. Only rarely were the networks she described captured in institutional histories or newspaper accounts, which focused on the work of men in businesses, government, and formal institutions.

Juliette was part of a group of families that made Chicago not just a place where money was gained (and lost) but also a setting where urban life could flourish. Her life reminds us of the broad reach of informal networks, the "kinship and credit ties that emanated from New York and New England" and transformed Chicago into an urban place. These families came to Chicago not only to make money, but also to create a society.[8]

Early Chicago civic culture was dominated by private associations that women like Juliette could participate in even though they had no independent political status. This privatism meant that personal connections held considerable sway over public issues ranging from police and fire protection to schools, orphanages, and hospitals. A small state and a small formal market offered space for women to exert some influence.[9]

Civic culture, which today we often equate with political culture, was then far less tethered to government. It emerged from the efforts of households to create the services and organizations that would replicate a society familiar to migrants from the Northeast. Because of this, Juliette's limited individual political rights mattered less to her than we might expect. She was part of a public sphere that emerged more as an extension of households than from any level of government. She viewed civic culture not as sharply different from her home but as expanding outward from it. In Juliette's view, women's role, as expressed by her contemporary Catharine Beecher, was to be "first in the family, then in the school, then in the neighborhood, then in the world."[10] This fluidity allowed Juliette Kinzie to play an important role in Chicago's early civic life. Without women like her, Chicago would have remained a small settlement far longer.[11]

Traditionally, historians have told the story of Chicago's early rise by looking at the speculators who boosted real estate. Almost all of this speculating was done by men, leading historian Bessie Louise Pierce to suggest in 1937 that early Chicago "was preeminently a man's city." Their work was indeed vital to the city's economic growth, but Chicago also grew as an actual community, not just as parcels of real estate. This entailed the work of building houses, creating schools, and founding key institutions. Yet even when Pierce discussed the emergence of a "fabric of society," she still focused almost exclusively on the work of men.[12]

Juliette's life reveals that the growth of Chicago did not flow solely from the success of the real estate market. Instead, it rested on a group of men and women who created households that together laid the foundation of Chicago as a city. Juliette and John Kinzie's substantial brick house is emblematic of this process. Although the couple built their home from profits gained in real estate speculation, it was not a speculative venture. The house was initially an ostentatious display of wealth, but it was also an anchor that steadied a large extended family through the ups and downs of the business cycles.

Within houses like this, there took place the work of social reproduction—of raising children and fostering communities—that was so much a part of the family claim on women.[13] Households made possible the rise of Chicago, just as surely as it rested in real estate speculation and federal investments. Household work was not ancillary to the task of city building but an essential part of it.

And it was work that men and women did together, largely outside the formal market.

Losing Chicago

While Juliette and her cohort were shaping civic culture in early Chicago, the rapid advance of industrial capitalism was altering the landscape of both the public and the private spheres. After 1848 railroads, industrialization, and immigration transformed Chicago into one of the nation's largest cities. Corporate capitalism shifted business away from homes and into boardrooms. Households became less important as the growth of factory work and consumer goods moved more and more into the formal market.

Juliette discovered that good economic fortune was a destructive force that erased much of her family's achievement. She and other early Chicago residents saw their vision for the city overwhelmed by a new class of entrepreneurs, as well as by thousands of immigrants from Ireland, Germany, and Scandinavia.[14] She watched as the neighborhood she had helped create vanished under rail lines, grain elevators, and shanties and as the societies organized in her parlor grew more formal and less open to women.

Alongside the rapid economic and demographic change in Chicago, the 1850s brought a deep political divide that led the nation to war in 1861. Juliette's family, like many others, was deeply enmeshed in the sectional conflict that was the Civil War. While most of her male relatives served the Union, her son-in-law was a Southern officer. Her brother-in-law commanded Union troops off the coast of Georgia in 1862 when her daughter and granddaughters were living just a few miles away in Savannah. The Confederate commander there waggishly suggested he should tie Nellie to the highest church steeple to keep her uncle from attacking the city. When necessary, Juliette mined personal connections on both sides of the war; she prevailed on President Lincoln to get trunks filled with tea, coffee, children's clothing, and other household items for her daughter through Union lines. After her sons had been seized as Confederate prisoners, daughter Nellie appealed directly to Jefferson Davis to gain their release.

The Civil War brought a greater role for government as it reached into families to recruit soldiers and disrupted kin networks that crossed regions. It also placed the fight for broader individual rights squarely in the national consciousness.[15] Although Juliette defined herself as part of a society of households, by 1865 this vision was increasingly anachronistic. She was unable to adapt to a changed world; indeed, adaptation was beyond her ability. Juliette grew more and more out of step with the modernizing, rights-focused world as Chicago developed into an industrial powerhouse.

Across her lifetime, Juliette Kinzie witnessed the dramatic western expansion of American society as well as seeing more and more of the business of everyday life move from the informal household economy to the formal market. In three roughly chronological parts, this book traces that evolution through her experiences and those of her family as Chicago grew from a small outpost to a burgeoning city of more than 300,000. Part 1 examines Juliette's life in the 1820s and 1830s as she evolved from an easterner to a westerner and established a Chicago home. Part 2 considers the rapid rise of Chicago and its civic culture during the 1830s and 1840s and into the 1850s, as Juliette's house became a center for civic culture. Part 3 focuses on the late 1850s and 1860s, characterized in Chicago by rapid growth, industrialization, and the sectional divide.

Recovering Juliette Magill Kinzie through a careful consideration of her experiences and writings provides us with a richer, deeper view of Chicago before the Great Fire of 1871. The story of her family highlights the tension between individual entrepreneurial progress and the communitarian vision that underlay the city's early civic culture. Perhaps the most powerful symbol of this lost world was the house she helped design, built with some of the first bricks made in the town. A Chicago landmark in 1835, it represented both success in the market and private civic engagement. But by the time Juliette died in 1870, the house was surrounded by factories and the homes of working-class immigrants; it burned to the ground the following year, along with much of her neighborhood. Juliette's story would be all but forgotten save for her writing, which now offers us an opportunity to recover part of this lost Chicago and her place in it.

PART 1

Building at Cass and Michigan,
1806–36

1

....

Chicago and Middletown

Juliette Magill was twelve years old in 1818 when Chicago first influenced her life. President James Monroe appointed her mother's younger brother as Indian agent at Fort Dearborn. Dr. Alexander Wolcott Jr. was a keen observer of new places and a prolific correspondent. Soon Juliette's "highest delight" were her uncle's letters describing his home and his life in "Indian country." From nine hundred miles away in Middletown, Connecticut, she began to imagine Chicago long before she saw it.[1]

In return, Juliette wrote lively letters to her uncle Wolcott. He thought of them as "really conversations" that reminded him of pleasant evenings he had spent at her "dear mother's cheerful fireside." He asked her to write "as often as you can afford." Letters became the lifeblood between family members, who shared gossip, news, and musings on the events of the day. They were read over and over, often aloud; many included humorous anecdotes, wordplay, and teasing references to moments shared. They kept the family circle strong.[2]

Juliette began to envision Chicago from Wolcott's descriptions: it was a small village of a dozen or so houses surrounding Fort Dearborn, an outpost in Indian country that held about 160 soldiers.[3] Wolcott's neighbors included Potawatomi families and many mixed-race households of fur traders. The Beaubiens, Chevaliers, and Ouilmettes were métis families of French traders and their Indian wives. Businesses and families were closely intertwined, with houses as the center of activity.

John and Eleanor Kinzie lived across the Chicago River to the north of Fort Dearborn. He operated a trading outpost from the house where they raised four children. John, their oldest son, was serving a six-year indenture with the American Fur Company at Mackinac Island, Michigan, but younger son, Robert, helped his father in the fur trade. Daughters Maria Indiana and Ellen were both at home. The family welcomed Wolcott into their sociable household. The Kinzies' circle also came to include John Crafts, an American Fur Company agent originally from New England. They entertained one another with good food and good company and looked after each other. In one letter Wolcott reported that they were all going to Crafts' outpost at Bridgeport "to eat roast goose with brandy sauce."[4]

While Wolcott described Chicago as an "odd, out of the way place," he also admitted that he was "daily becoming more attached" to it and contemplated a more permanent life there. Wolcott set about establishing a household, planting corn, and raising cattle, chickens, and milk cows. He improved his rudimentary dwelling by adding a kitchen, a stove house, a blacksmith's shop, a council house, an office, a corncrib, a smokehouse, a poultry house, and a milk house. As he wrote to Juliette and other family members, "I intend to make it one of the most convenient and inviting little spots in the country."[5]

Alexander Wolcott was fast becoming an unofficial settler at Chicago as well as a local representative of the federal government. He worked alongside the officers and soldiers at Fort Dearborn.[6] As Indian agent, he was involved in negotiating cessions from area Indians, but he was also charged with protecting them from unscrupulous traders and settlers. These official duties often conflicted, especially because of his friendship with local traders like John Kinzie and his preparing for a permanent settlement at Chicago by making improvements and putting land into farming.

While he settled into Chicago, the Potawatomi and their allies were being pushed to cede millions of acres of land and move west. Wolcott looked forward to the time when all this land would be open for American settlement, but he also pitied the Potawatomi. Less with contempt than with dismay, Wolcott came to view them as "despicable wretches" who were fast losing their lands and livelihoods. Unlike some American officials in the west, he sought to protect the Indians under his agency as best he could while still promoting American conquest. He worried particularly about dishonest traders who sold liquor on credit in order to take advantage of their already harassed Indian customers through "mean and rascally tricks" like overcharging or watering down alcohol. Decades later, Juliette expressed a similarly sympathetic yet paternalistic view of "our native brethren" for the "wrongs they have received at the hands of whites," in language reminiscent of her uncle's letters.[7]

Although Juliette came to know a great deal about Chicago, it was not well known to other Americans on the East Coast. This began to change in 1820 when Lewis Cass, governor of Michigan Territory, led an expedition officially charged with locating the source of the Mississippi River. Alexander Wolcott accompanied the group as its doctor. They gathered information to use in future treaty negotiations for further Indian cessions, as well as for American settlers who would then come into the region. Henry Rowe Schoolcraft, tasked with geological and mineralogical surveying, sketched several of the places they visited. Wolcott wrote to Juliette about Schoolcraft's landscapes, encouraging her to continue her own sketching. Juliette must have pored over her uncle's descriptions as well as Schoolcraft's 1821 book on the topography, natural history, and mineral wealth of the region.[8]

Schoolcraft's description of Chicago was particularly appealing to farmers and speculators looking for a new start in the west. He wrote that "the country around Chicago is the most fertile and beautiful that can be imagined" and that Chicago would become a "great thoroughfare" for the entire country. Wolcott agreed; he felt that the rich region would provide a new home for his eastern family as soon as the local Potawatomi were forced to relinquish their lands.[9]

Indeed, the American government sought cessions from the Indians almost immediately. In 1821 Wolcott hosted Governor Cass, Schoolcraft, and Robert Forsyth (John Kinzie's nephew and Cass's secretary) in Chicago as they negotiated with more than three thousand Potawatomi. Though Cass opened the conference by suggesting that it would "probably be many years before the country will be settled by the Americans," he pressed the Potawatomi to cede their lands east of Chicago. Over the protests of many of those assembled, Potawatomi leaders turned over five million acres of "choice lands." The local market would soon extend beyond the fur trade into real estate.[10]

During these negotiations, Schoolcraft was "seized with bilious fever," likely malaria, which Wolcott, the only physician in the area, treated. When Schoolcraft was well enough to travel, both men went east. Wolcott consulted with federal officials at Washington, DC, and made an extended visit to Middletown.

Middletown

The heart of Middletown was a colonial-era common along the Connecticut River, surrounded by churches and the houses of the most prominent citizens, which included Juliette's grandfather Alexander Wolcott Sr. His daughter Frances, widowed and the mother of a young daughter, married Arthur W. Magill, the son of her father's business partner, in 1805. The couple's first child was Juliette, born September 11, 1806. Over the next sixteen years, six more children were born: William, Mary Ann, Arthur, Henry,

Alexander, and Julian. Juliette's extended family was large and close; she later wrote about a fictional holiday celebration where "breakfast was hardly over before hosts of cousins and friends, to whom due notice had been given, began to arrive."[11]

Juliette received her early education informally within these households. She learned the myriad tasks women were expected to perform, including cooking and preserving most of the food the families ate. She became a skilled baker, known for her cakes and muffins, and learned to cook over open fires as well as on stoves. Juliette also became a skilled seamstress who could make bedsheets, underwear, and infants' diapers as well as work pants and shirts. She also mastered finer work for women's dresses, sewing most of her own clothing by hand; like one of her fictional characters, Juliette had "the means of always appearing in a tasteful and appropriate manner" in her homemade wardrobe.[12]

Juliette was part of a generation of literate New England women. In families like hers, where sons received advanced education, daughters often learned from their brothers' tutors. Women were educated to be good mothers and companionable wives. Juliette was especially privileged because during her childhood she had access to her grandfather Wolcott's large library. Her mother taught her early lessons there, and her uncle Wolcott tutored her in Latin. Juliette became fluent in French. She had lessons in art and became an accomplished pianist. Her family believed that the "expense of a piano" and a musical education prepared a young woman "to make her own living, should the necessity arise."[13] Juliette was being readied not only to be a good wife and mother, but to be able to support herself as a music teacher if need be.

While much of Juliette's childhood was spent within the Magill and Wolcott households, Middletown, standing between New Haven and Hartford, was not an isolated village. Founded in 1650, by 1806 it was the largest city in Connecticut and a busy international seaport on the Connecticut River. Merchants and sea captains made their living by trading in rum, molasses, and enslaved people. So while the Magill and Wolcott households were largely self-sufficient, they were ensconced in a market economy defined by commercial capitalism.

Indeed, Juliette's other grandfather, Arthur Magill, was a sea captain. His sisters married "three Bermuda devils," the Williams brothers, who worked with Magill in the Caribbean trade. Captain Magill likely trafficked in enslaved people, since the slave trade was not entirely abolished in Connecticut until 1848. Juliette grew up in a world where bound labor, both enslaved African Americans and white indentured servants, worked within family households.[14]

Soon after Juliette was born, Middletown's successful trade was threatened by federal policies, especially the 1807 Embargo and the end of the external slave trade in the following year. Both disrupted the Caribbean market, which never regained its previous prominence. As a result, Middletown's economy languished as nearby rivals grew rapidly. By 1820 Hartford and New Haven had doubled their populations while Middletown's lagged.

Middletown also underwent wrenching changes caused by a mix of religion, politics, and business. Both the Wolcott and the Magill families were Episcopalians. Juliette was baptized on December 28, 1806, at Holy Trinity Church, where her family rented a pew and supported the church's many activities. The families held Sundays sacrosanct as a day when "no business can be transacted." Beyond church attendance, family meals, and visits, writing letters was one of the few pursuits "wholeheartedly sanctioned for the day."[15]

As Episcopalians, the Wolcotts and Magills dissented from the Congregationalism that was then Connecticut's state religion. They supported the local Congregational Church through tax dollars and the Episcopal Church through their donations. Religion and politics became intertwined when Thomas Jefferson and his supporters pushed for disestablishment of state religions across the new nation. Juliette's family joined the Jeffersonians in Connecticut and fought successfully for a new state constitution breaking the state's tie with religion.[16] After 1818 all congregations relied on the voluntary support of families.

Disestablishment also "proved good politics" for the Magill and Wolcott families. Alexander Wolcott Sr., a Yale graduate who trained as a lawyer, was appointed by President Jefferson as the Middletown collector of customs. Middletown merchants, who were mostly Federalists, protested angrily to Jefferson, but Wolcott kept the post. His influence continued through the presidency of James Monroe into the 1820s.[17]

During the trade disruption caused by the Napoleonic Wars, Wolcott invested in an early industrial enterprise with Captain Arthur Magill Sr., who had retired from the sea. In 1810 they founded a woolen mill, the Middletown Manufacturing Company, "one of the first, if not the first manufactory" in the United States to use steam power. They transformed a large brick sugarhouse along the river into an enterprise that produced forty yards of broadcloth each day. Juliette's father, Arthur W. Magill, joined the company too and took a leading role after his father died in 1812.

Juliette would later remember this shift to factory production with some disapproval, longing for a time when "women spun, and wove, and knit what they wanted to wear, without being beholden to their neighbors to do it for them." Yet the early success of the operation allowed Juliette a privileged childhood. The company prospered during the Napoleonic Wars, which kept cheaper British cloth from American consumers. With the end of war in 1815, the Atlantic trade resumed, and inexpensive British goods overwhelmed the US market, imperiling nascent American factories. The Middletown Manufacturing Company could not compete with less expensive woolen imports and faded away.[18]

The family sought other opportunities tied to the federal government. Alexander Wolcott Jr. headed west to Chicago as a US Indian agent, intending to explore western places that were expanding. When President Monroe approved the charter of a Second Bank of the United States in 1817, Alexander Wolcott Sr. got Juliette's father the plum position of cashier at the Middletown branch. The appointment did not sit well with Connecticut Federalists, who were willing to destroy the town's enterprises rather than see them in the hands of their political enemies.[19] They watched Arthur W. Magill carefully, waiting for an opportunity to bring him down.

As cashier, Magill managed the bank's daily operations. For his family, and for the nation at large, things went well for a time. Magill, buoyed by ready money, made unsecured loans to himself, family members, and friends. He began construction on a massive brick mansion.[20]

The hope that the bank would help to keep capital and currency stable crumbled in 1819 as cheap British manufactured goods and declining agricultural exports led to a banking collapse and years of hard times. This downturn was felt particularly in cities and towns like Middletown that were tied to trade and manufacturing. To shore up the national bank, its directors forced the branches to redeem notes "issued to themselves and various insider friends."[21]

Magill got caught short. Unable to cover the overdrafts he had allowed to himself and his friends and family, he was accused of embezzling $66,548.60 from the Bank of the United States. He lost most of his assets, including his house and the remnants of the woolen mill, while his Federalist opponents relished his spectacular fall. The *Boston Daily Advertiser* wrote in early November 1820, "Certain *delicate* facts have just been disclosed relating to the affairs of the United States' Branch Bank at Middletown, and that in consequence, the Cashier, A. W. Magill, is removed." Soon after, Magill was arrested and sent to the New Haven jail. There he wrote hopelessly that he expected "to remain confined up in this place til the day of Judgement."[22]

Jailing debtors was not uncommon at this time. For the Magill and Wolcott families, however, it was an act of public shaming tinged with political retribution. Alexander Wolcott Sr. was furious with his son-in-law for embarrassing his daughter as well as his extended kin and business networks. He rewrote his will to exclude Magill from his estate, setting up a vehicle by which his daughter

Fig. 3 The federal-style house that Arthur and Frances Magill completed in 1821 at 625–31 Main Street in Middletown, Connecticut. Juliette lived there only briefly before financial setbacks forced her father to give up the property. Since 1832 the building has housed a boys' school, a boardinghouse, and most recently a community health center. Photo by Ann Keating.

would inherit money that her husband could not control. Despite this, the Wolcott family did not disown Magill. They took care of his children, wrote him letters, and helped secure his 1821 release.[23]

From Chicago, Juliette's uncle expressed deep dismay. Alexander Wolcott Jr., like his father, blamed Arthur Magill for deceit and misdirection. Long-simmering mistrust surfaced when Magill wrote accusingly to his brother-in-law, "you see how well I know you." His anger was most acute when thinking about his sister and her children, who lost their home and their standing in Middletown. Wolcott closed on an irate note, suggesting that Arthur might wish to move to Indian country, where "it is the law among these nations that every man shall have the privilege of throwing away (as they call it) his wife whenever it suits his pleasure."[24]

Juliette was an impressionable young woman; she later created a fictional father who was ruined by the financial collapse in 1819. The character was seized by the economic panic that "brought blessings to many, but to some it brought ruin." Juliette wrote that her character, like her father, "struggled on for a while, collecting the shattered remnants of his fortune, and striving to make a new beginning."[25] Her life would be shaped by recurrent upswings and subsequent downturns of the volatile American economy. Like many whose families had been deleteriously affected in 1819, Juliette came to see that a household economy and the support of extended family offered a safety net in an unpredictable world.

Chicago Visitors to Middletown

By 1821 a visit from her uncle must have been a wonderful distraction to Juliette, even if it was a thorn in her father's side. Wolcott came to Middletown with a large contingent from Chicago that included Henry Schoolcraft, Ellen Marion Kinzie, and at least one officer from Fort Dearborn, Lieutenant Lewis Nelson Mason. Ellen's sister, Maria, may also have accompanied the group.[26]

In Middletown they saw an old town with houses, businesses, schools, and churches built along traditional streets. The Connecticut city also had established institutions and local government, a customs house, and a branch of the national bank. In contrast, in Chicago there were no streets, and the few houses were oriented toward the river. There were no churches or schools. Fort Dearborn provided the center of activity and a reminder that the area was still part of Indian country. Still, Chicago's growth seemed imminent, while Middletown faced an uncertain future.

For a sensitive young woman like Juliette, these visitors must have made quite an impression as they sat before the fires in family parlors on cold evenings. No longer limited by letters, Uncle Wolcott and the others regaled Juliette and her family with tales of their adventures. Wolcott described the Chicago Treaty negotiations, and Schoolcraft may have shared more of his expedition sketches with Juliette, providing models for her own drawings.

This was also Juliette's first encounter with a member of the Kinzie family who would figure so prominently in her life. Ellen Kinzie, born in Chicago in 1804, had grown up in Indian country, a world Juliette could only imagine. No doubt her Chicago stories were endlessly fascinating. Juliette learned about Ellen's family, including her older brother, John, who had two years of service remaining on an indenture to the American Fur Company at Mackinac.

Ellen's presence in the group reflected an already strong personal connection between the Wolcott and Kinzie families. Seventeen years old, in Middletown Ellen attended school, impossible to do in Chicago. The Wolcotts got better acquainted with her, and Ellen got to know the family. A romance was blooming between her and Juliette's uncle, despite the fourteen years that separated them. They married soon after returning to Chicago in summer 1822.[27]

Watching their romance, fifteen-year-old Juliette saw marriage as a way out of Middletown and on to Chicago. She set her sights on the visiting Lieutenant Morris, but after a flirtation, he returned to Chicago alone. The following year, Uncle Wolcott wrote with the news that Lieutenant Morris, whom Juliette "insisted upon having for a husband," had left Chicago and married someone else. Wolcott did not think Juliette was seriously upset; he advised, "There are as good fish in the sea as ever were caught."[28] He encouraged her to cast a wide net, but the idea of marrying someone from Chicago had been planted.

Juliette's parents began their own plans for moving west. Her mother thought they would "be much more happy" away from Middletown. She was tired of the gossip and recriminations against her husband and her family in this place that had been the center of her life. However, Alexander Wolcott cautioned that no matter where they settled, there would be neighbors "whose delight it is to lessen the sum of human enjoyments and increase the stack of human miseries." Still, he encouraged his sister to move, reminding her that family ties would survive: "You will not go so far but that I can follow you."[29] Geography would not keep them apart.

In 1822 the Magill family moved, but only a short distance west, to a cottage along the Hudson River near the town of Fishkill, New York. Across the river from their new house was the US Military Academy. During the summer, Juliette sailed across to West Point several times a week to socialize with the young people who gathered there. It was a wonderful change from the straitened circumstances they had faced in Middletown.[30] Her uncle teasingly complained that Juliette no longer wrote: "I suppose that she is too busy thinking of her ugly cadets."[31]

In 1823 Juliette attended Emma Willard's Troy Female Seminary, just up the Hudson River near Albany. The Wolcott family valued education highly, but her parents may also have wanted to divert her attention from all those cadets. It seems likely that her uncle paid her tuition, since her father remained mired in debt. Daughters of two of his western colleagues, Michigan governor Lewis Cass and Detroit judge Solomon Sibley, attended the seminary during these years, so Wolcott certainly was familiar with the school.[32] In a later work of fiction, Juliette wrote about a beloved uncle who "had watched over every step of her life, and helped her mother to train her for usefulness and happiness."[33]

Emma Willard's Troy Female Seminary had opened in 1821 as the first institution in the United States dedicated to higher education for women, which Willard argued would raise the "female character." She included subjects traditionally offered only to young men: mathematics, philosophy, geography, history, and science. By attending Emma Willard's academy, Juliette joined a small group of young women who had access to advanced education. Elizabeth Cady Stanton was among the most prominent to graduate from the school in these years. Catharine Beecher, just six years older than Juliette, grew up in Hartford, just north of Middletown along the Connecticut River. In 1823 she opened a seminary like Willard's to educate young women, including her sister, Harriet.[34]

Though she attended the school for only a year, Juliette was greatly influenced by it. Willard's emphasis on geography and history informed her later writing. Juliette's approach to marriage, education, and religion were also shaped by Willard, who stressed "the subservience of all human beings to God." She did not see "it a peculiarity to our sex, to be under human authority" but instead suggested that everyone served other people. Of course her female students, while subservient, were also privileged members of American society. Willard believed education would make her young women better marriage partners and mothers. On completing their studies, they would better serve their households and communities. Juliette embraced Willard's hierarchical view, which matched much of what she had learned within her family and in the Episcopal Church.[35]

Imbued with this outlook, Juliette accepted her place and obligations within her home and community. She did not call for equal rights for women or other subservient household members. Instead, she worked to identify and fulfill her responsibilities. Like her mother, Juliette did not rebel against the hierarchy that tied her inexorably to a husband or a father but instead turned to home and religion for guidance on her remit within her world. She accordingly expected others, including the enslaved people in her household, to be content with their place.

Emma Willard emphasized a woman's choice of a spouse as the "defining decision, the most important one a woman would make." But she also reminded her students that when they married they received "protection and support" from their husbands and so must "yield obedience" to them.[36] There was real tension between this one independent choice and the general subservience of women. As one 1820 observer noted, once married, wives "subject themselves to his [their husbands'] authority." Inspired by her time at Willard's academy, Juliette understood that courtship was a serious undertaking, the search for a worthy husband.[37]

Beyond her mother and Emma Willard, Juliette was influenced by her step-grandmother, who had married Alexander Wolcott Sr. in 1807. Lucy Waldo Wolcott had an independent fortune and owned a townhouse near the Boston Common. When her husband died in 1828, Lucy returned to Massachusetts and welcomed Juliette for long visits. As a wealthy widow, she was the head of her household and enjoyed considerable independence. Indeed, one friend noted that it was difficult to move Lucy Wolcott "from any purpose which she had once formed."[38] Juliette came to see the power a financially independent widow could wield. In her grandmother's parlor, she also met potential marriage partners from the leading families in Boston.[39]

During the late 1820s, Juliette's parents moved again, to New Hartford, New York, a small mill town near Utica along the newly opened Erie Canal, which attracted New England families seeking better economic opportunities. Because of his experience running the Middletown Manufacturing Company, Arthur Magill apparently found work in a local textile mill. The family lived in a comfortable brick house and were members of St. Stephen's Episcopal Church.[40] Juliette's older half-sister, Frances Homan, married Hiram Higby, from a prominent local family.

Juliette later described a fictional town that seems drawn from her recollections of New Hartford: "The houses of the little town stood principally upon one street, as in most country villages, from which a few green lanes stretched out." Although Juliette painted an idyllic view, her family continued to be plagued by financial and legal troubles. Arthur Magill's creditors still pursued him as court cases continued against him. It was said that he "ever had been, and still is, an utter bankrupt." New Hartford turned out to be only a temporary respite.[41]

Chicago

While Juliette moved around during the 1820s, her uncle Wolcott settled at Chicago. After marrying Ellen Kinzie, he boasted that she was "becoming quite a notable housewife under the superintendence of her mother who . . . is the most furiously industrious woman that I ever saw."[42] Soon he wrote that Ellen had become "fat and hearty," and within a few years the couple had two children. He nicknamed his son Natty Bumppo after the main character in James Fenimore Cooper's *The Last of the Mohicans* (1826), a book the Wolcott and Magill families devoured. They relished Cooper's romantic American tales whose settings moved from New York to the Great Lakes, much like their own family.[43]

Ellen and Alexander Wolcott worked within their self-sufficient operation on the north side of the Chicago River across from Fort Dearborn.[44] As their family grew, they continued to make improvements to the house, although Wolcott noted that the "architecture [was] not quite that of the Parthenon." The rambling Wolcott house became the center for family from both Chicago and Connecticut. Alexander and Ellen looked to ease the burden on his sister Frances by taking care of her children; between 1821 and 1828, they welcomed two of Juliette's siblings for extended stays. He enjoyed teaching them, readying Juliette's brother William to enter college as well as imparting the rudiments of farming.

Ellen and Alexander Wolcott thus supported not only their own children but nieces, nephews, and younger siblings. In doing so, they created a western center for their families, especially after Juliette's grandfather died in 1828. Wolcott wrote to his sister that his "highest ambition seems to be to be snugly settled alongside of you." Juliette's uncle was certain that within a few years settlers would pour into the region and Chicago would become the great depot "for inland commerce." He encouraged all their eastern relatives to come west when the Indians had "left this country" because the land was "good, plenty and cheap."[45]

After the elder John Kinzie's death in 1828, the couple also welcomed Ellen's mother, her half-sister Margaret Helm (and son Edwin), her sister Maria, and her younger brother Robert to live with them. As well as being a major householder, Alexander Wolcott was the leading public figure in Chicago, especially during the stretches when no companies of soldiers were assigned to Fort Dearborn. With the death of his father and father-in-law, he also increasingly functioned as the head of both the Wolcott and Kinzie families.

John Harris Kinzie

Missing from the family hearth during the whole of the time Alexander Wolcott served as Indian agent at Chicago was John Harris Kinzie, his wife's elder brother. After finishing his five-year indenture with the American Fur Company at Mackinac Island, Michigan, in 1823, the younger John Kinzie became a company employee at Prairie du Chien, Wisconsin. During his two years along the Mississippi River, he devoted himself to mastering the Ho-Chunk language and developing relationships within tribal villages. John's knowledge proved invaluable in treaty negotiations undertaken by the US government in 1825. Michigan territorial governor Lewis Cass headed the delegation; his secretary was Robert A. Forsyth, the same Kinzie cousin who had been present at the 1821 Chicago treaty negotiations. Although the conference stalled on many issues, Cass was impressed with John Kinzie's deep knowledge of Indian languages and customs and offered him a staff position. He quickly accepted the offer, seeing more opportunity with the federal government than with the American Fur Company.[46]

After an initial posting among the Wyandots in northwest Ohio, Kinzie soon was dispatched back to Wisconsin as an interpreter for Thomas McKenney, the US Indian Department head, as he continued negotiations with the Ho-Chunk. The Ho-Chunk felt ill served by the federal government and were unwilling to cede rights to nearby lead mines. Indeed, Ho-Chunk warriors had recently attacked several groups of Americans investigating mines in their territory, and more hostilities seemed likely. Besides his language facility, Kinzie had the confidence of many Ho-Chunk leaders, who often called on him "to stand by their side during their *talks* with the *big knives* and tell them whether what was said was truthfully interpreted."[47]

John's knowledge and contacts contrasted with those of Thomas McKenney, who headed the negotiations. McKenney was on only his second trip west and necessarily relied on the local expertise of men like Kinzie. (Juliette later created a fictional commissioner who said of the knowledgeable westerner modeled on John Kinzie, "I shall squeeze him as I would a lemon!")[48]

McKenney encouraged a delegation of Ho-Chunk to travel east in 1828 to impress on them "a sense of the power and superiority of the United States." John Kinzie accompanied the group, which also included Governor Cass and John's cousin Robert Forsyth. This was quite likely the first time John Kinzie had visited the East Coast. Like Indian delegations before them, they met with federal officials in Washington, DC, and toured cities including Boston, New York, Baltimore, and Philadelphia. They inspected "forts and battleships, visit[ed] arsenals, and watch[ed] parades and artillery demonstrations," all to show the Ho-Chunk the might of the bellicose United States.[49]

In every city, the delegates attended special events and performances. In New York they met with General William Henry Harrison, whom some of the Ho-Chunk remembered battling in the War of 1812. The delegation saw an ascent of a manned balloon as well as many theater productions. They stayed at some of the best-known establishments in the country, including the Indian Queen, then "Washington's finest hotel." Newspapers across the East covered their progress, especially marking their unfamiliarity with urban life. One article noted that while the trips impressed "some untamed young savages," the "wary collected old chiefs" simply re-sponded, *"American foolish!"*[50]

In the course of their travels, John Kinzie got to know the Ho-Chunk representatives even better. He later described the delega-tion head, Naw-Kaw (Walking Rain), as having "a broad, pleasant countenance," while noting that the elder leader Day-kau-ray's "perfectly neat, appropriate dress, almost without ornament and his courteous demeanor . . . all combined to give him the highest place of consideration of all who knew him." One of the few women in the delegation was the wife of Wau-Kaun-zee-Hah (Yellow Thunder), who was known after the trip as "Mrs. Washington."[51]

The official highlight of the trip was a meeting with outgoing president John Quincy Adams at the White House on November 29, 1828. Sixteen Ho-Chunk warriors in full regalia entered the room one by one to shake the president's hand. The guests were served Madeira and macaroons. As Naw-Kaw addressed the president, John Kinzie translated his words "first into French and then into English." He said, "Father, a cloud has been between us. It was thick and black. I thought once it would never be removed. But I now see your face." After these pleasantries, the Ho-Chunk requested the release of their imprisoned warriors. President Adams agreed only to commute their death sentences, so long as the Ho-Chunk agreed to sell to the United States lands "that had been the source of the recent troubles." While "stunned" at the request, the war-riors agreed to open negotiations. Governor Cass, with Kinzie's help, would finalize a treaty in 1829 under which the Ho-Chunk relinquished 1.76 million acres.[52]

As a reward for negotiating this massive cession, Lewis Cass became secretary of war in the new administration of President Andrew Jackson.[53] John Kinzie was appointed the subagent sta-tioned at Portage, Wisconsin, in recognition of his crucial role in the process. With Cass as a mentor in Washington, DC, and with his extensive knowledge of the west, at twenty-five years old Kinzie was a young man with a bright future.

2

....

The West

Despite their connections to Chicago, John Kinzie and Juliette Magill did not meet there. Their introduction came in the parlor of her cultured grandmother, Lucy Wolcott, probably in late 1828 when the Ho-Chunk delegation stopped in Boston.[1] Her grandmother's house in Franklin Place was designed by Charles Bulfinch and was one of sixteen three-story townhouses along a crescent that included the city's first garden square. It was near churches, theaters, the statehouse, and the Boston Common. Some of the city's most elite families lived in the townhouses and entertained each other in beautifully appointed rooms.

Among Lucy Wolcott's neighbors was Henry Sargent, a painter whose subjects included *The Dinner Party* (1821) and *The Tea Party* (1824), both now part of the collection of the Boston Museum of Fine Arts. These two paintings were likely based on his own dining room and parlors in Franklin Place. *The Dinner Party* includes only men, elegantly attired in high white cravats and dark frock coats. In *The Tea Party* the men are simply ciphers facing away from the painter, with a focus on elegantly attired women in empire-waist

Fig. 4 Henry Sargent, *The Tea Party*, about 1824 (Photograph copyright 2019, Museum of Fine Arts, Boston).

dresses, turbans, feathers, and elaborate shawls. The walls are papered and painted in deep, rich colors and hung with large mirrors and paintings. Candelabras adorn the fireplaces and tabletops, while lush carpets and fine furniture fill the rooms.[2]

Although Lucy Wolcott's parlors may not have looked just like these, this was her neighborhood. Imagine John Kinzie stepping into one of these parlors and encountering Juliette Magill. He was a handsome young man, with dark hair and kind eyes, well dressed in fittingly fashionable eastern clothing. But he was a westerner in manner and speech and would certainly have stood out from the other men in the room. Though he was not uncultured, his upbringing was shaped by his mother's British roots, his French and métis neighbors, and the Indians he lived and worked among. He was also something of a celebrity, since the touring Ho-Chunk delegation was being covered by the Boston papers.

In contrast, Juliette was comfortable if not entirely at ease in this world. She moved in elite Boston circles based on her grandmother's wealth but remained the daughter of a disgraced debtor. Knowing her lifelong interest in fashion, it is easy to imagine her well dressed and ready to make conversation about the latest books, performances, or political news. She had more than a passing interest in John Kinzie. For years she had read letters filled with Chicago, the Kinzie family, and Indian country from her uncle Alexander Wolcott and his wife, Ellen. In turn, John must have heard much about Wolcott and his extended kin in Connecticut, especially in letters from his mother and his sister Ellen.

In many ways it is no surprise that Juliette Magill married John Kinzie. Their marriage cemented kin and business ties that her uncle Alexander Wolcott had fostered for more than a decade. By 1830 Wolcott was strongly encouraging his eastern family to move west for economic opportunities and family unity. Moreover, for Juliette the west had long "possessed a wonderful charm" in her imagination.[3] John Kinzie appeared in her grandmother's parlor as the embodiment of her romantic fascination with the west.

John H. Kinzie's early life was a sharp contrast to Juliette Magill's. Born on July 7, 1803, just outside Detroit in British territory, he spent his childhood in and out of the Indian country of the western Great Lakes. Juliette, born three years later, grew up in the tight orbit of Middletown, Connecticut, whereas John's family moved to Chicago before his first birthday. His father, also John Kinzie, a silversmith and fur trader, created an outpost across the Chicago River from the newly established Fort Dearborn. John had an older half-sister, two younger sisters, and one younger brother. Juliette had an older half-sister and six younger brothers. Whereas Juliette lived in one of the largest towns in New England, John passed his early childhood in a small trading outpost in Indian country. Juliette was in and out of her grandfather's fine library; John played in and around the fort.[4]

In both their households, people worked together to provide the necessities of daily life. Yet while men and women worked alongside each other, they were not equals. Grandfathers, fathers, or uncles headed most households, and everyone else fit in according to a loose hierarchy based on family connection, gender, race, and class. Both John and Juliette were closely familiar with the institution of slavery; it was deeply ingrained in their worlds. John grew up in a home where young métis women of French or British and Indian descent served as servants and housemaids to a large extended family. His father held several enslaved men during his time at Chicago.[5] Juliette's family also kept black and white servants, some of whom were enslaved or bound in some way.

Both John and Juliette grew up connected to extended family through letters and long visits. Cousins, aunts, and uncles often joined and left their households. In return, they felt welcome in the homes of their relatives, whether in Detroit or Boston or Chicago. Both John and Juliette began their education at home, tutored by family members, but Juliette was also able to attend established schools near her home. There were no schools at Chicago; it was a "scramble" for John to receive an education at all. He was delighted to find a spelling book in a tea chest shipped to his father. One of his cousins taught him to read from the few books available at home.[6]

Despite these differences in their educations, both Juliette and John were lifelong readers. Juliette's family had access to her grandfather's large library and often read together during long evenings. John honed his interest in books during his years in Mackinac, where Mrs. Robert Stuart (the wife of his supervisor) tutored him and shared books, helping to make him "the equal of many whose youthful years had been trained in schools."[7]

Both Juliette and John showed a facility for languages and a love of them. Juliette studied Latin as a young girl. She could read and write in French as well as converse. John learned French from his métis neighbors at an early age, as well as the related Algonquian languages of the Odawa, Potawatomi, and Ojibwa. The two also shared a deep appreciation of music. In Middletown, Juliette learned to play the piano well and took voice lessons that only marginally improved her singing. Still, she sang and played in church choirs and recitals. John had enjoyed the fiddle music and dancing of métis culture from his early years at Chicago. His father played the fiddle for his family; at Mackinac, John found a métis woman to teach him to play, and he practiced "during the long isolation of the winter months."[8]

Beyond Juliette's family, the local Episcopal Church was the principal institution of her early years. She attended several services each week as well as many social events. Organized religion was central in public life. In contrast, there were no churches in Chicago during John's childhood. Only occasional religious services were held at Fort Dearborn. Juliette also lived in a town where musical and theater performances were part of public life. In the Chicago of John's childhood, there were no "evening entertainments" or "shows," even from traveling troupes.[9] However, the seasonal rhythms of the fur trade provided ready diversions. John's father operated his business from their home, and the family was busy with a steady stream of French and métis traders, as well as Potawatomi leaders, who brought news and conversation from far and wide.

Both had experienced trying times. John was nine years old at the time of the Battle of Fort Dearborn in August 1812. His father, busy trying to negotiate the peaceful exit of federal troops from Fort Dearborn across Indian country to Fort Wayne in Indiana, put his family in a large bateau. Under the protection of two Potawatomi men, John's family and household servants saw the battle from a distance. While dozens of US soldiers and members of their families were killed by Potawatomi warriors, the Kinzie family drifted safely near the mouth of the Chicago River. After the war, John's father made an unsuccessful bid for appointment as the US Indian agent at Chicago and found it difficult to support his family.[10] John was indentured to the American Fur Company, the largest private corporation in the United States, but the fur trade was in decline in the western Great Lakes region as the supply of beaver and otter skins dwindled and trappers moved west across the Mississippi River.

For Juliette, 1819 was the year that brought real calamity to her family. Before then her grandfathers had launched one of the first woolen mills in America, and her father held a choice position with the Second Bank of the United States. But then Juliette's father was fired, was jailed, lost the family home, and endured public humiliation. Both John and Juliette grew up amid great uncertainty and wild economic swings, but household economies offered some protection from the vagaries of a small and volatile formal market.

These differences and similarities must have intrigued John and Juliette as they courted. John traveled east at least one more time before their August 9, 1830, marriage in New Hartford, New York. We know little more than this. In her short biography of John Kinzie (written after his death), Juliette stated simply that "in 1830 he married." It is likely the wedding took place at St. Stephen's Episcopal Church, a congregation established by Connecticut migrants like the Magills. Juliette's parents and siblings were in attendance.[11]

When John came to upstate New York for his wedding, he was on official business as the subagent to the Ho-Chunk at Portage, Wisconsin. He would stop in Detroit after the ceremony to fill a large wooden box with $18,000 in silver that constituted the first of thirty annuity payments made to the Ho-Chunk in return for their 1829 land cessions. Juliette brought a larger load: boxes filled with furniture, china, and books. She intended to transplant a New England household into Indian county. Her proudest purchase, perhaps underwritten by her grandmother Wolcott, was a Nunns and Clark piano that would be with her until the end of her life.[12]

Together they created a playful, loving household, filled with music and lively conversation. John was a storyteller, and Juliette wrote fiction and nonfiction based on his tales. They worked together and showed respect for each other's talents as well as real affection.[13] But theirs was not a modern marriage of equals; just a few months after their wedding, Juliette wanted to accompany John on a trip but he refused her. She long remembered her husband's decision, but she did not cross him.

Despite this inequality, their marriage was a long one based in mutual understanding and cooperation. John, without a religious affiliation before marriage, joined his wife in the Episcopal faith. He also consulted Juliette on household investments. John recognized her good sense and business acumen, noting in an 1834 letter to his brother-in-law that "wifey is smart." Because John was so frequently away from home, Juliette grew comfortable making decisions for the household in his absence. She achieved a great deal of latitude within a patriarchal structure.[14]

Above all, John and Juliette shared an intense loyalty to family, which would bind them together over the years. The pair also worked hard to develop and maintain a family reputation that was above reproach. This sensibility came from both their birth families. In a rare letter, the elder John Kinzie encouraged his oldest son to work hard and develop a good name that was "better than wealth."[15]

The pair's differences did not disappear. Juliette was far more judgmental than her husband. She was wary of the motivations of people beyond her close circle of family, congregation, and friends. In contrast, John was quite trusting and willing to believe the best of others and was always looking to help those in need. Many times over their marriage, Juliette became annoyed with her husband's credulity. When a clerk stole money from John's office, Juliette wrote to her daughter in exasperated tones, "Of course, your father suspected nothing." Still, in the next sentence she defended John against newspaper accounts that cast aspersions on his character. Her frustration did not boil over beyond her immediate family.[16]

But all this was in the future in September 1830, when Juliette

and John traveled west. An ebullient Juliette relished every moment of the trip west, where she would become a resident of a "distant land, with its vast lakes, its boundless prairies, and its mighty
forests." For years it had been the center of her imagination; now it
"was to be [her] home!"[17]

Into the West

The couple went west not to Chicago but to Wisconsin, where John
was stationed. They stopped at Detroit, which Juliette found picturesque: "The quaint and venerable mansion of the Governor stood,
as did many another, delightful, old-fashioned residence, a little
below the town, on the banks of the broad, beautiful river." Detroit
had some of the familiar trappings of an established city, including
government buildings, hotels, churches, and schools. Steamships
came and went, and streets were "filled with officers in uniform,
the ladies in their most fashionable attire; humbler citizens in their
holiday garb."[18]

After a time, Juliette and John boarded a small steamship headed
west. Few American women traveled this route, which more often
carried government officials and military officers. The ship made
a brief stop at Mackinac Island, where Juliette met many of the
people who had been so important to John during his indenture
with the American Fur Company, including Mr. and Mrs. Robert
Stuart. As they left the island, Juliette was moved by the new can-
vas before her, where "there was no sign of living habitation along
that vast and wooded shore." At Green Bay, in what is now Wisconsin, John and Juliette transferred their most precious possessions,
including her piano, into a smaller boat. The last leg of the journey
to Fort Winnebago was up the Fox River.[19]

Arriving in Portage, Juliette set to housekeeping in what she
saw as a wilderness. There were few options for accommodations at
Fort Winnebago. Initially they accepted two large rooms in the officers' quarters adjacent to the commander, Major David E. Twiggs,
and his wife, Elizabeth. The rooms were furnished with large, un-

wieldy pieces, but John and Juliette were grateful to have them. They lightheartedly named an enormous wardrobe in the apartment the "Davis" after Jefferson Davis, the young lieutenant who had built the ungainly pieces.[20]

With the help of servants and extended family, Juliette tried to create a home that met eastern standards. She unpacked her trunks, sewed her carpets together, and cooked the first of many meals in her own home. Juliette kept a tally of what was in her storeroom at any moment; she was always looking for foods for her household. Because supplies were often short at Portage, she had brought barrels of eggs and butter as well as salt pork and flour. In Detroit she had preserved fruits and meats to bring west.

There was no Indian Agency House at Fort Winnebago when John and Juliette arrived, but they had been promised a congressional appropriation for a new dwelling. Unfortunately, repeated requests to Congress went unanswered, and the arrival of new officers at the fort left them scrambling. John and Juliette first moved into an old log barracks, but the structure leaked, and Juliette resorted to "wearing my straw bonnet throughout the day." When funding for a blacksmith's house was approved, the bachelor holding that post let the Kinzies have it.[21]

Workmen came from Prairie du Chien to build the house—with a parlor and two bedrooms on the ground floor and two chambers under the roof as well as a separate log kitchen. It was not large, but it seemed "quite a palace" after the leaky barracks. Before work on the house had proceeded very far, however, John had to travel to Detroit. He expected construction to be on hold while he was away, but Juliette challenged the workers to finish the job. When he returned, John was surprised but delighted to find the building completed.

When Congress finally authorized funds for an agency house at Portage, John and Juliette planned an even more substantial building. Craftsmen came from distant St. Louis, and lumber and brick for fireplaces had to be transported long distances to a hilltop overlooking the Fox River outside Fort Winnebago. The high ceilings, plastered walls, gracious fireplaces, and staircase all showed close attention to detail. The large windows let in light, and a substantial entry hall served as a waiting room for those on agency business. The parlor and dining room were painted and wallpapered. At the rear was a large kitchen where the hearth included an oven, so the family was able to bake bread and cakes. Upstairs were two large bedrooms with fireplaces and two smaller ones. Although it was expensive, John noted that "the house is well built, the work inside is plain and substantial and very convenient for a family." Juliette was house-proud and filled it with the furniture, wall hangings, carpets, knickknacks, china, and books that she had purchased in Boston, New York, and Detroit.[22]

Juliette needed servants to maintain this household to her standards. She made several "fruitless attempts" at hiring before leaving the East, then tried at Detroit and again at Green Bay to find a "servant-woman" willing to accompany her to Portage. The commander at Fort Winnebago, who was originally from Georgia, offered Juliette the services of Louisa, "a young colored girl" in his household. Although Juliette seldom, if ever, used the word "slave," it is likely that Louisa was enslaved. Indeed, US Army officers regularly brought enslaved people into free regions like the Northwest Territory. Juliette did not object to bringing slavery into her home, but she found Louisa "irregular and unmanageable," especially when she refused to take religious instruction and to sit quietly with the family on Sundays.[23]

After a time another servant "from the South" joined the household. Harry, "a Negro boy" (whose age was not clear), was "transferred" from the Kinzie household in Chicago to John Kinzie in Portage. Juliette wrote that when Harry came to Illinois from Kentucky, his "position became somewhat changed—he could be no more than an indentured servant." That is, on moving into the Northwest Territory, where slavery was prohibited, enslaved people like Harry were coerced into signing lifetime indentures that kept them bound to their old masters. Thus Harry reported that he still

Fig. 5 The Indian Agency House in Portage, Wisconsin, was completed under the direction of John and Juliette Kinzie in 1832. Owned today by the National Society of Colonial Dames of America, the building has been on the National Register of Historic Places since 1972. Photo by Betsy Keating.

"felt as if he belonged, in a measure, to Master John." Bondage and subservience were difficult to root out.[24]

The métis men and women who lived and worked in the trading outposts of the western Great Lakes region made up another pool of servants. Language, customs, and dress all distinguished them from Americans from the East Coast or even those like John Kinzie who had grown up in Indian country. Eventually Juliette replaced the recalcitrant Louisa with a "tidy, active little French servant" who was the métis wife of one of John's assistants. Juliette also brought the young daughter of Archange and Antoine Ouilmette, who had long been neighbors of the Kinzie family at Chicago, as a "little *bound-girl*." Josette was only ten, but she helped in the household, and Juliette provided her with a rudimentary education.[25]

Having made a home, Juliette set about creating a life familiar to "a true daughter of New England." She provided her household with food, clothing, bedding, and other necessities. She brought with her knitting work, embroidery, pencils, paper, and of course books. Sitting in her parlor, with her furniture and tools, she did many of the same things she would have done in Connecticut. Yet here there was no local Episcopal congregation for services and fellowship; Juliette made do with her prayer book. She later remembered being "cheered by the consolations of this precious book in the midst of the lonely wilderness."[26]

Nor were there schools or formal entertainments. Instead, the families of the officers at Fort Winnebago became companions and confidants, sharing the hardships of life at the remote garrison. Elizabeth Twiggs, wife of the commander, became a close friend. They soon created "the happiest little circle imaginable . . . although far away in the wilderness." The wife of another officer at the fort remembered weekly musicals at the Kinzie home as well as horseback rides through the countryside.[27]

A Ho-Chunk World

Juliette learned much about life in what she saw as the "wilderness" simply by watching her husband work. John conducted business from a room in their house, so Ho-Chunk representatives were regularly in the hall waiting to see him. Juliette did not even have to leave her home to learn a great deal, and she was a most interested observer.

John was responsible for US relations with the Ho-Chunk along the Fox River, just as Alexander Wolcott served among the Potawatomi at Chicago. As agents, they controlled when and where annuity payments were made as well as tribal access to the federal government more broadly. John Kinzie was the face of the federal government to the Ho-Chunk on the Fox River. In Wisconsin it was a particularly fraught time to be that representative as the US government sought more and more land cessions from Indians, who grew more hostile to the American presence as the pressure grew. Also, President Andrew Jackson had recently signed the 1830 Indian Removal Act that made the forced relocation of Indians east of the Mississippi national policy, signaling even more changes to come.[28]

Often US agents were appointed who had little knowledge or understanding of life in Indian country. This had been true for Juliette's uncle at Chicago, but it was not so for her husband, who had deep knowledge of regional Indian culture. Growing up, young John learned to speak with, and listen to, the many Potawatomi, Miami, and Odawa men and women who came to his father's fur trading outpost or to Fort Dearborn and the nearby Agency House. John's intense interest in Indian languages and customs had also been stoked by the experiences of his mother, Eleanor. She had been taken captive by the Seneca in western Pennsylvania during the Revolutionary War and had "so completely learned their language and customs as to have forgotten her own." Later John had encounters with a wide range of Indians from the western Great Lakes region during his time at Mackinac.[29]

By the time he was stationed at Portage, John had mastered the Ho-Chunk language—part of the Siouan language group and quite different from the Algonquian dialects he had learned as a youth. He compiled a dictionary of the Ho-Chunk language that was organized by parts of speech. It also contained the "words and music to several songs," indicating his interest in understanding the broader culture and outlook of the Ho-Chunk. He shared his knowledge with Juliette, who was eager to learn.[30]

The Ho-Chunk were linked by language to western tribes, but by the time John and Juliette encountered them, they were encircled by Menominee to the north, Potawatomi to the east and south, and Sauk to the west. The Ho-Chunk around Portage were farmers, raising corn, beans, and squash. They also collected wild rice and tapped sugar maples, hunted for beaver and other game, and fished the local waters. Women were farmers and gatherers while men were hunters and warriors. They lived in matrilineal villages of 100 to 150 people, in wigwams generally larger than those of their Algonquian neighbors. Across most of the seventeenth and eighteenth centuries, the Ho-Chunk had regular interactions with Europeans through trade, missionary activity, and marriage. They had integrated into their daily life goods traded for furs, including tobacco, kettles, needles, knives, weapons, and cloth. Indeed, they were dependent on these trade goods, and the US government used this dependency to help gain land cessions.[31]

Juliette did not just experience living in this world; she made careful observations of what she saw. She was finally experiencing what she had only read and heard about. There is no record that she took notes about the people, places, and events she saw in Wisconsin, but *Wau-Bun*, the book about these experiences that she published more than twenty years later, is filled with very specific stories.

Told in the first person, the vivid stories that Juliette related about Wisconsin in the 1830s are very much a memoir, a primary source about her experiences. She augmented her written description with a series of drawings of the rivers, forests, and lakes that were the setting of her adventures. Her descriptions show a reliance on her husband's deep knowledge of Ho-Chunk culture. The couple shared an empathetic eye for describing Ho-Chunk individuals and their broader culture.

Among the first Ho-Chunk Juliette met were the ones who had traveled east with her husband. She had heard a great deal about Naw-Kaw and Day-kau-ray. Now she met them as individuals who had moods and opinions and interjected themselves into her life. Juliette got to know Cut-Nose (Elizabeth), a daughter of Day-kau-ray who had married a Mus-qua-kee man who came to live with her family according to Ho-Chunk customs. When Cut-Nose refused to move to her husband's tribal home along the Mississippi River, he mutilated her face and left her. By the time Juliette met her, she was an older woman suffering from rheumatism. Juliette was most sympathetic to her story and offered a remedy that "afforded her almost entire relief." In thanks, Cut-Nose brought her a fawn that Juliette kept as a pet.[32]

Juliette also met Mrs. Washington, who had accompanied her husband to the White House as part of the 1828 delegation. She "had a pleasant old-acquaintance sort of air in greeting me," Juliette wrote, "as much as to say 'you and I have seen something of the world.'" She sometimes visited with Juliette at her home with other Ho-Chunk women. On one occasion Juliette proudly served some freshly made crullers over which she had grated a "goodly quantity of white sugar." The women took the cakes but would not eat them; they thought the sugar was salt. Juliette did not know her guests were familiar only with brown sugar; one of her Ho-Chunk guests bravely tasted the cakes, bridging the cultural divide.[33]

Juliette slowly became attuned to the everyday life of these women as they gathered rice and made rush matting for the floors of their homes while older women watched children and took care of dogs. Juliette later wrote with an ethnographic eye about their clothing, foodways, child rearing, and other housekeeping practices. She was fascinated by the unfamiliar division of work among men and women. For instance, she was surprised that when the Ho-Chunk set up camp, "the master of the family, as a general thing, came leisurely, while the woman, with the mats and poles of her lodge upon her shoulders, [carried] her papoose, if she had one, her kettles, sacks of corn, and wild rice." Juliette came to see that ideas about gender roles and even "women's rights" were bound by culture as much as biology.[34]

Religion and education were subjects Juliette observed closely. Feeling keenly the lack of institutions, she sought a missionary to minister to the garrison. However, she was less sanguine about missionary activity in Indian country. Juliette noted the divisiveness that Catholic and Protestant missionaries created within the trading centers. Nor was she convinced that missionizing among the Ho-Chunk would be successful: "As a general thing, they do not appear to perceive that there is anything to be gained, by adopting the religion and custom of the whites."[35]

Missionaries often established schools that would "civilize" Indian children. Juliette respected Day-kau-ray's perspective: "We think that if the Great Spirit had wished us to be like the whites, he would have made us so." He did not send his children for a missionary education. Nor did Juliette rebut Day-kau-ray's view, even in her private writing, seeming to recognize the ethnocentrism of mission work.[36]

Very few American women ventured into Indian country, and even fewer had the time or talent to write about it. Juliette's time with Emma Willard and her enchantment with her uncle's letters prepared her to be a most thoughtful observer. John Kinzie also fostered a sympathetic, personal view of their Ho-Chunk neighbors, sharing his deep knowledge with his wife. On talking with the couple in later years, a traveler noted that they "are the only persons I have met with who, really knowing the Indians, had any regard for them."[37]

Juliette and John Kinzie witnessed the US government's expropriation of vast tracts of Indian country east of the Mississippi. Indeed, John was an active participant as the Ho-Chunk ceded substantial tracts of their lands between 1829 and 1833 while he was their agent. But the couple were unlike many Americans who saw westward expansion as destiny, with tribes divesting "themselves of portions of their territory by their own free will." They did not believe these transactions were made possible by "God in his providence"; they criticized treaty negotiations where liquor and debt unduly influenced deliberations. The couple worried that future generations would judge whether the "foundations of an empire" thus laid would "prove stable and sure."[38]

This is not to say that Juliette and John did not embrace the superiority of American culture. When a visiting Ho-Chunk friend "borrowed" a conch shell from their parlor, Juliette was deeply disappointed, blaming her friend because "she was partly civilized and knew better." That is, the Ho-Chunk woman was familiar with American customs, exposed to "civilization." She knew the correct manner of behavior and could be judged more harshly. However, in a later work of fiction, Juliette seems more equivocal. A US official impatiently looked forward to a time "when the whole of our magnificent country will be open to the footprints of civilization" and "the bloodthirsty savages who now so fearfully jeopardize their lives and property can be transferred to some far remote region." In response, a young métis woman responded: "Savages? Bloodthirsty? And who sir, made them such?" Juliette questioned whether "a judgement is not perhaps laid in store" for her American countrymen for "all the injustice permitted" against "a people to whom the gentler arts of life could in time have been taught."[39]

Change at Chicago

While John and Juliette were settling into Portage, Chicago was emerging as a center for American ambitions. The opening of the Erie Canal in 1825 dramatically expanded the range of migrants into the western Great Lakes region. The election of President Andrew Jackson had strengthened the United States' reach into the Indian country remaining east of the Mississippi River. Land became real estate as speculators and settlers indulged a seemingly insatiable thirst for property.

In treaties from 1795 to 1816, the US government had demanded a corridor of land from the mouth of the Chicago River at Lake Michigan southwest to the Illinois River. In 1827 it granted the state of Illinois land along the proposed canal route.[40] Two years later the Illinois legislature appointed a commission to survey and sell land to finance construction of the Illinois and Michigan Canal. The planned canal heightened the importance of Chicago, since it would link the Great Lakes to the Mississippi River. The Erie Canal had cut the travel times from New York City to Chicago by two-thirds, from six weeks to two weeks; this canal would work similar magic with space and time.

In 1830, the year Juliette married and came west, the canal commissioners hired James Thompson, a St. Louis surveyor, to survey the northern endpoint at Chicago. No individuals could own land until this first plat was done, leading one historian to suggest that the map marked "the beginning of Chicago as a geographical locality."[41] Real estate became the base for Chicago's growth. The river was squarely in the center of the plat, only three-eighths of a mile square. The original survey did not reach the lake. Kinzie and Madison Streets served as the northern and southern boundaries, with State Street to the east and Des Plaines Avenue to the west. That first plat set out basic characteristics of Chicago: the grid that defines the city began here. James Thompson laid out streets sixty-six feet wide that remain today.[42]

Those who lived within the initial plat purchased lots for property they had long claimed but not owned. Those who lived outside the initial plat could make a preemptive claim of 160 acres with the federal government. The homes of Alexander and Ellen Wolcott and the Kinzie family were outside the initial plat, and both families made such claims. These land sales represented a monumental transfer of resources (and wealth) from Indians to the US government and then quickly to individual American families. The Wolcott and Kinzie families gained this land simply by being in place at the time of the initial sale.

Alexander Wolcott made one of the first real estate purchases beyond the Thompson plat in September 1830: Block One on the north side of the river, which included the property under the US Agency House. Soon the Kinzie family claimed over 100 acres of land just east of Wolcott's property and outside the canal lands. Juliette's mother-in-law, Eleanor, pressed her son Robert to claim the full 160 acres that the law allowed. Robert replied, "Mother, we have just got over 102 acres—more than we shall ever want, or know what to do with."[43] Soon the Kinzie and Wolcott families together owned most of the land along the north side of the Chicago River from the lakefront to the north branch of the river.

Both families had anticipated Chicago's rise. Long before his death in 1828, John's father had "foretold its eventual prosperity and importance."[44] Alexander Wolcott, a later arrival, was also an early booster. As Indian agent, he had carefully monitored the federal government's moves in the region and made a preemptive claim as soon as he could. Wolcott was positioned to be a leading figure as Chicago. Unfortunately, within weeks of his return from southern Illinois, where he had registered his land claim, Juliette's uncle was taken mortally ill with some contagion, perhaps typhus. In a matter of days, Wolcott, his two young children, and several other Chicago residents had died, throwing "a gloom over all the different branches of the social circle."[45]

John Kinzie hurried to Chicago without Juliette, though she desperately wanted to accompany him. He felt he needed to move as quickly as possible to comfort his sister and mother. Alone in Portage, Juliette accepted her husband's decision, but "sad and dreary were the hours of his absence, notwithstanding the kind efforts of our friends to cheer me." Just married, filled with plans to join her extended family in the west, she felt this death as a deep blow. Decades later, Juliette wrote about this sad time in *Wau-Bun*, mourning the loss of "that noble heart, so full of warm and kindly affections."[46]

Months later Juliette finally made her first visit to Chicago. In March 1831 she and John traveled overland on frozen paths through Wisconsin. Across five chapters of *Wau-Bun*, she chronicled their experiences as well as her first impressions of Chicago and its residents. Juliette also drew sketches of places they saw besides Chicago, which would be included as engravings in her 1856 book.

As Juliette remembered, "Chicago was not, at the period of my first visit, the cheerful, happy place it had once been" because of the death of her uncle and other residents. It must have been extremely disconcerting to visit in these circumstances the settlement that had long been the center of her romantic attraction to the west. Juliette stayed in Chicago for two months, and she found the weather matched the gloomy mood set by her uncle's death: "inclement and stormy . . . only twice, during a period of two months, did the sun shine out through the entire day."[47]

Even though land sales were under way, what Juliette saw on this first visit looked very much like the little community her uncle had described in his letters. Chicago remained a métis trading community where mostly mixed-race families lived in houses that "sprawled in seeming disorder" and "followed the meanderings of the river's branches, rather than sitting smartly in neat platted rows." Real estate and landownership were still abstractions. There was no indication of the grid of streets created by the Thompson plat and little sense that the property claims of the Kinzie and Wolcott families would amount to much anytime soon. Even the most substantial structure except the fort, the Sauganash Hotel, sat in the middle of one of the newly platted streets because its proprietor, Mark Beaubien, "didn't expect no town."[48]

Only about one hundred people lived outside Fort Dearborn. Juliette found the settlement "remarkably free of institutional trappings associated with American town life," such as churches, schools, or newspapers. Business took place at the fort or in a few taverns, but mostly within households. A tight network of kin and neighbors took responsibility for the care and protection of its residents.

Life at Chicago was very foreign to Juliette, but still she enjoyed her stay. She remembered horseback riding through woods on the north side of the Chicago River. She described the "thick boughs" along the makeshift bridle path, where "projecting branches of the shrubs impeded [their] path." Just a short distance away from the main stem of the river, there were no streets or even clearly used routes. She was taken with firing a pistol, something that had not been part of her everyday life. Juliette was less impressed with a rather disheveled itinerant Methodist preacher who mangled his words and seemingly did not hold with the maxim that "cleanliness is a part of holiness"; she stayed home at the US Agency House rather than attending more of his services.[49]

Juliette spent much of her time at Chicago getting to know her mother-in-law, Eleanor Kinzie, who enthralled her with stories of her years with the Seneca. Eleanor also regaled Juliette with stories of the Battle of Fort Dearborn and early life at Chicago. All of this helped her to know better her new family and the world she had entered. During these cold, wet spring months of 1831, Juliette heard many of the stories that would become the basis of her work as a Chicago historian. Her 1844 account of Chicago history was based on Eleanor's recollections, as was the later *Wau-Bun*.[50]

Eleanor Kinzie's focus on early Chicago history may have been sharpened by the family's imminent departure from the place. Alexander Wolcott had made the US Agency House at Chicago the center for extended family, but with his death the "family circle was to be broken up." His widow, Ellen Wolcott, moved to Detroit, while John's mother, stepsister, and young nephew moved to Portage to live with him and Juliette. Juliette helped her mother-in-law pack up after nearly thirty years in Chicago. John's younger brother, Robert, was the only immediate family member who remained at Chicago.[51]

Juliette's extended family had also lost its anchor at Chicago. Juliette's parents, as well as her half-sister Frances and Frances's husband, Hiram Higby, were in the process of moving from upstate New York to northeastern Illinois when Alexander Wolcott died. Without him, Chicago was no longer the new western home they had envisioned. Instead, both the Kinzies and the Magills looked to John and Juliette, who had a stable position and a home, to succeed Alexander as the head of their families. John and Juliette welcomed everyone in Portage, including various cousins from Detroit and St. Louis, at what Juliette remembered as the "little india-rubber house . . . [that] contrived to expand itself" with every new inhabitant. Also, John's sister Maria moved to nearby Fort Howard (Green Bay) after her husband, Lieutenant David Hunter, was transferred from Fort Dearborn.[52] With John's help, Juliette's brother Arthur took a position in the fur trade at Green Bay, which allowed him to visit Portage regularly in his travels. Julian, Juliette's youngest brother, then nine or ten, came to live at Portage, and Arthur and Frances Magill made plans to join their children there.[53] Their outpost in Indian country was now the center of a large extended family.

The Black Hawk War

While Kinzies and Magills moved toward Portage, more American settlers streamed into the Chicago region. They claimed land and began farming fields that had long been cultivated by Indian women. Although Ho-Chunk, Potawatomi, and Sauk had ceded these lands to the US government in treaties, for decades they had continued to farm, hunt, and maintain traditional villages there. The arrival of American farmers brought conflict as some Indians tried to hold fast to lands that had been taken from them in often questionable circumstances. In spring 1832, conflicts escalated when the Sauk warrior Black Hawk and more than a thousand men, women, and children returned to Saukenuk, their summer village and farm fields on the east side of the Mississippi River near what is now Rock Island. Violence ensued when they found American settlers farming fields that had been theirs. Militia groups from across Illinois, including one led by Abraham Lincoln, organized to support American settlers at Saukenuk. The US Army also quickly mobilized a force under General Winfield Scott. When the Sauk tried to surrender, they were fired on, and Black Hawk's contingent fled farther north into Wisconsin, to territory still held by the Ho-Chunk.[54]

John Kinzie acted quickly, trying to keep the Ho-Chunk under his agency from joining Black Hawk. John hoped his presence among the Ho-Chunk would "act as a restraint upon them." He went from village to village, trying to persuade Ho-Chunk leaders to remain neutral. Most needed little persuasion, knowing how disastrous war could be for their people. Indeed, only one of the warriors who had traveled east with John supported Black Hawk.[55]

However, the threat of a wider alliance among the Ho-Chunk galvanized the US Army units at Fort Winnebago and Fort Howard. John thought his family should leave Portage and take refuge at Fort Howard. Juliette objected, but later she remembered, "It was in vain that I pleaded to be permitted to remain." This was not the first or the last time that Juliette would submit to the will of her husband despite strong feelings to the contrary. Her obedience was not silent; John's decisions did not go unchallenged. Yet John thought Juliette needed to be removed to safety: by July 1832 she was three months pregnant.[56]

John arranged for Juliette and his family to travel to Green Bay accompanied by his brother-in-law Lieutenant David Hunter. They journeyed along the Fox River in an open boat that John had fitted up. The group arrived safely but found Fort Howard in an uproar over the threat of cholera and rumors that Black Hawk lurked nearby. As Juliette recalled it, they seemed trapped by "the savage foe on the one hand and the pestilence on the other!"[57]

So when Juliette received word from her husband that Black Hawk had crossed the Wisconsin River well to the south of Portage, she quickly arranged to return home without consulting him. This was a pattern over the course of their long marriage. Juliette seldom directly crossed her husband, but she often operated independently during his frequent absences. The group did not encounter any hostile Ho-Chunk on their return to Portage, but their boat capsized over rapids in the Fox River. When they finally arrived at Fort Winnebago, "a more happy or thankful party has seldom been assembled."[58]

The formal end of what came to be known as the Black Hawk War came on August 2, 1832, when several hundred Sauk men, women, and children were killed at the Battle of Bad Axe. Those who survived the attack by US forces faced Sioux warriors across the Mississippi. Only about 150 of the original band survived, including Black Hawk, who was captured and taken to Prairie du Chien. Soon after, John accompanied Ho-Chunk chiefs to meet with government officials at Rock Island. They agreed to open negotiations for lands east and south of the Wisconsin River—what would become known as the 1833 Treaty of Chicago. The Ho-Chunk quickly lost control of much of the land they had held for generations. John was sympathetic to their plight but nevertheless helped to expropriate their land.[59]

While hundreds of men, women, and children died in the

battles, many more succumbed to cholera and starvation. Cholera, a highly contagious waterborne disease, was greatly feared because death often came within hours of symptoms that included cramps, diarrhea, and vomiting. The epidemic came to Detroit and Chicago on ships with American troops. When Juliette learned that cholera had arrived along the Mississippi River at Rock Island, she worried because her husband was there. John did indeed contract the disease on his journey home, but he was nursed back to health by friends among the French trading community.[60]

Hunger remained a longer-term threat. The war with the Sauk had disrupted the regular planting and harvesting seasons, leaving many Ho-Chunk villages with little or no food in the fall of 1832 and winter of 1833. The people had to rely on food distributed by John Kinzie on behalf of the US government, which was very slow in coming. Although Juliette carefully collected "every remaining particle of food" after their meals "to be given to some of the wretched applicants," there was not nearly enough to provide for all in need. Her Ho-Chunk neighbors felt betrayed by the government that John and Juliette represented. Juliette took to keeping her doors and windows shut, but her neighbors' "wretched faces would peer in above, to watch us." One day Juliette saw the "pretty daughter" of a Ho-Chunk elder appear at her window. The young woman "did not beg, but her countenance spoke volumes."[61]

In January 1833, in the midst of this suffering, Juliette gave birth to Alexander Wolcott (Sandie) Kinzie. After his birth, Ho-Chunk mothers that Juliette knew rushed in when a door opened and "grasp[ed] the hand of my infant . . . imploring 'his little brother' for food." One young Ho-Chunk woman, Agatha-Tomah, who had recently lost her own child, came to congratulate Juliette on Sandie's birth. When Agatha-Tomah looked at him, "she spoke some little words of tenderness, which showed that her heart was full." Juliette could not help but cry for the losses of her Ho-Chunk friend.[62] What should have been a most happy moment was marred by the awful suffering around them. Not until early spring did additional food supplies for the Ho-Chunk reach Portage.

All during this long winter, the Kinzies and their neighbors tried to assess the future. The Ho-Chunk who lived south along the Rock River moved northward, closer to Portage, as their lands were ceded. They made new villages along the west bank of the Wisconsin River about twenty to thirty miles south of Portage, as well as along the Baraboo River. Because of this, John Kinzie expected his outpost to become a permanent full agency, serving the long-term needs of the Ho-Chunk. The new Agency House was a significant marker of the presence of the United States in the region and bolstered John's expectations. But Juliette was haunted by the suffering the Ho-Chunk women and children around her had endured. The west was no longer simply a romantic vision—it was also a miserable, dangerous place.[63]

3
....

Property

The year 1833 marked a crossroads for John and Juliette Kinzie. John, at thirty, had a deep familiarity with the Indian country of the western Great Lakes region. He knew the land and traveled with ease in a world without established transportation systems and routes. He knew more than a dozen Indian languages and had close relationships with many Ho-Chunk, Potawatomi, and Odawa people. His immediate supervisor, Michigan territorial governor George Porter, described John as "one of the most valuable men in the Indian Department."[1]

Juliette was a woman of twenty-seven who had spent most of her life in the East, but she was no longer naive and untested. She had lived more than two years in Indian country, giving birth to her first child and surviving the Black Hawk War. Her husband had been absent a great deal, and Juliette had proved her mettle by not just enduring but thriving in trying circumstances. Now she lived with her extended family in a substantial new house in Ho-Chunk country. The west was no longer an imagined world; it was her home, filled with all life's suffering and joy.

Juliette and John were not movers and shakers who shaped the economy and public policy. Instead, they led one of many families looking to improve their circumstances, weighing whether to stay and put down roots or move on to seek new opportunities. Individually, any one of their decisions did not change the course of history, but taken together their story is indeed that of the United States, not from the top down or the bottom up, but from the middle.

The region they lived in was on the brink of momentous change, moving from Indian country to American territory. Setting a course for the future during this unsettled time was not simple, but they had more options than their Ho-Chunk and métis neighbors, who would increasingly be forced to move west of the Mississippi River. Initially John and Juliette looked to improve their situation while staying in Portage. John hoped that a full agency (not just a subagency) would be established at Fort Winnebago. The attendant promotion not only would increase his responsibilities and prestige, it would also nearly double his salary to over $1,000 a year. Being a full agent also had particular meaning for John, since his father had made an unsuccessful attempt to be promoted from subagent to agent at Chicago.[2]

Governor Porter endorsed the plan to promote John; all that was needed was the approval of Secretary of War Lewis Cass, who knew John personally. But Cass was a stalwart ally of President Jackson and the Democratic Party, while John supported the Whig Party. As Juliette later commented about Secretary Cass, "All the world knows how chary his exertions [are] in behalf of those who are not of his political creed." And John's uncle Thomas Forsyth, dismissed from his longtime post as Indian agent to the Sauk for criticizing President Jackson's Indian policy, could no longer help his nephew. The proposed promotion did not come through.[3]

Instead, Governor Porter offered John the post of subagent and interpreter at Detroit, a well-established town where he had family and political connections. Moving to Detroit would let John continue to use the knowledge and skills he had honed in Indian country while removing his family from danger. Juliette was not unhappy with this prospect, since she had found Detroit "picturesque and attractive . . . genial, refined." Her Magill relatives were eager for her to leave Wisconsin; Juliette's father encouraged them to move to the "better climate at Detroit and a little nearer the center of the earth."[4]

Toward Chicago

Juliette joined her parents in Detroit in 1833, along with several Kinzie family members, but it was only a temporary stop "while making arrangements for a permanent settlement at Chicago." When John's family packed up all their "heavy articles" and left Chicago in 1831, there was one possession they could not take with them: the real estate they had claimed.[5]

Decisions made in Washington, DC, and in New York reshaped the direction of John and Juliette's lives. With the end of the Black Hawk War, the federal government eyed the survey and sale of vast lands in the region. In Chicago, already the endpoint for the proposed Illinois and Michigan Canal, the General Land Office had begun selling property after the 1830 Thompson survey. Additionally, the federal government began harbor improvements to the Chicago River at a time when other proposed western projects languished.[6]

Related to these federal moves, powerful New York investors focused on Chicago. General Winfield Scott, on his return to New York from the Black Hawk War, noted that "Chicago stood at a critical location for trade in the new country." He shared his positive assessment with wealthy New Yorkers like John Jacob Astor and Daniel Jackson, who knew the west from their involvement in the fur trade and more recently in real estate speculation in Ohio, Michigan, and Indiana. Arthur Bronson, whose father had been an investor with Astor, hoped to make his fortune in the booming real estate market in Chicago and its hinterland.[7]

Bronson met the Kinzie and Wolcott families in 1833. Soon after the birth of Juliette's first child, her mother-in-law journeyed to New York City, accompanied by her younger son, Robert, seeking treatment for a facial cancer that western doctors had been unable to cure. In New York she consulted physicians recommended by her sister-in-law Alice Haliburton, part of a wealthy New York family. Through his aunt, Robert Kinzie gained access to powerful circles of investors. At some club, reception, or parlor, he and Arthur Bronson met. Bronson, eager for information about Chicago real estate and its prospects, expressed an interest in purchasing some of the Kinzie family lands for as much as $5,500.[8]

Stunned by the sum, Robert quickly wrote to his brother John about Bronson's interest in their unsurveyed land. John traveled to Chicago in February 1833, accompanied by his brother-in-law Lieutenant David Hunter, who controlled the adjoining parcel that Alexander Wolcott had initially purchased. They turned to surveyor Joshua Hathaway Jr., a new arrival in Chicago, to plat what became known as Kinzie's Addition. John Kinzie paid for the work and walked the ground with the surveyor, who laid out the lots and streets that turned the claim into real estate. The Kinzie family could now sell lots to investors like Bronson.[9]

It is ironic that western real estate would draw the Kinzie family out of the orbit of Indian country. Juliette lamented the treaties that divested the Indians of their "council-fires, and graves, and hunting-grounds . . . compelled to accept some remote, desolate tract, too worthless to tempt the white man."[10] But it was through such treaties that her family came to own a central parcel of land at Chicago. Their long tenure in Chicago would rest on this paradox—uneasy, but quintessentially American. Not only were John and Juliette Kinzie choosing to move from Indian country to an American world, their decision also shaped the work John would do in the future. His deep knowledge of the Ho-Chunk and Potawatomi would be only marginally useful in this American financial world. As much as John knew about Indians, he knew little about American business and its risks. He had never been an entrepreneur, nor had he worked outside Indian country.

In 1833 these two worlds were shoulder to shoulder at Chicago, so at first John did not so much abandon his work in Indian country as add real estate speculation to his activities. After supervising the survey of Kinzie's Addition, he stayed in Chicago to prepare for the treaty negotiations that would officially end the Black Hawk War. He moved into the US Agency House, long the home of Alexander Wolcott, making improvements in anticipation of the dozens of officials and thousands of Potawatomi and their allies expected in late summer.[11]

Meanwhile Arthur Bronson journeyed to Chicago, accompanied by fellow New York investor Charles Butler. John welcomed them and shared his recent survey. Bronson purchased two lots abutting the Chicago River for $700. This was more than John's salary for the entire previous year, when he had risked life and limb during the Black Hawk War.[12]

Shortly after Bronson and Butler left Chicago, more than six thousand Potawatomi and their allies arrived for negotiations with the US government. John had a full house for weeks during the deliberations. By the treaty the Potawatomi and their allies ceded five million acres that included much of northern Illinois and southern Wisconsin. The Potawatomi in the Chicago area agreed to move west of the Mississippi River. The treaty also included a large payout (more than $175,000) to non-Indians with claims against the Potawatomi and their allies. John, his mother, and his siblings each received $5,000 to resolve claims that dated to the War of 1812. Coupled with the sale of their lands over the next few years, the Kinzie family amassed wealth quickly on the transition from Indian country to American territory.[13]

During most of 1833 Juliette and her young son lived in Detroit, surrounded by Kinzie and Magill relatives, including Juliette's parents. When John's mother, Eleanor, died in New York early in 1834, Juliette and her mother traveled east with one-year-old Sandie and ten-year-old Julian, Juliette's youngest brother, on a trip that included a "splendid large steamer" and a difficult stagecoach ride. After a visit to Middletown, they made their way to New York City, where John joined them.[14] Together they attended to Eleanor's affairs as well as to Chicago business.

While in New York, John and Juliette arranged publication of a map of Kinzie's Addition. On Bronson's urging, John commissioned Peter A. Meisner to create a lithograph of Hathaway's survey. *Chicago with the School Section, Wabansia, and Kinzie's Addition*, the first published map of Chicago, provided a graphic representation of their hopeful dreams. The colored map included the original 1830 plat, the federal holdings around Fort Dearborn, the large school section set aside to fund public education, a small triangular subdivision just north of the juncture of the branches of the Chicago River, and Kinzie's Addition. The map was made on six kinds of paper including individual sheets, on rollers and in leather cases. The intention was not only to sell lots in Kinzie's Addition but to promote Chicago as a whole.[15]

The couple sent the printed map to potential investors and boosters; John wrote to one, "[My] wife sends you a plat of our section." They left copies with Arthur Bronson to pass along "to persons who will feel an interest in the growth and prosperity" of Chicago. David Hunter shared prints with his New Jersey family and their wealthy friends. They also sent a lithograph to US secretary of war Cass. Finally, John and Juliette took copies of the map back to Chicago, where they advertised its availability in the *Chicago Democrat*, noting that it was "beautifully executed."[16]

All these efforts brought Chicago and its prospects to the attention of a national audience. The high quality of the printed map suggested a promising future for the town. Boosters and speculators poured into Chicago. John noted that the town had "become of late a place of great notoriety—property immensely valuable and great sales made within the last fortnight." As Bronson and other easterners purchased property from the Kinzie family and others, John rose quickly as one of Chicago's leading businessmen. He was elected to serve as the second town president, building a wharf, warehouse, and store.[17]

Although married women did not have the right to buy and sell

Fig. 6 *Chicago with the School Section, Wabansia, and Kinzie's Addition* (1834) is based on a survey commissioned by John H. Kinzie and completed by Joshua Hathaway Jr. This was the first published map of Chicago, printed in New York City by Peter Meisner for John H. Kinzie. Chicago Historical Society, Newberry Library, Graff 1817.

property in most states, Juliette was closely involved in her husband's investments. She wrote letters that he signed and made copies of deeds and other documents. Years later Juliette remembered minute details of specific transactions. John recognized her as an important part of his real estate business. He saw himself as the representative of a household rather than as an individual operating in business and society.[18]

Juliette's keen recollection of real estate transactions also rested on state law that required wives' acquiescence to the sale of real property that could affect their dower rights, that part of their properties reserved for widows. Indeed, wives did not just give their consent but were interrogated apart from their husbands by an officer of the court.[19] In this process, Juliette interacted with some of the most prominent speculators. Her signature appeared on many transactions between Arthur Bronson and her husband. She came to know Bronson from encounters in law offices and courts as well as in parlors and at receptions. John regularly closed his correspondence with Bronson with social greetings like "Mrs. K joins me in best regards to you and your family." Among the other eastern investors was William Butler Ogden, who came to oversee the interests of his brother-in-law Charles Butler. He became a close neighbor of the Kinzie family.[20]

The 1835 Removal

The arrival of speculators like Ogden was emblematic of a broader demographic shift that accompanied the transformation of Indian lands into real estate. The people who had long called the Chicago region home now found themselves without a place in it. Until 1833 Potawatomi families made up a great proportion of the region's population; just two years later, the US government began a forced removal. In 1835 more than seven hundred Potawatomi men, women, and children walked to reservation lands across the Mississippi River in Iowa. The following year, another thousand people were moved west by government officials. The Potawatomi fields were almost immediately taken up by American settlers, who planted corn.

The small population at Chicago also changed rapidly. When Juliette visited in early 1831, she described a modest métis trading outpost at Fort Dearborn. Many residents—including the Ouilmette, Mirandeau, and Beaubien families—were deeply interrelated with the Potawatomi villages around Chicago. Over generations they had intermarried, melding Indian and Euro-American culture and traditions. They congregated around Wolf Point, at the confluence of the north and south branches of the Chicago River, and maintained a community that valued "harmony . . . leisure . . . hospitality, [and] generosity."[21]

As the Potawatomi were pushed west, the métis residents of Chicago faced their own challenges even though they were not forced to leave. The removal still tore many families apart as well as destroying the fur trade that had been the base of the economy at Chicago. Some, like Jean, Mark, and Madore Beaubien, maneuvered warily through the emerging American economy and society, running taverns, finding government positions, and living on treaty largesse. But most found they were increasingly unwelcome at Chicago, marked as "the miserable race of men" who predated the Americans. They were no longer at home as eastern newcomers sought to make Chicago a great American city.[22] Very quickly, eastern families like the Doles, Newberrys, and Ogdens, as well as Irish, German, and Norwegian immigrants, replaced the Ouilmettes and Beaubiens and the Potawatomi farm families that had long held the region.

The Kinzies held a privileged place in this demographic transformation. They had been a part of the older métis trading culture, but because they were white and descended from the British, not French, colonial world, they had more choices. John Kinzie's marriage to Juliette Magill, a member of an educated New England family, added to the family's legitimacy in the new order. They could become an accepted part of the new American city.

Indeed, the couple were leaders in the "Americanization of early Chicago society," a role that Juliette highlighted in her historical writing as well as in her drawings of those early years.[23] She was well aware of the significance of this moment, later writing ambivalently about the expropriation of Indian lands. However, she displayed neither much interest in nor much sympathy for the passing of the métis society at Chicago. Instead, she deliberately downplayed—and even erased—the presence of earlier families except for the Kinzies. In later years she described her husband and herself as the "grandfather and grandmother of Chicago."[24] In doing so she asserted that the area's history before her arrival had little to do with the city that emerged after 1833.

Chicago's population grew quickly. By 1837 the city had 4,000 residents. The population doubled by 1844, and by 1847, 28,000 people lived there, a sevenfold increase over a decade. Roughly half the migrants were from the Northeast, with almost as many immigrants from Europe.[25] Early on this population skewed young and male, with fewer children and older adults than in eastern communities. It is easy to see why Chicago in the 1830s might be characterized as a man's city.[26] But the migration into Chicago was also shaped by extended families, with women at the center. Even more than in eastern communities during these years, Chicago and other western towns relied on households and the men and women within them. Juliette and John Kinzie, like many other couples, worked in concert to build a life and a community. It was not a man's city after all.

Households, not individuals, negotiated not only the dramatic demographic shift of these years, but also the transformation of land into real estate. While we often think about private ownership as the bedrock of individual rights, real estate ownership also rested on a household world. A household head purchased land and held it not as an individual but as a representative of his family. This was certainly the case for John Kinzie, who worked closely with Juliette during these first years in Chicago. Together with other households, they were creating an American city.

The Kinzie Household

As the young family settled into life at Chicago, John also continued to work as an Indian subagent. The couple went "to considerable expense in repairing and improving" the old Agency House, and "there were pleasant, happy hours passed under its odd-shaped roof." However, the house stood literally "in the street" of the newly platted Wolcott's Addition. Rather than move the house, sometimes called "Cobweb Castle," the family planned a substantial new residence on one of the new streets.[27]

John and Juliette Kinzie built one of the first brick houses on the western edge of their North Side addition. John Van Osdel, an early architect, singled out their home as "one of just a few dwellings that made any pretensions to architectural adornments."[28] The house became a testament to their vision of home as a center for family and civic life. It was a real estate venture, but it was much more. It became the center of a vibrant household world for more than three decades.

As a married woman, Juliette could not purchase this house, but she certainly shaped its design and style. It looked nothing like the Kinzie "mansion" where John and Eleanor Kinzie had lived. Instead, it bore a strong resemblance to the three-story brick federal-style house that Arthur Magill had built in Middletown. Juliette paid minute attention during the construction. Thirty years later, she still remembered how many bricks were used to build it.[29]

The family moved into the house in September 1835, just after the birth of their daughter Eleanor (Nellie) Lytle. It was one of the largest residences in Chicago, with spacious parlors and a dining room, and it remained so for more than a decade. A third story contained bedrooms for family and guests, with additional space in the attic for more family and servants. Nellie remembered that her mother "had a way of making things homelike and attractive" with books, mementos, and china brought from the East as well as newly purchased furniture, carpets, and draperies. For Juliette, setting up the Nunns and Clark piano in her home was a moment of "great joy." It had already endured several moves; now it had a special place in the new parlor.[30]

The family home faced south at the corner of Cass and Michigan Streets, with the home of Robert and Gwinthlean (Gwinney) Kinzie just to the east. As Nellie remembered it, "The two yards, comprising a whole block between them, made a children's paradise. A large green lawn about forty feet deep ran across the front of the garden, with a circular bed filled with flowers in the center." A picket fence ran all around the garden.[31]

They had only a few neighbors, among them William B. Ogden, who built a large house in the center of a four-acre plot a little more than half a mile to the north. Naming the property Ogden's Grove, architect John M. Van Osdel designed a large wooden house that, like the Kinzies' house, featured a long piazza and was surrounded by gardens. Other neighbors soon included attorney Isaac Arnold and Walter Newberry.[32]

Much of what was used within John and Juliette's large household in the 1830s and 1840s was produced at home. Juliette's myriad skills kept costs low as (with the help of servants and family members) she grew and processed food and made clothing. The couple cultivated an extensive kitchen garden and orchard that included plum trees, pears, apples, peaches, apricots, and nectarines along with grape trellises, raspberry bushes, and strawberry beds. They kept chickens and cows, which were left to wander into the neighboring prairie during the day. The property also held a small smokehouse, where the Kinzies cured their own hams and bacon.[33] Most of the time the household had a hired man, responsible for hauling in "great casks" of drinking water from Lake Michigan. He took charge of the Kinzies' horses and cart and did other outdoor tasks including maintaining the icehouse during the winter with frozen blocks taken from the Chicago River.[34]

Like many of their neighbors, John and Juliette were thrifty. John supervised the garden, and Juliette made jams, jellies, syrups, and wines from recipes learned from her mother and her mother-in-law. She and her husband could mend shoes and harnesses.

Juliette explained, "I learned when I was a young girl to make shoes as *an accomplishment*."[35] She made most of her family's clothing, with the periodic help of a seamstress. They sewed everything from undergarments to dresses for Nellie and shirts for John and the boys. Juliette was known for her fine stitches. For their few purchases, she kept a detailed record of household expenses, noting proudly that she knew "every pound of starch or soap—the smallest item that is used in the family and exactly how much."[36]

Juliette maintained an orderly house. She was proud when a visiting relative remarked, "How pleasant it is here . . . you do keep a clean house."[37] Although Juliette had a cook who made the daily meals for the large household, she supervised closely and did much of the baking herself. While her children were small, Juliette also employed a nurse to look after them. She generally had one or two servants who did daily cleaning and serving, depending on the family's income as well as the need. Initially most of these servants lived in rooms under the eaves.

Juliette expected a great deal from servants. She worked long hours alongside them, keeping clothing, cookware, carpets, and curtains clean. Together they whitewashed the house, the interior walls, and the fences. In one of her novels, Juliette described a household in the midst of a "Dutch cleaning" with "carpets hanging upon the fences, chairs, tables, and sofas filling the piazza, or even, for want of room elsewhere, set out upon the grass in front, beds and mattresses upon the roof, blankets and woolen garments sunning in the open windows." Inside two servants were scrubbing parlors, and another was whitewashing the dining room.[38]

Although the work Juliette did in her household evolved over time, it did not change as dramatically as the ethnicity of her servants. At first they were frequently métis women. There were also black men and women, formerly enslaved and now serving long indentures. Into the late 1840s, the Kinzie household included indentured African Americans, some old and infirm, who had long been in the service of the extended family.[39]

As time went on, more of her servants were immigrants from

Germany, Scandinavia, or Ireland. Juliette held a relatively positive view of Germans, even learning their language in order to work more closely with them on household tasks. In contrast, she had little positive to say about the "paddies" who came into her household. Juliette complained that "these Irish [were] so stupid" that she had to provide close supervision to get tasks done.[40] When several of her Irish servants left together, she bemoaned "the deceit of those Romanists." She was quick to ascribe intemperance and all that came with it to the Irish as a group. Once when John fell and scraped his face, Juliette wrote that "he looked very much like some tipsy Biddy O'Callahan after an Irish wedding."[41] Still, some of the servants with the longest tenure were Irish, and the population of Irish in the surrounding neighborhood was growing.

Family

The house was not just a site for producing goods; it was also the center for social reproduction. Juliette gave birth there to five more sons: John Harris in 1838; Arthur Magill in 1841; Julian Magill in 1843 (died in infancy); Francis William in 1844; and George Herbert in October 1846. Across the garden, Kinzie cousins Gwinthlean, Maria (Posey), David Hunter, and John joined a family compound that was filled with laughter, music, and games.

All these children were born at home, and Juliette nursed them when sickness or accident struck. In 1839 six-year-old Alexander (Sandie) took a sip from a bottle left in an empty house a couple of blocks away. Despite the efforts of doctors and of Juliette herself, "the poison had done its work." Sandie died at home, in the arms of his distraught mother. Her husband, who had been away on Indian affairs business, came home to the terrible news. For decades afterward, John would "hastily leave the room if his name was accidently mentioned."[42]

A few years later, Francis (Frank), born in 1844, became a family favorite, "a lovely little fellow with the sweetest disposition . . . soft dark eyes and yellow curls." When not quite two years old, he followed his nurse into the kitchen, where washday was in full swing. While the nurse and cook were momentarily distracted, Frank fell into a washtub filled with boiling water. Juliette heard the commotion, hurried to the kitchen, cut off his clothing, and covered his burned body with a homemade ointment. She spent the next two years nursing him, walking the halls at night and singing to distract her son from the pain. The couple's last child, George, was born just as Frank recovered his health. Juliette doted on her young sons, but her delight in them was tempered always by fears of death or injury.[43]

Beyond their own children, Juliette and John welcomed extended family, especially young people. John's sisters Margaret and Ellen made long visits from Detroit. Their sons, Edwin Helm and Kinzie Bates, both lived with the Kinzie family for years at a time. When John's sister Maria and her husband, David Hunter, were on leave from his army postings, they often stayed at the Michigan Street house. They had no children of their own but took a lively interest in their nieces and nephews.

Juliette and John also welcomed many Magill and Wolcott relations. Juliette's parents lived with her and John for long periods.[44] Arthur Magill worked as a clerk in John's offices for more than a decade, and for a time the Magills lived in a nearby house that likely belonged to their son-in-law.[45] Juliette's father greatly appreciated this support, and he praised his daughter as "kind, dutiful, and affectionate."[46]

Two of Juliette's brothers, Alexander and Julian, also lived at the Michigan Street house. Like their father, they both came to work for John Kinzie.[47] Julian began living with the Kinzies shortly after their marriage; in many ways John and Juliette were his surrogate parents. The couple also opened their home to five of Juliette's young cousins. Alexander, Henry, and Caroline Wolcott "spent their youth" at the Kinzie house after Juliette's uncle died. Alexander became a surveyor, while Henry worked for some years in the commission business. Caroline (Carrie) lived in the Michigan Street house until her marriage.[48] Two more cousins who lived there were Elizabeth (Lizzie) and Frederica (Freddie) Williams. Their mother, one of Arthur Magill's sisters, sent them to Chicago when she was widowed. Juliette's daughter, Nellie, described Lizzie as her "adopted sister."[49]

The Kinzie and Magill family assembled at Chicago was distinctive in its size, but in other ways it was typical of these years. Many other families, particularly from New England and upstate New York, made similar migrations. One woman stoically described her family's relocation to Chicago as "the removal."[50] Gurdon Hubbard encouraged his New England relatives to emigrate. George Dole and his brother persuaded their Rumsey nephews and nieces from Geneva, New York, to join them. William B. Ogden drew his mother, brother, and sisters to Chicago.

These families also encouraged neighbors and friends to come to Chicago. Juliette and John were no exception. Among the Middletown families who came with their support were E. K. Hubbard and his wife, Elizabeth Sebor DeKoven, one of Juliette's childhood friends. The women remained fast friends for the rest of their lives and spent many happy times together as their children grew up in Chicago.[51]

Children, both John and Juliette's own and many young relations, were the center of the Michigan Street house. John gave special attention to their only daughter, Nellie. Whenever she had any trouble, she was sure that her "papa" would "do what he can." The children roamed the open prairies on horseback in the summer and went ice-skating and sledding in the winter. Nellie described herself as a tomboy who loved to play with her brothers. She remembered being "a famous marble player" whose "wonderful collection of alleys and moss agates" was "greatly coveted by her brothers John and Arthur." The children also spent hours in the garden, using a tiny woodshed "as a playhouse." A gate in the fence was a passage between their house and their neighbors' (first their cousins and later the Butterfield family).[52]

The Kinzies had many pets over the years. Dogs were a regular part of their household, roaming the garden and grounds. They were useful protectors, but they also caused many humorous incidents. When the first sidewalk was built in front of their house, Neptune, their big Newfoundland dog, could not accept the public access it offered, and "for weeks and for weeks never allowed anyone except members of the family to walk on it." Indoors, the family kept a parrot. The bird spent considerable time in the parlor and learned many words by repeating snatches of conversation. Since John often referred to Juliette as "wifey," the parrot frequently repeated the term to family and guests.[53]

In spring and summer, John and Juliette gave parties for their family, neighbors, and friends to mark the ripening of strawberries or plums from their garden. In winter, they hosted "candy pulls" after evenings of sledding and skating. There was good food and music, with John playing his violin, accompanied by Juliette on the piano. Their guests listened in the parlor or from out on the piazza. These entertainments were "very popular," especially with the young people, who enjoyed dancing and socializing during summer garden parties.[54]

Many of the young people who lived with John and Juliette married and established their own households in the neighborhood. Cousin Lizzie Williams married Mark Skinner, another lawyer from New England. Juliette's brother Julian married Laura Rumsey, part of a powerful extended family related to the Doles.[55] These large families, who shared a unitary vision of a good community, created informal networks that became the base of Chicago civic life.

Becoming a Historian

Juliette grew up reading novels like James Fenimore Cooper's and western travel accounts like Henry Schoolcraft's, sparking her imaginative longing for the west. As an adult, she had high praise for British authors like Charles Dickens and William Thackeray as well as for Jane Austen and Charlotte Brontë. Thus John and Juliette fostered a household where storytelling and reading had a central place. The Michigan Street house had a library, and the family read books, newspapers, Episcopal publications, and popular magazines like *Godey's Lady's Book*. The family read aloud from current and classic literature; they especially enjoyed works by Dickens, from *The Pickwick Papers*, first published in 1836, onward. They came to know the fictional characters in many popular novels so well that they gave acquaintances nicknames tied to their favorites. For instance, their next-door neighbor Mrs. Butterfield, who was prone to "amusing mistakes and speeches," became known as Mrs. Partington, a character in a popular novel who shared those characteristics. They also read children's books and poems with titles like *Cowslip, or More Cautionary Stories* and "Quarrelsome Children."[56]

During Juliette's lifetime, there was a dramatic increase in reading materials available to American households as inexpensive editions proliferated. Juliette regularly entertained family, friends, and visitors by reading aloud or listened to others read. She enjoyed discussing stories from newspapers and magazines as well as the latest fiction. Juliette judged people she knew by the books they liked or disliked. She questioned Julian's taste because he disliked *Pride and Prejudice*. Fictional characters also offered a shorthand for referring to events and people. For instance, in a letter to her daughter she described someone as being like Frank Churchill, a character from Austen's novel *Emma*.[57]

Writers who came to the city sought out the conviviality of Juliette's parlor, often bearing letters of introduction. The Kinzies' hospitality "captivated the hearts and won the commendation" of visitors, including Fredrika Bremer, Harriet Martineau, Charles Fenno Hoffman, and Frances Kemble.[58] Bremer said the Kinzie family offered her "house, and home, and friendship, and every good thing." She described the house as a "pretty villa" that hosted congenial evening gatherings. For the benefit of their visitors, members of the family read from Juliette's stories of early Chicago. Bremer found that Juliette wrote "with facility and extremely well," noting that some of her accounts were "full of cruel and horrible scenes; others, also touchingly beautiful, and others again, very comic."[59]

Another visitor to the Michigan Street parlors was Joseph N. Balestier, a young lawyer who arrived in Chicago from Vermont in 1835. He quickly worked to amass a fortune, making as much as $500 a day in the speculative real estate fever of those years. He courted Juliette's niece Caroline Wolcott, spending agreeable evenings in Juliette's parlor listening to stories of early Chicago. Balestier used these stories, as well as the accounts of other early Chicagoans like Gurdon Hubbard, to construct an oration on the history of Chicago that he delivered to the Chicago Lyceum in 1840 and later published as a pamphlet.[60]

Perhaps the publication of Balestier's address encouraged Juliette to gather her own written accounts of Chicago history in the early 1840s. In explaining her decision to publish *Narrative of the Massacre at Chicago* in 1844, Juliette wrote that it came "at the solicitation of many friends, and to avoid the possibility of its unauthorized appearance in print." This suggests that her historical accounts were already well known and that she feared they might be used without acknowledgment. But she wrote mostly to preserve "for the children . . . a faithful picture of the perilous scenes through which those near and dear to them had been called to pass." Regardless of her motives, the publication of the stories brought her a larger audience.[61]

Juliette Kinzie wrote even while raising a large family and running a substantial household. She wrote after the loss of her firstborn son, when she still had small children underfoot. She stole time from other duties (the family claim) and gloried in "the comfort of writing" as a distraction from daily responsibilities.[62] Juliette's writing was done in the library or the parlor, often with family members around her. They were well aware of her efforts and supported them as best they could. Juliette regularly read passages aloud to John, gauging from his reactions what needed revision. Nellie watched her mother intently. While her mother wrote,

Nellie created her own series of illustrated short stories. Writing, like sewing or cooking, was something she learned by modeling her mother's daily activities.[63]

In 1844 Juliette brought a "small letter-page half-bound blank book" filled with five chapters of handwritten history to Robert Fergus, a small publisher. He set the type, then she "read, revised, and approved the proofs" in his Clark Street office. He published it as *Narrative of the Massacre at Chicago*, with its author listed as anonymous, though John H. Kinzie held the copyright. Only later would Juliette publicly claim the work. Still, with this publication she became a historian, and its authorship was no doubt clear within her circle.[64]

Her book recounts the events surrounding the August 15, 1812, battle between hundreds of Potawatomi warriors and a US Army contingent marching along Lake Michigan near what is now Eighteenth Street. Juliette's history rests on the recollections of two women: her mother-in-law, Eleanor Kinzie, and her sister-in-law Margaret McKillip Helm. Both had charge of their children and other members of their household during the battle.[65] Thus, unlike most accounts of military engagements, Juliette's history is written from the perspective of women and focuses on families and their experiences. The first chapter opens months before the hostilities: a cheerful family scene in the Kinzie house describes children dancing to their father's violin as they await their mother's return from a sick call. But Eleanor brought the frightening news of an Indian attack in retribution for William Henry Harrison's attack at Tippecanoe, Indiana, just months before. The account moves forward to the battle itself, highlighting the bravery of Juliette's father-in-law, John Kinzie. But it also recounts the heroism of women like Archange Ouilmette, a neighbor who sheltered Margaret Helm and a US soldier in her home during the fighting.[66]

The influence of Juliette's time in Wisconsin among the Ho-Chunk, as well as the general sympathies of the Kinzie family, are central to this account. The Potawatomi were not simply the enemy; they were individuals who aided the Kinzies as well as regular soldiers and their families with "more kindness than was to have been expected from an enemy in most cases so merciless."[67]

By 1844 the Potawatomi and métis traders were already becoming a distant memory in Chicago. By publishing her work, Juliette put the Kinzie family in the center of an early history, staking a claim to their importance by making them the focal point in Chicago's transition from an isolated outpost in Indian country to a thriving American city. Her claim to primacy rested not only on this history, but on the civic culture she helped to create and foster during these years.

PART 2

Creating a Civic Culture, 1834–56

4

....

Culture

Juliette and John made their fortune between 1833 and 1837 as the Chicago region transitioned from Potawatomi to US control. The couple were among the wealthiest Chicagoans. They built a large house on Michigan Street, full of family and friends. Their ambition was not just to establish a western beachhead for their extended family, however, but also to be city builders.

Although Juliette had come west into Indian country, by 1834 she was intent on creating an urban place that would be well integrated into American society. She created a home that could easily fit into Middletown or Boston, filled with eastern-style furniture and accessories. She also looked to create a western version of American urban culture by organizing and supporting a rich array of societies and institutions. Juliette and John saw themselves as founders of a new place that emerged at the end of Indian country.

Perhaps nothing embodied this vision better than the two portraits the family commissioned in 1837 from James F. Wilkins, an English painter living in Peoria, Illinois. One was of their five-year-old son, Alexander, proudly well dressed, while a second shows a luminescent Juliette in white satin with their young daughter also fashionably dressed. The paintings suggest the foundation of a lineage at Chicago that future generations would admire. They look like eastern portraits; there is no sense that until very recently their lives had been closely tied to Indian country. The portraits embrace the conventions and expectations of wealthy Americans. The viewer is privy to Juliette's smooth satisfaction with success, reflected in the untroubled smiles of mother and daughter and the rich folds of their expensive clothing. The paintings were displayed proudly in the Kinzie home.[1]

Juliette and John Kinzie's household was not alone in wanting to create a new civic culture for Chicago. This foundational generation included men like William B. Ogden and Walter Newberry, but also women like Frances L. Willard, Eliza Chappell Porter, and Eliza Clark Garrett. Men and women knit their households together to create a new public sphere at Chicago that closely resembled that found in eastern cities and towns. It also grew seamlessly from the growing commercial economy in the city, especially the commodities trade, transportation, and banking, which were dominated by just a few families. The Newberrys, Doles, and Rumseys were among the families that developed under the leadership of women, through their households and informal networks as well as through more formal societies and institutions.[2]

Juliette Kinzie had grown up in a town with a rich civic life based in churches, schools, and other groups. Her parents and grandparents had accepted responsibility not only for their own households and businesses, but also for a wider community. Although she could not participate directly in politics, Juliette embraced a "republican liberalism" rooted in the idea that there is a common good. Women like Juliette were fundamental to maintaining places like Middletown and creating places like Chicago. New York investors like Arthur Bronson and Charles Butler understood the importance of women in city building, especially "in the beginning to give character to the society."[3]

From her Michigan Street house, Juliette worked alongside

Fig. 7 Oil portrait of Juliette Kinzie and her daughter Nellie (Eleanor Lytle) about 1838, by James F. Wilkins. A second oil painting was completed at the same time of Sandie (Alexander Wolcott), Juliette and John's oldest son, who died in 1839. Image from the Collection of the Girl Scouts of the USA. Used by permission.

her husband in many ventures. Besides caring for her family, she hosted countless gatherings to consider community concerns. With her husband, she embraced a civic stewardship resting on the idea that successful families owed a "dual obligation of time and money to communities in which they have prospered." Families like the Kinzies worked to create a social and cultural infrastructure in Chicago that rested not on the market or the limited local government, but on an extension of their household world into a public sphere.[4]

St. James

Organizing religious institutions was among the very first efforts made by this group of Chicagoans. Although there had been missionary activity in the region for over 150 years, it was in the early 1830s that the first Roman Catholic church and five Protestant congregations were organized (with the first Jewish congregation following in the next decade). The Kinzie family "served as the center of the small community of Episcopalians in the new settlement." St. James was organized in 1834 by John Kinzie and nine other men. John and Juliette donated two lots for the church, directly across the street from their house. Among the first congregants were Juliette and her mother, Frances Magill.[5]

Juliette helped to enlist the Connecticut Episcopal missionary society to sponsor Rev. Isaac Hallam as the first pastor of St. James. Hallam, married and with a large family, understood the central role of women in households and in his congregation; he especially highlighted their efforts in his annual reports to the Diocese of Illinois. Juliette helped to organize a ladies' sewing circle that raised funds for a substantial church building, rectory, organ, and bell. This group not only organized bazaars to fund the construction of their church but also created a new society of "educated, refined, and wealthy persons." They regularly gathered in Juliette's pleasant parlor across from the church.[6]

While the rectory was under construction, the pastor and his family stayed at the Kinzie house; for decades afterward, the house was the Chicago base for visiting Episcopal bishops and clergy. The church was built of the same brick as the Kinzie house; they remained among the few brick structures in a largely frame city. One nineteenth-century history described the congregation as "the Kinzie church society." Within a few years, Juliette and John could

Fig. 8 Sketch of St. James Episcopal Church, which stood on the west side of Cass Street (now Wabash Avenue) between Michigan (now Hubbard) and Illinois Streets, directly west of the Kinzie house on land donated by the family. The first Episcopal congregation in Chicago worshipped there from 1837 to 1857. Chicago History Museum, ICHi-176156.

look out the west windows of their house directly at the church entrance and monitor the comings and goings.[7]

John and Juliette supported the church for the rest of their lives, crossing Cass Street for services many times a week. Their daughter, Nellie, was among the first infants baptized there. Although John had not grown up in the Episcopal Church, he became an active member of the vestry of St. James. Although the congregation was led by male ministers counseled by an all-male vestry, in the 1840s a new pastor disdainfully noted that Juliette Kinzie was "the ruling female spirit" of the congregation. The clergyman found the situation demeaning and sought to "put her down," bluntly arguing that "either I or she would be rector." He was gone within a year, while Juliette continued her work from her parlor.[8]

Juliette played a central role in early church services as well, leading the singing despite having "a most croaking, unmusical voice." Perhaps knowing her limitations, Juliette "got up the choir," which initially consisted of her three cousins Freddie and Lizzie Williams and Carrie Wolcott, who all lived at the Michigan Street house. Laura Rumsey, the niece of Mr. and Mrs. George Dole and the future wife of Julian Magill, was the organist.[9] In addition, Juliette taught the older children in the Sunday school held in the church basement while Mrs. George Dole managed the younger ones. Dole and Kinzie children were in attendance through the 1840s.[10]

Other St. James families built substantial houses on large lots near the church, so a neighborhood of fellow congregants, family, and friends developed. One visitor described the area as "pretty villas, some of them large and elegant, built with great taste, and surrounded with well-planted gardens."[11] Juliette and her family maintained a regular round of social calls, receptions, and parties in their own home and those around them.

Some of the activities the couple and their neighbors hosted in their parlors laid the groundwork for related organizations. Like many Protestant churchwomen, Juliette belonged to her congregation's sewing circle, which made clothes for the needy or to raise funds. The group met in its members' parlors, socializing as they sewed. Like similar groups in cities and towns across the North, their sewing circle was informal yet strong enough to step up when crises arose.[12]

For instance, in 1835 a family was shipwrecked along Chicago's shoreline. A doctor "made personal appeals to all the ladies in the neighborhood, for provision for their needs." Juliette and her sewing circle responded quickly and made frequent visits to the family with food and supplies. Later that year, so as to be better prepared for such appeals, a group of such women from different congregations organized Chicago's Dorcas Society. It combined a more formal agenda of helping those in need with gatherings "in each other's homes to chat and share the warmth of human companionship." Juliette later wrote a short story about the inner workings of a Dorcas Society, using her knowledge of this powerful informal women's network.[13]

Both John and Juliette saw education as a key to their children's financial, religious, and personal future. Juliette wanted their children to have the opportunities she had in Middletown, while her husband sought for them the formal education he did not receive. After her arrival in 1831, Eliza Porter Chappell opened one of the community's first schools in the basement of her husband's Presbyterian church. Other "family" schools followed, often tied to a specific congregation; Chicagoans supported these "semiprivate" schools through subscriptions and donations. Families who were able paid tuition, but fees were waived for those who could not afford it. Embedded in such a system was a growing recognition that the community had a duty to educate all children. Over time, Chicago's local government took increasing responsibility for building and supporting a school system.[14]

The first "public" school in Chicago, organized in 1833, still collected tuition from parents who had the means to pay. It held classes in a privately owned building whose other tenants included several Protestant congregations, making it almost indistinguishable from a private school. Frances L. Willard, who had been recruited to help develop the public school system in 1836, was disheartened by the lack of progress and left after a few years. But other women came and, following national trends, soon outnumbered men among teachers employed in Chicago. Juliette and John supported both the emerging public and the private school networks with their tuition dollars as well as volunteer efforts, especially as their children grew older.[15]

The Lake House

John and Juliette knew the importance of a hotel to their city's prospects. They both worried that taverns like the Sauganash Hotel presented visitors with "appalling confusion, filth, and racket." They wanted "a commodious public house" that would provide space for their neighbors as well as represent Chicago to travelers. Their models were the refined hotels in eastern cities. John Kinzie gathered a group of local investors who pooled $100,000 to construct a fine hotel just east of the Michigan Street house along the Chicago River. Over the next few years, Kinzie came to own a controlling interest in the operation.[16]

Opened in 1836, the Lake House was the largest hotel in the west; for visitors arriving by steamboat, the four-story brick building surrounding an open courtyard made an imposing first impression. From the observatory on the roof, there was an uninterrupted view of Lake Michigan from three sides. The main story included a large dining room that could be divided with folding doors to provide a private space for women before and after meals. There was a stagecoach office, a reading room, a billiards room, and a barroom with Michigan Street frontage that was lit at night with sperm oil chandeliers. The third floor had sixty-three bedrooms and sitting rooms. Two large garrets on the fourth floor housed servants' bedrooms. The basement on the ground level contained two large kitchens, a washroom, and an ironing room as well as a barbershop and wine cellar.[17]

The hotel was "the pride of the city and the admiration of strangers." Locals frequented it, including the officers at the gar-

Fig. 9 The Lake House hotel and the Rush Street bridge over the main stem of
the Chicago River, sometime before the 1871 Chicago fire. Engraving by Francis
Dare (1930). When the Lake House was first built, it had an unobstructed view of
Lake Michigan. By the time of this photograph, factories and warehouses stood
between it and the lake. Keystone-Mast Collection, UCR/California Museum of
Photography, University of California, Riverside.

rison, circuit court judges, canal contractors, and lake captains.
Among the early guests were English writer Harriet Martineau,
US senator Daniel Webster, General Winfield Scott, and President
Martin Van Buren. When James Silk Buckingham visited, his party
found the Lake House to be "equal to that of any house we had bed
with since leaving Baltimore."[18]

Juliette's influence can be seen in the appointment of James
Russell, a Middletown native and an early supporter of St. James
Church, to take charge of the hotel. Juliette no doubt played a role
in furnishing the Lake House. With expensive mahogany furniture in the parlors and dining rooms and all manner of linens and
tableware, the hotel distinguished itself inside and out from the
rough taverns and public houses that had heretofore served visitors to Chicago.[19] The hotel was one of the few places where recent
eastern migrants felt at ease outside their own homes. Within its
rather opulent rooms, they organized societies, held meetings, and
entertained guests.

By 1836 a North Side neighborhood was emerging with the help (both organizational and financial) of Juliette and John. The area was not yet intensely urban; the Kinzies were aware that theirs was an unfinished and raw place. Fredrika Bremer, the Swedish writer who stayed with the Kinzie family, noted that while John and Juliette were immensely proud of Chicago, they could "see deficiencies and [could] speak of them properly."[20] Although Bremer saw a modesty in John and Juliette's view of "their city," they were also immensely proud of what they had accomplished by then. It turned out to be a brief moment of triumph. The 1837 Panic ushered in a very different era for the couple as well as for Chicago. Instead of remaining the social center of the city, the Lake House became a symbol of the hubris of its early residents.

1837 and Its Aftermath

John and Juliette were at the center of initial efforts to create urban institutions and spaces, including the incorporation of Chicago as a town in 1833. John was elected first president of the town board. He oversaw the first municipal ordinances, which dealt with obstructions and nuisances in streets and sidewalks and with controlling markets, horse racing, gambling, and disorderly conduct. The range of concerns reflected the difficult transition under way, from métis trading center to eastern-influenced city.

As the population grew, residents, including John Kinzie, drafted a charter for a city government that was affirmed by the Illinois State Assembly in 1837. In the first election for mayor of Chicago, John Kinzie ran against his neighbor William B. Ogden, who had been in the city for only two years.[21] Ogden ran as a Democrat, enlisting the support of immigrants and workers. His opponents described him as "a transient speculator," despite his substantial North Side house. Kinzie, who had helped to organize the Whig Party in Illinois, emphasized the need for more plank roads and other improvements. In a close election, Ogden became Chicago's first mayor. John was a gracious loser, but Juliette harbored long-term resentment against the man who had beaten her husband. Their attention soon was diverted in the face of a devastating economic panic.[22]

The crash that came in 1837 was in many ways eminently predictable. It was precipitated by an international financial crisis, and western speculators were hit particularly hard as banks closed and land prices collapsed. Months before the panic, Harriet Martineau had visited Chicago and predicted that "a bursting of the bubble must come soon. The absurdity of the speculation is so striking."[23] However, some of those involved in the local real estate market were not so aware of the inevitability—until it struck them. When the state of Illinois, nearly bankrupt, halted all work on the Illinois and Michigan Canal, real estate prices dropped precipitously. For a while John and Juliette appeared to weather the crisis because of the large fortune they had accumulated. They had not had to borrow money for their home, for their investment in the Lake House, or for John's business. They also still held real estate parcels in Chicago and across the region. But as the depression deepened, John's forwarding and commission agency became moribund, as did many other businesses. Most of John and Juliette's Chicago relatives, friends, and business partners (especially if they carried any debt and did not have wealthy backers) suffered business setbacks and bankruptcies. Chicagoans were learning hard truths about depression and business failure.

In need of cash to keep the Lake House open, the couple turned to Arthur Bronson for a $9,000 loan, putting up as collateral their interest in the hotel as well as other real estate. Juliette cosigned for the mortgage and was involved in the negotiations with Bronson as a visible and knowledgeable counsel to her husband. Indeed, she figured prominently in Bronson's decision to make the loan. In a world with no credit ratings, businessmen had to make evaluations based on their knowledge of debtors, society, and business. Bronson judged the couple "meritous" and found Juliette an "interesting wife" as he evaluated his risk. But the couple was unable to pay either principal or interest, and in March 1841 Bronson filed to foreclose on the loan.[24]

Like other suffering Chicagoans, the Kinzies took advantage of a recent Illinois debt relief law that slowed down foreclosure actions by out-of-state residents. An enraged Bronson appealed the case to the US Supreme Court. His personal friend Chief Justice Roger Taney ruled the Illinois law unconstitutional, noting that a state legislature could not assign "new conditions injurious and unjust to the mortgagee."[25] John and Juliette lost their interest in the Lake House. Although Bronson would recoup his loan, John Kinzie never again wielded as much economic influence in Chicago. Emblematic of the Kinzie family's fall, the Lake House foundered and was eclipsed by South Side establishments like the Tremont Hotel (but not before Bronson had profitably sold out).

The direct intervention of the US Supreme Court in ruling against the debt relief law placed John and Juliette within the national political and economic power structure. The Kinzies, in common with many westerners and members of the middle class, certainly held some privilege within this system. However, they had little power compared with men like Arthur Bronson who influenced politics and the economy through personal, family, and growing corporate connections. Bronson could address a letter to his good friend Roger, while Kinzie had no such powerful acquaintance.[26]

John Kinzie's tangled relationship with Bronson was further complicated by the election of Whig president William Henry Harrison in November 1840. John and his brother-in-law David Hunter, as well as men like Abraham Lincoln, were among the early organizers of the Whig Party in Illinois. Although Juliette could not vote, she actively campaigned for Harrison. The Kinzies were elated with his election for personal as well as political reasons. David Hunter went to Washington, DC, to make the case for patronage appointments for John and himself. Hunter was commissioned a paymaster in the army, and he pressed for John's appointment as registrar for the US Land Office at Chicago.

Curiously, Arthur Bronson promoted John's appointment despite their ongoing litigation. In a letter to the secretary of the treasury, he highlighted his long relationship with Kinzie and noted that he was "a gentleman of untarnished moral character" and "an excellent accountant" who was an active Whig. Bronson described Kinzie as a businessman made "poor" by "the late reverses." Whether Bronson hoped he could seize Kinzie's future salary in lieu of the bad debt or genuinely wanted to help the beleaguered family is not clear.[27] Regardless of motivation, the appointment, which was granted, offered the Kinzie household a lifeline but once again changed the course of John's career.

As head of the Land Office, John supervised a staff of clerks and surveyors who continued to sell federal property to private investors and farmers. While still subject to political turnover, John now relied on patronage appointments to protect his family from the worst vagaries of the American economic and business cycles. The steady salary allowed them to maintain their home on Michigan Street. Never again would they accumulate debt as in 1838, nor would they ever again control a fortune.[28]

John settled into relatively safe salaried positions even while other Chicagoans took risks that brought them great wealth. The development of railroads, banks, and the Board of Trade, coupled with nascent industrialization and ongoing real estate speculation, fueled Chicago's rapid rise. Families who were positioned to take risks by investing in these opportunities accumulated fortunes. William B. Ogden purchased real estate during the downturn and invested in key industries, especially railroads. Walter L. Newberry made a fortune in real estate and as a merchant banker. Julian S. and George F. Rumsey launched businesses in the grain trade, meatpacking, railroads, and banking. Many were neighbors, fellow congregants at St. James, and friends of the Kinzie family. John and Juliette watched as many grew rich in ways that were impossible for them.[29]

Although John and Juliette were able to stay in their home, financial reversals forced many of their family members to return east or move farther west. Robert and Gwinthlean Kinzie sold their substantial home and joined the Potawatomi in Kansas, and David and Maria Hunter followed US Army postings. Juliette's brother Alexander left to farm in LaSalle County. Cousins Henry Wolcott and Caroline Williams Balestier left for New York City. Never again would Chicago be so full of Kinzie and Magill family members.

But John and Juliette's substantial Michigan Street house remained an anchor in an uncertain world. Despite many public and private hardships, they found great happiness at home. Juliette noted that it was in this place that she concentrated her "tenderest cares and interests." John emphatically told his wife, "we shall never leave this spot which we love . . . we shall never find a pleasanter home."[30]

Civic Culture

Juliette and John continued to support institutions that met the needs of their growing city, but they were no longer able to make leading financial contributions. Juliette's work with her congregation led her to broader work across the city. In 1842 a Ladies Benevolent Society was formed as an umbrella organization for individual church groups.[31] This network developed social service infrastructure, complementing the work of local government.

The Ladies Benevolent Society found innovative ways to raise money. In 1844 it received the proceeds of one particularly successful fund-raiser—the performance of a "phenomenal pig" that amazed audiences with its "intellectual wonders" learned "under the tutelage" of its owner. Juliette and other women grew adept at organizing fairs. A typical one in 1849 was held in Market Hall, with long tables of food and other items for sale. The women sold Atlantic Ocean lobster and chicken salads, oysters, turkey, and sandwiches. They also sold coffee and cakes, while their children offered musical entertainment. Daughter Nellie remembered that despite a "very busy life," her mother devoted "an immense amount" of time to this sort of charitable and philanthropic work. Juliette showed her good sense and keen organizational skills as a leader in many of these efforts.[32]

Many women were motivated to transform their world by religious conviction, emerging from the evangelical revivals of the era. They increasingly saw themselves not only as mothers, but as reformers and activists acting on their faith. While Juliette did not embrace this evangelicalism, she shared with these women a growing sense of standing in civil society, having a place in public life emanating from their households.[33] John and Juliette continued to devote themselves to St. James. The family was particularly close to Rev. Robert H. Clarkson and his wife, Meliora, after their arrival in 1849. The two families worked together on services, rehearsals, classes, meetings, and fund-raisers. They organized soup kitchens and Christmas dinners for the poor as well as offering food and clothing to people who appeared on their doorsteps. Even the children helped at church fund-raisers by providing small performances.

While showing Christian charity to poor neighbors, Juliette also betrayed an intolerance for what she saw as unfortunate behavior. She believed, as did many of her neighbors, that intemperance and poor work habits led to poverty. When she helped her congregation feed over a thousand people in a single day at a soup kitchen, Juliette dwelled not on the charity of the act, but on the hope that the kitchen would soon close and the "beggary cease."[34]

Perhaps the chief challenge to Chicago's young and fragile social service infrastructure was the arrival of cholera during the warm months of every year from 1849 to 1854. Some 50 percent of those infected died within a few days, their skin turning blue gray from extreme, rapid dehydration. Several of Juliette's servants succumbed. Then it struck her six-year-old son Frank, the youngster who had survived being scalded as a toddler. The boy, such a lively presence in the household, "was taken ill one afternoon and died the next morning."[35]

At first Juliette and her neighbors responded to the contagion within their households, leaving the larger concerns in the hands of local government. But soon the small county poorhouse was filled to overflowing with the sick and their family members. The cholera epidemic made clear the limited ability of the new institutions to respond to crises. There were no regular hospitals or corps of nurses; local government aid was intermittent or lacking altogether. The only assistance that could be relied on came through family, friends, and religious institutions. Since local government remained small, by design and by default, private efforts relied on the work of both women and men. Juliette was among a generation of women who organized and operated not only their own households, but the first institutions that took responsibility for orphaned children and the sick.[36]

The city government created a temporary cholera hospital each year, but more permanent responses came from religious groups. The Roman Catholic Sisters of Mercy founded a hospital in what had been the Lake House. The Illinois General Hospital of the Lakes, renamed Mercy Hospital in 1852, was the first institution of its kind in Chicago. Modeling it on these efforts, Rev. Clarkson and his wife founded St. James Hospital near the Kinzie house. Both Juliette and John devoted considerable time to nursing the sick there, as many women did. In addition, their household provided "huge caldrons of broth" to the hospital through many summers of epidemic. Throughout her life, Juliette also took an active part in fund-raising and in equipping the hospital.[37]

John and Juliette also supported St. James Hospital as an alternative to "popish" care. They, along with many of their more affluent neighbors, blamed the spread of cholera at least in part on immigrants' squalid living conditions. They worried about the Irish shanties that bookended the Kinzie home and St. James Church and were deeply suspicious of the growing Roman Catholic population and its institutional presence in Chicago. Juliette saw both as threatening her vision of a civic culture based in Protestant volunteerism. Indeed, by the 1850s the growing Catholic presence challenged the Protestant hegemony of that first civic culture.

John and Juliette's denominational concern manifested itself after it became clear that children orphaned by the cholera out-break had nowhere to turn except the almshouse. After the Mercy Sisters, under Mother Agatha O'Brien, established the city's first orphanage as "a haven for children who had lost their parents in the epidemic,"[38] the couple joined in creating an analogous Protestant institution. The Chicago Orphan Asylum was supported by lead-ing residents who had helped to found the city's first Protestant churches. Although it operated as a Protestant institution, the Chi-cago Orphan Asylum was open to all children regardless of race, ethnicity, or religion. The first child admitted was a Swedish girl whose parents had died of cholera; more than a hundred orphans lived there by 1853. Almost half were surrendered by parents who could not care for them.

John was among the male directors who founded the institution, and Juliette became the first director of the women's board. The women took on the day-to-day tasks needed to create the home.[39] For more than three years, Juliette gave her considerable talents to this effort as a housekeeper, nurse, mother, and fund-raiser. She and the other female directors not only supervised internal affairs but also solicited funds and supplies. They divided the city into dis-tricts, and each woman assumed a share of the work and responsi-bility.[40] This kind of organization made good sense to someone like Juliette, who organized her world outward from home to church to neighborhood and the city beyond.

The women canvassed the city for supplies, supervised staff, and managed admissions and placements as well as hosting din-ners and sponsoring fund-raisers. Juliette called on neighbors to provide food and goods that could be sold (from fancy needlework to artwork to cakes and pastries). Some items were made within church sewing circles and donated to the cause. Juliette also orga-nized benefit performances, including a musical in 1849. Three years later she helped to raise more than $1,000 through a fair with entertainment and food that people bought, plus $600 in outright donations.[41]

The female directors met at least once a month—initially at

churches and then at the asylum itself. Under Juliette's leadership the women created committees on health, diet, instruction, wardrobe, bedding, and general order and cleanliness. All these areas were ones that Juliette and her fellow directors dealt with daily in their own homes. Moving to a citywide level was a difference of degree, not necessarily of experience. But at the same time, Juliette and the others also honed new organizational skills.[42] Juliette's efforts for the asylum slowed only after it was relocated south of downtown.

As with the Chicago Orphan Asylum, the officers and members of many new cultural societies, organizations, and institutions in Chicago were often all male, masking women's participation. For instance, the Chicago Athenaeum was organized in 1836 with a mission of cultural uplift. Among its leaders was John Kinzie, and all thirty-eight of its official members were men. They met for debates, lectures, and performances. Yet the organization was not a male-only one: women, including wives like Juliette Kinzie, were invited to participate and were part of the operations even if they were not visible in the records.[43]

This was particularly clear in another organization John Kinzie was a member of, the New England Society—a social club for New Englanders. John was born in Detroit, but he joined the society because Juliette was Connecticut-born. He even served as an officer, representing Juliette's home state. The men took part in the annual December celebration of the landing of the Pilgrims, an event hosted by women.[44]

The couple also helped organize a group called the Old Settlers Society, whose members had arrived in Chicago before 1840. It is little wonder they were prominent participants. For the Kinzies it was an opportunity to revel in the glory of bygone days. The Old Settlers Society and the New England Society were ways that established families like the Kinzies could continue to play a leadership role even as they lost ground to wealthier Chicagoans.[45]

Another organization that Juliette and John supported was the Chicago Historical Society. Founded in 1856, the society set about collecting and preserving materials from the city's short past. The organization was modeled on groups like the New-York Historical Society and the Massachusetts Historical Society. Juliette attended the annual meetings of the Chicago Historical Society before the Civil War, listening to addresses given by members on historical subjects. Although the officers and membership rolls show only men, women played an important part, organizing and attending lectures and discussions. In its early years, the Chicago Historical Society often met in the homes of its members. John and Juliette Kinzie were among those who hosted the evening meetings, constituting "a self-appointed elite who were recognized by others as prominent citizens and social leaders."[46]

Since women like Juliette seldom left documentation of their participation, historians have often ignored their early presence in such organizations; yet it is clear that John represented not just himself, but his household. They were her groups as well as his, and Juliette certainly felt at ease within them. For instance, at a November 1859 meeting of the Chicago Historical Society, Juliette was a key participant in a discussion on "a need for a high-toned and creditable periodical in Chicago as a vehicle for the production of our many literary people." Indeed, she agreed to write to publishers she knew to identify someone to launch it.[47]

Shaping a Legacy

By this time Juliette was the city's most successful author. Three years before, in 1856, her *Wau-Bun: the "Early Day" in the North-West* had been published by Derby and Jackson in New York and in 1857 by D. B. Cooke in Chicago. This was a much more ambitious effort than her *Narrative of the Massacre at Chicago*. Identified on the title page as "Mrs. John H. Kinzie of Chicago," Juliette understood the book "might have been more modestly put forth under the name of a third person," but she did not want to remain anonymous as she had in 1844. Instead, she became a public persona in her own right, a national author from Chicago. She was part of a generation of women who saw literary careers as an acceptable way of gaining fame and even fortune. Of course Juliette did so as John's wife, tying even her writing to her place in a household.[48]

The book itself was ambitious; thirty-eight chapters that combined history, travelogue, ethnography, and family reminiscence. The ordering of the chapters is whimsical; readers are taken from one story to another with little sense of chronology or geography. Juliette seems to have considered only readers' entertainment when setting the order. She may have envisioned *Wau-Bun* as being read aloud in a parlor on a winter's evening, the way the stories long had been told in her own home. Unfolding before readers or listeners was a mix of experiences, places, and people, each chapter a story of the Kinzie family in Indian country. Juliette wrote from material she had long collected from family journals, letters, and stories as well as from her own life.[49]

Much of *Wau-Bun* recounts Juliette's experiences in Wisconsin and Illinois before 1833. Her firsthand accounts offered a compelling look at the region while it was still controlled by the Potawatomi, Ho-Chunk, and other tribes. Other chapters consider the experiences of her mother-in-law and father-in-law as young people in the west. Juliette's portrayals of Indian country are sympathetic views that emphasized the individuality of Indian men and women.

Because of its fanciful arrangement and romantic tone, *Wau-Bun* has sometimes been mistakenly identified as fiction, but Juliette intended the book as a history that would affirm the "truth and reality" of the Kinzie family's claim to primacy in Chicago. She accomplished this in a set of related chapters that include material drawn directly from her 1844 *Narrative*. With this addition, Juliette set out to define a foundation story for Chicago that properly acknowledged the role of her family.[50] Her history of Chicago began in 1804 with the arrival of John and Eleanor Kinzie, the same year the US government completed Fort Dearborn. Whatever happened before was simply a prequel. This allowed Juliette to acknowledge and then quickly diminish the earlier presence of others like Jean Baptiste Point de Sable, now widely understood to have been Chicago's first settler. She shrewdly interjected race into her dismissal of his claim to primacy by repeating what she had heard from area Indians: "the first white man who settled here was a negro." She assumed that her largely white readership would then simply discount his importance.[51]

Juliette also skillfully downplayed the handful of métis families at the small trading outpost that emerged during the 1790s. Their houses, gardens, and outbuildings already dotted the riverbanks when Fort Dearborn was founded. In *Wau-Bun*, Juliette ignored them when she enumerated the residents of Chicago she encountered in her 1831 visit. By narrowing her field to "white inhabitants," Juliette overlooked even the Kinzies' longtime neighbors Antoine and Archange Ouilmette, who had lived alongside Point de Sable during his years at Chicago.[52]

Perhaps more effectively than writing earlier settlers out of the history, Juliette drew them out of it. One of the lithographs she had prepared for *Wau-Bun* included her sketch of the home of John and Eleanor Kinzie on the north bank of the Chicago River, directly across from Fort Dearborn. The dwelling had been built by Jean Baptiste Point de Sable, a fact Juliette did not mention. She based her drawing on her in-laws' historical descriptions as much as on her own 1831 observations; it appeared to be quite isolated and well tended. Her idealized view of the Kinzie "mansion" with "a fine, well-cultivated garden" gave no hint that just to the left sat the Ouilmette home or other buildings beyond it. Not including them meant her readers never saw them.[53]

Once Juliette had established the Kinzie claim on Chicago's founding, she turned to the heroic role her father-in-law, John Kinzie, played in the battle of August 15, 1812. This material had already been published in 1844, but now she focused on John Kinzie as the founder of Chicago. Juliette argued that although her father-in-law did not live to see "the eventual prosperity and importance" of Chicago, he had long predicted its rise and indeed was essential to it.[54]

Wau-Bun was widely read and discussed in Chicago, capitaliz-

Fig. 10 Photograph of the lithograph of the "Kinzie mansion" based on a sketch
by Juliette Kinzie and included in *Wau-Bun*. Jean Baptiste Point de Sable built
the house and trading outpost in the 1790s along the north bank of the main stem
of the Chicago River east of what is now the Michigan Avenue Bridge. The Kinzie
family lived there from 1803 until sometime before 1828. Mrs. John H. Kinzie,
Wau-Bun: The "Early Day" of the North-West (Chicago: Caxton Club, 1901), 151.

ing on an increasing interest in the city's recent past. Indeed, at a
meeting of the Chicago Historical Society after the book's publication, John Kinzie noted the bevy of well-wishers who surrounded
Juliette: "Wife, I believe you are pretty popular."[55] The *Chicago Tribune* recommended Juliette's book, noting that "all classes of readers . . . will greet warmly *Wau-bun*." The reviewer thanked her for
"giving it to the public." It provided an opportunity for new and
old Chicagoans alike to know "the men and women who were pioneers. . . . [O]ne likes to take up such a book, to read it."[56]

Juliette had intended *Wau-Bun* as an introduction to the city
and its history as much for East Coast readers as for Chicagoans.
Wau-Bun was reviewed nationally, including in the *New York Herald*, which "recommended it strongly to the favor of our readers. . . . [I]t deserves to rank with the best sketches of the sort that
have as yet been published." The secretary of the Massachusetts

Historical Society was "well-entertained" by the copy Juliette sent to Boston, and the Michigan Historical Society endorsed the book for public school use. The book was popular with Juliette's many acquaintances and friends in Chicago and across the country, especially those from her old haunts in Middletown, Fishkill, Boston, and New Hartford. She was heartened by the "many compliments from old friends."[57]

Wau-Bun also had British readers. In September 1860 the young Prince of Wales, oldest son of Queen Victoria who would become King Edward VII, stopped in Chicago on his trip across the United States. One of the royal aides had read *Wau-Bun* and wanted to meet the author. When an invitation came to meet the prince at a private reception, Juliette could not resist. Although the event received newspaper coverage, she also carefully crafted a story about their meeting that she shared with her daughter:

> Of course, I did not offer my hand, but curtsied. He however put forth his, and shook your father's cordially. . . . The papers do not report correctly my reply to his polite remarks. . . . I only spoke of his mother and the place she had in our hearts and that her children were dear to every American Mother for her sake. He looked pleased and touched. As if he realized he was not merely a prince but a son also. . . . I laughed and said I supposed he was anxious to see the Grandfather and Grandmother of the 110,000 people who were welcoming his party.[58]

Juliette very much encouraged the idea that she and her husband were that grandfather and grandmother. Long after John and Juliette were central actors in Chicago's economic life, they focused on creating a foundation narrative where the Kinzie family was central. They did so not only with the publication of *Wau-Bun*, but also through visual cues that would remind Chicagoans and their descendants of the primacy of the Kinzies.

A Visual Legacy

John and Juliette used the newest technology to solidify the Kinzies' standing in Chicago society. After viewing an exhibition of Alexander Hesler's daguerreotypes in 1854, they commissioned portraits of themselves and their children. These photographs were of value to their family but also provided a record for posterity. Hesler encouraged this view of his work as beyond "the mere gratification of the present. We should remember that we are working for future generations."[59]

Perhaps with this in mind, in 1856 Hesler took what is now one of the oldest surviving landscape photographs of Chicago. The image looked north across the Chicago River, with the abandoned Fort Dearborn at the center. The image told an important story. In the foreground was what remained of the fort, which was soon to be torn down; across the river behind it was the Lake House. In 1856 the hotel was long past its prime, but its well-proportioned and tasteful brick construction contrasted with the even older fort. Beyond the Lake House are a scattering of houses, churches, and other buildings. Among them one is clearly visible: the three-story brick Kinzie residence.[60]

The composition of this photograph is intriguing. If Hesler's only object was to capture an image of the fort before it was torn down, he had many angles to choose from. He chose one that highlighted the Kinzies' mark on the city. The perspective showed Chicago's past as a United States military outpost and its more recent history as a young commercial port anchored by the Lake House and substantial homes like the Kinzies'. The photograph was displayed in Hesler's gallery, offering a visual representation of the history of Chicago that Juliette and John embraced, in which the Kinzie family was instrumental.[61]

The couple also supported portrait painter George Peter Healy, who came to Chicago in 1855 on the invitation of William B. Ogden. Healy recognized the city as a place of opportunity for a portrait

Fig. 11 Fort Dearborn is in the foreground of this 1856 photograph by Alexander Hesler. Looking north across the Chicago River, the Lake House is to the right, and in the distance on the left is the Kinzie house. This is one of the earliest extant photographs of Chicago. Chicago History Museum, ICHi-176155.

painter even as he described it as being at "a somewhat rough stage. Like an overgrown youth whose legs and arms are too long for his clothes." Healy was supported by "the old settlers," among them the Kinzies, and made "kind friends . . . at this happy time." There were many newly wealthy families in Chicago who thought a portrait by one of the leading painters of the day would help ensure their place in society. They could afford to pay the hundreds or even thousands of dollars that Healy charged.[62]

Although Juliette and John were no longer among the wealthiest people in Chicago, they got to know Healy, who lived with his family just a few blocks from the Michigan Street house. As their neighbors began to commission portraits, they decided to invest in a full-length portrait of their daughter, Nellie, who was almost twenty and still unmarried. She was their pride and joy, and the

Fig. 12 Photograph of the full-length portrait of Nellie Kinzie Gordon painted by George Peter Healy in 1856. Chicago History Museum, ICHi-168746.

portrait was a way to claim a place for her among Chicago's elite. In the portrait, Nellie wore a stunning pale yellow gown with a tight bodice and low neck. The painting hung in the Kinzie parlor alongside the earlier portrait of Juliette and her daughter. Young Juliette and Healy's Nellie show the same confident air. The portrait was

Fig. 13 This 1856 portrait of Juliette Kinzie was painted by George Peter Healy (Joe Byrd collection). Long in the possession of the Gordon family, the portrait is now on display in a parlor of the Juliette Gordon Low Birthplace in Savannah. Image from the Collection of the Girl Scouts of the USA. Used by permission.

prized by her parents and well received in Chicago. Healy long remembered their "pretty and lively daughter," whose portrait he borrowed for public exhibitions.[63]

Although they could ill afford it, John and Juliette also commissioned small portraits of themselves. Both look kindly and smile slightly. John looks content and happy, but Juliette's countenance

Fig. 14 This 1856 portrait of John Kinzie was painted by George Peter Healy (Joe Byrd collection). This portrait and the one of Juliette Kinzie had been sent to Savannah just weeks before the 1871 Chicago fire. Image from the Collection of the Girl Scouts of the USA. Used by permission.

suggests a woman who has endured despite challenges and suffering. It is a view dramatically different from her 1837 portrait: the decades had taken their toll. The pair are dressed simply in dark colors, in contrast to the pale yellow of Nellie's gown. John wears a nondescript formal suit, while Juliette has chosen a high-neck dress softened by a lace collar fastened with a brooch. Perhaps most intriguing is a blanket draped at her right hand: it looks much like a blanket from the Indian trade. If it is, the portrait creates a visual reference to *Wau-Bun*, published at the time Healy did the portrait.

Juliette and John had long used images and visual cues to shape perceptions of Chicago and its history. In the 1830s, when they had considerable wealth, they used their published plat of the Kinzie Addition, their substantial Michigan Street residence, St. James Episcopal Church, and the Lake House to help establish Chicago's urban claims and confirm their own part in them. The Wilkins portrait of Juliette and Nellie bespoke the wealth, elegance, and ease to be found in the city, a counterpoint to the brash, loud image of early Chicago. Through their buildings, paintings, and publications, the Kinzies shaped perceptions of Chicago within their families, for contemporary society, and for later students of their era.

5

....

Industry

John and Juliette fostered the development of a neighborhood filled with families and institutions that extended their household beyond their picket fence. A friend sketched that neighborhood in 1848, showing the slowly emerging urban character of the area more than a decade after construction of the Kinzie house. It remained the largest residence on the north side of unpaved Michigan Street, but the dominant structure was St. James Episcopal Church. In a city of frame buildings, the "brick city church" and the brick Kinzie house were linked in a slowly urbanizing landscape.

While Juliette and John Kinzie stayed in the house, the neighborhood around them changed dramatically after 1848. Where once there had been only a few neighbors and open land for grazing cows and horses, Michigan Street began "to look quite business-like."[1] Indeed, the Kinzie house was in the center of an extraordinary transformation as Chicago began its rise as an industrial and commercial behemoth. The year 1848 brought many new technologies and innovations. The first telegraph linked the city with the rest of the country, and businessmen organized the Board of Trade.

Fig. 15 A sketch of Juliette's neighborhood in the late 1840s looking east along
Michigan Street (now Hubbard), with St. James Church in the right foreground
and the Kinzie house to the left and farther east. Juliette Kinzie to Nellie Kinzie
Gordon, Easter 1858, Gordon Family Papers, University of North Carolina
Archives.

More than twelve years after the start of construction on the house,
the Illinois and Michigan Canal opened, to great fanfare, linking
the Great Lakes to the Mississippi River; John was appointed the
canal toll collector. The first railroad was under construction, with
many more to follow.

These developments radically reshaped the Kinzies' neighborhood. Just one block east of the house rose an enormous structure
that blocked any view of the Chicago River. It was a steam-powered
grain elevator much taller than the Lake House or any of the church
steeples and employing hundreds of workers for much of the year.
The elevator—"the dustiest in all the worlds"—deposited a thick
film over Juliette's house and garden.[2]

This grain elevator was not a solitary structure. Going west
from the foot of Cass Street along the river stood one considerable structure after another. Less than a quarter mile west was the
two-story depot and substantial rail yard of the Galena and Chicago Railroad (later the Chicago and North Western), which had

Fig. 16 Close-up of
the Kinzie house
at the northeast
corner of Michigan
and Cass Streets
(now Hubbard and
Wabash), from
J. T. Palmatary's
bird's-eye view of
Chicago in 1857.

been spearheaded by William B. Ogden. The belching smoke and
the noise from the steam engines, brakes, and loading carried into
Juliette's parlor and gardens at all hours.[3]

To the east the Lake House, which only a few years before had
been the grand front entrance to Chicago, now looked like a construction site surrounded by lots filled with timber, stone, and
other building materials. Ogden encouraged Cyrus McCormick to
locate his factory for manufacturing agricultural implements in
the shadow of the Lake House. Soon the McCormick Reaper Works
expanded along the river.[4]

Such large workplaces attracted many employment seekers.
Between 1846 and 1851, the city's population nearly tripled, to more

than 34,000. By 1860 Chicago was a diverse city of over 100,000 people.[5] Many of the new residents were immigrants from Ireland, Germany, and Scandinavia, drawn to the Kinzies' neighborhood by the prospect of jobs. Groceries, taverns, and saloons soon dotted the streets. Many of the Kinzies' new neighbors were Roman Catholic and supported the construction of the large Church of the Holy Name a few blocks north. A wholly different neighborhood was grafting itself onto the one the Kinzies had helped create.

The streets were busy day and night. One visitor saw that even on Sundays "the shops were all open, and everywhere seen groups of Germans, smoking, jabbering, and drinking Lager beer to their hearts' content."[6] In 1855 Mayor Levi Boone, opposed to these immigrants' public drinking, enforced Sunday closing laws for saloons and increased license fees for tavern keepers. When German and Irish immigrants responded by massing at the Clark Street drawbridge, Mayor Boone raised the bridge to keep them from crossing the river and proceeding to city hall until he had a police force ready to meet them. When the police and militia fired on the crowd, a riot ensued.[7]

Depredations were joined by deprivation. Along the lake, some of the poorest immigrants built "miserable Irish shanties" on land they didn't own.[8] Infamously known as "the Sands," the area became a vice district. In 1857 Mayor John Wentworth, under pressure from neighbors like John Kinzie and William Ogden, had the police clear the land of all the squatters and illegal activity. But the shanties returned.[9]

There were other costs to this growth. Demands were made on the small city government to improve living conditions. During the 1830s and 1840s, city government had been narrow in scope— rudimentary fire protection and a limited public school system, as well as limited regulation of markets and nuisances. Expenditures were small and taxes were low. Now the city took on more responsibilities.[10] For instance, after the cholera epidemics, city officials worked to improve the water supply and introduced sewerage. Previously, acquiring potable water and managing human and animal

Fig. 17 Near North Side around the Kinzie house from J. T. Palmatary's bird's-eye view of Chicago in 1857: rail yards and grain elevator at the main stem of the Chicago River up Cass Street (now Wabash) past the Kinzie house, old St. James Church, and second St. James Church at Huron Street.

wastes had been largely in the hands of households. Then the city mandated raising street grades in densely populated neighborhoods, followed by installing water pipes and sewers. When the city laid these lines on Michigan Street in 1856, the Kinzie family lived temporarily at the Lake House to allow for modernization that included not only indoor plumbing but also gas lines.[11]

The service improvements within homes physically shifted the line between public and private, between the formal world of the state and the informal world of the household. Running water and flush toilets directly connected the Kinzie household to their neighborhood and to Chicago. While Juliette and John may have welcomed these improvements, with the expansion of city government to include water lines, sewerage, street paving, and policing, taxes and assessments on real estate grew substantially. These increases hit the Kinzies hard, since they still owned lots beyond those their house stood on, remnants of the original Kinzie Addition. During the 1840s these lots provided little income, but neither did they add much to their expenses. That changed in the 1850s; Juliette regularly complained about the "awful" taxes and assessments, which she knew would be "more than we like!"[12]

To meet the increasing tax burden, as well as to capture some profit from neighborhood development, on several of the lots John and Juliette built and rented out inexpensive frame structures. They hoped to take advantage of the rising real estate values as their neighborhood became denser and more heterogeneous.[13] Juliette was very much involved, seeing these properties as an extension of her household into the formal economy. She supervised the cleaning and upkeep of the units, helped to choose tenants, and often collected rents personally; she also kept careful track of income and expenses. Increasingly their tenants were Irish immigrants. Whenever Juliette had trouble with Irish tenants, she was quick to blame their ethnicity. In one case, when "miserable" Irish tenants left without settling their rent, Juliette and John promised themselves they would "never have another Irish tenant." But they soon broke that vow in their battle to cover the tax bills.[14]

A Modernizing Household

The family lived with the bounty of the seasons even as their relation to the market changed. Soon after they built their home, Juliette and John were enjoying strawberries from their well-cultivated garden, and they invited friends and neighbors to celebrations that centered on great quantities of the fruit. Juliette preserved dozens of jars of strawberries as well as making jam, saving some of that sweet June flavor for the dead of winter. By the mid-1850s, Juliette found she no longer had to rely solely on her own strawberries but could purchase berries raised by regional farmers; by 1858 she could buy strawberries shipped from Cincinnati.[15]

After the end of strawberry season, Juliette and her servants kept busy "pickling peppers, mangoes [bell peppers], yellow-pickles, tomatoes, onions, and cucumbers." Initially Juliette worked with glass jars of all sizes, but industrialization changed this as well. By the late 1850s, she had begun canning some of her preserves, taking advantage of tin cans manufactured more cheaply than glass jars. After Juliette had filled the cans, she had a tinsmith fasten on their tops for a small fee.[16]

Juliette also made sure her household had butter, eggs, and milk. Into the late 1840s, like many of their neighbors, the family owned a cow that grazed in the open fields around the Michigan Street house. But as railroad tracks, factory smokestacks, and shanties replaced those fields, Juliette got fresh eggs and butter from a tenant farmer in lieu of cash rent. Then peddlers began coming to her door, selling butter and eggs. Juliette chose those who brought produce "fresh from the country," now that her family lived in a denser, more urban neighborhood.[17]

Juliette's experiences showed how industrialization affected households directly. She spent her life responding to new products and methods, integrating them into her household as she could afford them and when she felt they improved daily life. Beyond food preparation, these changes were most readily apparent with clothing. Juliette was rightly proud of her traditional needlework skills.

She made most of the clothing the family wore, from pants and petticoats to "diaper-drawers" for her babies, made from a "half-square of fine cotton" into which she sewed a "ruffle at the place which goes round the leg."[18]

Juliette had learned to do all this work by hand, but by the late 1850s the sewing machine became part of her world. Although she did not own a sewing machine, Juliette hired a woman who had one to come to her house for several weeks and work alongside her making clothing. During a short burst of "furious exploits," the pair would make dozens of shirts, pants, and sheets. Juliette found that the "sewing machine is by no means the thing it is cracked up to be. It does not sew nicely." She found it fit only to make pants, common petticoats, and sheets.[19] Still, she continued to employ women with sewing machines to reduce the arduous work of running up seams for all the linens and other ordinary items.

Juliette had an increasingly wide choice of products available to her in the expanding commercial district south of the river along Lake Street. In fine weather, she traveled across the Rush Street Bridge and perused the many new shops and stores selling products from the region, the nation, and beyond. Over the 1850s, several horsecar lines offered an alternative to the family carriage in inclement weather. The Kinzie family had running accounts with stores that sold books, shoes, buttons and ribbons, cloth, tea, and coffee. Juliette was actively involved both in purchasing these goods and in settling household accounts. She kept meticulous records, especially as she purchased more goods and services over the course of the 1850s. She was proud that her family did "not spend one-half" of their earnings on household expenses.[20]

Educating Sons

Juliette and John were highly conscious of the rapidly changing economy; the uncertainty of these years made it difficult for them to direct their children's education and training. Having endured downturns in 1819, 1837, and 1857, they understood that the business cycles—tied to wars, government policies, and the vagaries of the market—made some people wealthy and left others mired in poverty. The couple sought stable and predictable paths for their children. Yet John's long apprenticeship with the American Fur Company did not provide a useful model in an industrializing city. Juliette had learned a wide range of household arts, from baking and canning to sewing and shoemaking, but many of these skills were growing obsolete in an industrial economy. How could they better prepare their children for the future?

These challenges were particularly acute for the growing middle class that the Kinzies were a part of. These were not the challenges faced by the city's working class, who took up the backbreaking work of building the canal, the railroads, and the city itself. Laborers did not have the means to obtain more than a rudimentary education for their offspring, and often they needed the wages of their teenage children to pay household expenses. In contrast, the wealthiest of Chicago's residents could groom their children at elite academies and finishing schools as well as through extended European travel. John and Juliette fit somewhere in between, searching for the best combination of training and experience to launch their children in business and society.

Over time the Kinzie children attended a range of schools: public and private, mixed and gender-segregated, day and boarding. They were part of a first generation of children educated in Chicago, and their parents were deeply involved in creating a broad infrastructure. The couple supported secular education as an adjunct to the religious training children received within their own household and congregation.

As Whigs, John and Juliette were committed to the expansion of public education not only for their own children, but for the broader population of Chicago. John served on the public school board during the 1840s and fought against the prevailing view that public schools "were only intended for paupers or those who could not pay for their children's schooling." As a show of support, for a time the couple sent their children to the public school at Ohio

and LaSalle Streets that most of the neighborhood children attended.[21]

Beyond Chicago, the couple supported a theological seminary
at Nashotah, Wisconsin, both financially and through regular visits to events there. When the Milwaukee diocese founded Racine
Academy in 1852, the Kinzie family and other members of St. James
supported it. Residents of Racine, along with regional Episcopalian
donors like the Kinzie family, constructed a large building "in an
oak grove, fronting on Lake Michigan." The next year fourteen-
year-old John and twelve-year-old Arthur enrolled there alongside
thirty other boys. John and Arthur took a classical course of study
that included mathematics, philosophy, Greek, Latin, English, and
natural sciences. There was a long tradition of classical education
in the Wolcott family, and Juliette hoped at least one of her sons
would attend Yale like her uncle and grandfather Wolcott.[22]

But John had little interest in continuing in the classics after
leaving Racine in 1857. He followed his fascination with the steam
engines that were transforming his neighborhood. Indeed, his first
memories included steamships docking at his father's Lake House.
He was not yet ten years old when the *Pioneer*, the first steam-
powered railroad engine, made its first run not far from his home.
The Galena and Chicago Railway built yards nearby along the river,
as did the Illinois Central Railroad. Steam engines were also introduced in early factories near the Michigan Street house. John took
an inordinate interest in the steam engines all around him.[23]

Juliette acknowledged her son's passion: "There was so much of
love for running an engine in his composition." Because there were
few academic programs in engineering in the United States, John
and Juliette tried to steer their son into a program in Europe. They
tutored him in French and German, hoping to improve the young
man's chances of acceptance, but he was entirely uninterested in
more formal schooling. Instead he took a series of jobs working
with steam engines, first with the Rock Island Railway. It was hard,
dirty work, and John soon "smashed his fingers, greased up his
wardrobe and wore out his muscles."[24]

The couple worried about their son's peripatetic career as well as about the hazards he faced; working with steam engines was dangerous. They witnessed the aftermath of several steam engine explosions. When a steamship blew up at a dock near the Kinzie house, Juliette reported that "the sight is a perfect wreck. . . . It is a wonder that more people were not killed or seriously wounded." Her concern was heightened because John was then working on another lake steamer, the *Lady Elgin*. But by the time the *Lady Elgin* sank at Evanston in 1860, drowning 287 people, John had already moved on to another position.[25]

When an entrepreneur, hoping to establish steam-powered bakeries in major cities, showered praise on their son's knowledge and skills, John and Juliette were lured into investing in his business. They hoped it would bring their son success, or at least stability. For a time Juliette touted the bread and crackers the bakery produced, but John soon tired of the clerk's work he was assigned and moved on to another railroad job.[26]

John and Juliette continued to support their son by providing him a home in Chicago. In early 1861 John introduced his parents to Elevanah Janes, whose family lived near Racine Academy. Unknown to his parents, Ellie and John had been sweethearts for years. Juliette found her to be "a pretty, amiable, sensible little person," although she did not see how her son could yet "afford to maintain a wife." The couple did not agree and were married just a few weeks later. They settled into the Kinzie home, and John began working with his father at the canal collector's office while continuing to look for other opportunities to work with steam engines.[27]

By contrast, second son Arthur chose to continue his education after leaving Racine Academy in 1857. He enrolled at Kenyon College in Gambier, Ohio. Founded in 1824 to train Episcopalian clergy, by the 1850s the institution enrolled a broader range of students. Arthur did well and opined that "Kenyon is the most gentlemanly institution he ever saw." Juliette was proud of his success in Greek and Latin. Here, perhaps, was her Yale scholar![28]

Juliette's dreams were dampened in late November 1859 when

Arthur came home and said he wanted to stay in Chicago to work for a railroad or become a farmer. His reluctance to return to Ohio may have been influenced by the financial problems his parents then faced, but there was also turmoil at the school. Students and teachers clashed over the strict rules as well as over religious instruction. Ultimately Arthur returned to Kenyon when Juliette's brother paid his tuition and expenses. Julian Magill argued that "it was simply returning a very small part of what had been bestowed on him at Arthur's age."[29]

Juliette remained hopeful that her youngest son, George, might become a clergyman. In 1858–59 he attended the local public Ogden School, where he regularly won prizes. In 1860 he enrolled at the preparatory school of the new University of Chicago. He traveled there on "the cars" (horse-drawn streetcars) along State Street south of the Chicago River. George attended the university for several years but never trained for the ministry.[30]

Rising Capitalists

Despite all Juliette's careful budgeting, the family was hit hard by the 1857 Panic and depression that affected all but the wealthiest Chicagoans. The Kinzies lost rents and other income and had to figure out ways to cut back on expenses. For workers the downturn had more dire effects—20,000 people lost their jobs in Chicago during the winter of 1857-58. This loss was even more painful because "artisanal work was disappearing and laborers crowded a market of low wages and few benefits" as wealth became concentrated in just a few cities and among the very top wage earners. Juliette and John certainly saw this in the streets of their neighborhood and at church services.[31] Many members of Juliette's church circle had acquired fortunes of global proportions. William Ogden and Walter Newberry amassed fortunes in real estate, railroads, and industrial investments. The Rumseys' affluence expanded with the Chicago Board of Trade, while John Turner's involvement with the Galena and Chicago Railroad ensured his wealth.

Like Juliette and John, their pastor Dr. Clarkson wrestled with the great fortunes being amassed by some of his congregation's leading families, especially as their wealth conflicted with central tenets of their faith. In the pulpit, he preached that many Chicagoans "worship the dollar more idolatrously than I could imagine men with reason and souls could do." Clarkson encouraged his flock to tend instead to the many needy families who lived "in shanties not too far from the lawns and greenhouses of the rich."[32]

Juliette, who had been on an economic roller coaster all her life, took Clarkson's words to heart. She wanted a refined life but rejected the extravagance around her that she could not afford. Her husband was happier with his life, surrounded by family in their old home. Juliette tried to content herself within a household that offered comfort but not luxury. She worked to make herself satisfied with "money enough to buy whatever was needed."[33]

Juliette was in some ways philosophical about her neighbors' great fortunes. She herself had experienced two periods in her life when she was among the most affluent in her circle. Before 1819 her father had been one of the richest men in Middletown, Connecticut, and before the 1837 Panic Juliette and John were among Chicago's wealthiest. But now they watched as a new generation of affluence emerged.[34]

By 1857 the Kinzie home, among the city's best and most spacious when new, was cramped within a burgeoning industrial district. Wealthier neighbors were moving away. One family moved to a larger, more elegant house after an extended European tour, renting their old house to Catholic nuns who constructed a "big frame building . . . for school purposes" in what had been "pleasant gardens." While this was better than a factory or warehouse, Juliette, ever wary of Roman Catholics, was dismayed by the change.[35]

Other affluent neighbors were moving, building anew, or refurbishing their homes. Juliette especially admired their fine lake views and beautiful libraries. Among them was William Ogden, who embellished his estate north of the Kinzie house with an extensive library, fine paintings, and furniture. Yet Juliette also coveted amenities like greenhouses that provided flowers, lettuce, and fruit during the winter. On one February visit, while snow and ice blanketed the world outside, Juliette enjoyed the warmth, scents, and colors of one indoor garden but could not avoid feeling envious.[36]

Juliette was more critical of the ostentatious display of wealth among some of her neighbors. Visiting Cyrus McCormick's new mansion, she disdainfully wondered why he "had not provided an inventory of furniture with prices left in some conspicuous place." She could barely contain her anger that their Episcopal bishop was dissatisfied with "a library on the first floor, glass doors, ten or twelve bedrooms, in short an elegant and complete establishment."[37] That a clergyman could dismiss such luxury as insufficient was beyond the pale.

Travel, as well as mansions and expensive clothing, became a conspicuous marker of great wealth. Leisure travel became a regular part of upper-class life as railroads and steamships offered more and more luxurious accommodations. Regular steamships carried whole families to Europe. But Juliette, once among the most adventurous, seldom left Chicago. Many of her neighbors left for months or even years, and a number of them gave up their houses altogether. Even Juliette's brother Julian spent years abroad, leaving her without his companionship and guidance. She saw each departure as "los[ing] another friend."[38]

Despite the rise of this elite, gossip remained a source of power for Juliette, even over the newly rich. One scandal concerned a very wealthy neighbor who was also a congregant at St. James. The young woman had a baby just six months after her marriage. Initially the family gave it out that the baby was premature and not expected to live, but Juliette saw the lie in that when the child was found to be "in every aspect like a mature nine month infant."[39] Yet Juliette tried to "think the best and most charitably." Although she assumed the child had been conceived before the wedding, she thought the family would have gotten more sympathy if they had not been so quick to censure others and had not "always judged by appearances and not with a righteous judgment." John tried to keep Juliette from making any public pronouncement on what she saw as hypocritical behavior, since it would do no good to alienate their wealthier neighbors.

John was generally a more forgiving, amenable member of his circle. He tried to soften his wife's judgmental views, at least outside their house.[40] While Juliette often heeded John's advice, she understood the power to shape "genteel society" that she and other women wielded through their parlor conversations. Gossip was not an idle game; it was central to a world where credit and business dealings still relied heavily on personal connections and family. In one rather dramatic case, Juliette remained in a state of high anxiety about some gossip and the alleged transgression behind it. She understood her responsibility: "I could realize now the position and sufferings of a juror sitting to receive evidence by which he is to acquit or pass sentence of death upon a prisoner.[41]

Another scandal that provided months of fodder for gossip concerned a sordid affair and very public divorce among neighbors who, Juliette regularly noted, were Presbyterians. The Burch divorce displayed the intermingling of moral, social, and economic standing. The case was covered by several New York newspapers, as well as the Chicago press, because the wife was from a prominent New York family. Isaac H. Burch had come to Chicago in 1845. He was a banker and an early investor in railroads, serving as a director of the Galena and Chicago Railroad, among others. His wife, Mary, was the niece of wealthy industrialist Erastus Corning. Burch's banking business flourished, at least in part because of the many social and family connections to the Cornings. Isaac Burch accused his wife of taking up with another man while he was away. Juliette found the whole thing scandalous, but it was even "worse because [Mary Burch] taught in the Mission Sunday School!!"[42]

The case was part of Chicagoans' daily life for months. Because of the heightened interest, the trial was moved thirty miles west to Naperville in order to get a jury less tainted by press coverage. One of Juliette's cousins wondered whether "the very devil reigned here in Chicago just now?" Many "of the most prominent ladies and gentlemen of Chicago" were called to testify as witnesses to the business and social standing of the estranged couple. While Juliette professed relief that she was not called to testify, she also was bothered that her perspective had not been solicited.[43]

Since Isaac Burch had sued for divorce, he had to prove his wife had transgressed. The jury was not swayed by his evidence of her infidelity, and she was acquitted. Juliette was dismissive of the reaction in Chicago, where "bells and rockets" were set off on the "arrival of a woman who under the most lenient construction had conducted herself as no wife should." Juliette decried the way the case had demeaned all married women, making "female and conjugal propriety a matter of perfect indifference." Still, she could not help discussing the case further, and she was not alone. A pamphlet presenting the misdeeds of the estranged husband sold briskly. It argued that Burch had maliciously maligned his wife's reputation after having exhausted her money and family connections.[44]

Through these turbulent years, Juliette and John remained strong supporters of St. James Church. They attended services several times a week and found solace in their faith as they mourned deaths and other losses. Their faith also offered comfort as Juliette began to suffer from several chronic ailments, including rheumatism and asthma. John worked closely with Dr. Robert H. Clarkson, their pastor from 1849 to 1865. Juliette told Nellie she felt certain there was no one "out of his own family that Dr. C loves as much as your father." When a rumor circulated, and was picked up by a local paper, that John and Juliette had sold their house, Clarkson reacted with "alarm." He breathed a sigh of relief on finding that the announcement was false, noting, "I do not know what we should have done here without him."[45]

Although the Kinzies did not leave the church, it soon left them. Increasingly, wealthy congregants found the church too modest, too close to industry and business, and too far from their new homes. Once substantial and imposing, St. James did not have space for High Church rituals that included a communion table, a robed choir, and stained-glass windows. In 1854 the congregation raised funds to buy property several blocks north, near William B. Ogden's large house and gardens. Ogden was among the group who raised funds to build a more impressive structure designed to stand favorably alongside the nearby Roman Catholic cathedral.[46] Although they had been the primary donors to the first church, the Kinzies could not make a large contribution for the second. The best they could do most years was continue to rent a pew, which was the minimum expected of members. Others stepped forward: Walter Newberry and other neighbors retired the $30,000 construction debt.[47]

The new church was completed in 1857. The relocation reflected the declining influence of the Kinzie family. After the dedication in January 1858, what once had been the "Kinzie church" now stood at a distance from the Michigan Street house.[48]

Juliette Responds

Juliette was over fifty at this time, and her health had been in decline for several years. During the humid days of summer, she had trouble breathing, likely exacerbated by the soot and smoke of nearby railroads and industry; when the weather turned cold, she suffered from rheumatism that kept her in bed for weeks at a time. John cared for her, making sure she had a good fire nearby to ward off her pain. He brought coffee and newspapers to her bedside in the morning. He also carried Juliette's letters to the post office and brought back correspondence, national newspapers, and magazines. Whereas Juliette stayed inside, John liked to work in the garden even in winter. One cold February day, Juliette watched from a window as her husband pruned his grapevines even though the ground was covered with snow and ice.[49]

John was his wife's regular source of local news. He was quick to oblige, coming home from the canal office at midday for dinner and bringing the latest tales, gossip, and letters. One day he brought a letter from Copenhagen from someone claiming kinship and needing money. When John contemplated offering help, Juliette chastised him, but generally conversation in their parlor and dining room was more companionable. Their parrot, Polly, was an endless source of anecdotes as well as being company for Juliette during the day.[50]

During the long hours Juliette was home alone, she turned more and more to writing. After the publication of *Wau-Bun* in 1856, she began work on her first fiction, her novel *Walter Ogilby*. The story line was a predictable romance, where the modest but comely heroine ultimately captures the heart of a worthy, well-educated, and wealthy young man. When *Walter Ogilby* was rejected by several eastern publishers, Juliette tried to stay optimistic by reminding herself that "*Jane Eyre* was rejected by seven different publishers. . . . I do not lose faith in my book, nor do I feel discouraged."[51]

Although writing was a solitary pursuit, Juliette regularly shared drafts with family and friends. She often read them aloud to her husband during long evenings in their parlor or on the piazza in the fading summer light. Juliette enlisted other friends and family as readers. Dr. Clarkson praised the manuscript, suggesting that "all that you made happen seems perfectly natural."[52] A friend on an extended visit amused herself by reading Jane Austen's *Persuasion* and then the *Walter Ogilby* manuscript aloud to Juliette. She opined that Juliette's novel was "exceedingly interesting and exquisitely written" and "that it must have great success."[53]

Juliette also read her draft to her longtime friend Elizabeth DeKoven Dyer, who, like Juliette, aspired to become a successful novelist. Although they were loyal and supportive friends, they were also fierce critics of each other's work. Juliette was clearly distraught when her friend nodded off as she listened to chapters from *Walter Ogilby*, but she conjectured that this might be payback for harsh comments Juliette had made on Dyer's latest story. Juliette wrote of her friend's manuscript: "There were parts that were worthy of Thackeray or Dickens and some that I would much rather have seen from their pens than from hers."[54]

Walter Ogilby, though set in the Northeast, allowed Juliette to wrestle with the modernization, industrialization, and growing individualism around her in Chicago. Among the novel's central themes were transience and mobility, embodied in the railroads just outside Juliette's door. Where once the trip between New York and Chicago had taken weeks, by the late 1850s it could be completed in just under two days. Juliette described railroads as "those ingenious contrivances for annihilating time, space, and human life." But her admiration was tinged with nostalgia for a past where people were more rooted: "As a general thing, people stayed at home in a humdrum manner, attended to their duties to God and their neighbor, and fancied that they were fulfilling exactly what they had been sent into the world for."[55] Juliette lamented the passing of a stable community as her neighbors traveled widely and moved away and as even her church abandoned her.

This mobility fostered an individualism that was bolstered by the growing dominance of wage labor. Juliette saw this both within her household and outside her doors. While she envisioned a household economy at the center of a good community, with family and servants working together for a common good, she increasingly faced recalcitrant help who did not embrace her worldview. A wider range of religious, class, and ethnic groups made ideas of a "common good" increasingly contested. In *Walter Ogilby* Juliette wrote dispiritedly about servants, black and white, immigrant and native, who did not accept their place at the bottom of the household hierarchy. She disdained "negroes [who] think they must put by work" for holidays of their own making. An employer was angry with a servant who "would go snoopin' round in closets and in trunks—every place that was not locked."[56] Juliette disparaged servants who had their own agendas counter to the needs of the household.

In Juliette's view the rise of the formal market—where households had to buy basic goods and pay wages—was eroding society. Juliette wrote nostalgically of a world where families lived "on their own farms and their children by them, without ranging all about the world to find a living." They sold their surplus crops, earning "money enough to buy whatever was needed, and a good bit more." Her characters found, as she did, that industry, railroads, and denser development made it difficult to keep cows and hens and to raise fruits and vegetables in the city. Through her characters she looked wistfully to a past where "women spun, and wove, and knit what they wanted to wear, without being beholden to their neighbors to do it for them."[57] Juliette had learned all these skills, but they were not necessary in 1850s Chicago. Instead, she needed cash.

In *Walter Ogilby* she lamented the poor working conditions for textile workers. She described the inhuman machinery where "greasy little boys, and . . . pale, weary-looking girls" sat "in a row, at a long board, on which was stretched a web of cloth." Her young heroine exclaimed, "What a life to lead. . . . to be chained down day after day to the same unvarying, uninteresting employment. It is enough to paralyze the mind—to destroy the faculties."[58] She was deeply troubled by the inhumanity of industrial work and the toll it took.

Juliette was particularly critical of middle- and upper-class women who no longer provided food and clothing for their households, leading them to shop, dress fashionably, gossip, and attend social events. She mocked young women who devoted too much time to studying the "comparative merits of a pink zephyr handkerchief and a blue one." Juliette showed real disdain for the overbearing character of a wealthy young woman who prided "herself upon her father's fortune, and her own fashionable education and acquaintances."[59] She reminded her readers that having money did not ensure good taste. It was only a short way from these fictional descriptions to her Chicago neighbors.

Juliette had little tolerance for the growing consumerism and individualism of American society. As an Episcopalian, she believed in societal hierarchies. She was not a supporter of revivals or evangelism. She was not an abolitionist, although she abhorred the excesses of slavery. She was not an advocate for women's rights, instead accepting traditional limits for women both within and outside the household. She did not advocate for the rights of wage laborers, though she wrote critically about industrialization, which degraded household work and promoted rampant consumerism. She remained an advocate for self-sufficiency in an increasingly consumer-driven society. Still, Juliette understood that the market was coming to dominate more and more of their lives. She may have wanted to retreat, but the need to launch their children and the troubling currents of national politics forced her and John to confront this new world.

PART 3

Losing Home and Neighborhood,
1857–70

6

....

Uncertain Future

During their years on Michigan Street, Juliette and John managed a hierarchical household that included a large extended family, immigrant and native-born household workers, and indentured servants including several African Americans who had been enslaved. In the worlds where the couple had themselves grown up, many members of their communities had been unfree, subject in one way or another to a head of household (a master). There were enslaved and indentured servants in the Connecticut households of Juliette's childhood, and John himself had served an indenture.

Over their tenure on Michigan Street, more and more Americans gained political and economic independence. Although the household world never disappeared, individualism and wage labor became more important as industrialization and modernization transformed Chicago.[1] Indentured servitude all but disappeared. Working-class white men gained full political rights, and the institution of slavery was abolished in more and more northern states. Still, women and children, even those who were wage earners, remained subject to their husbands or fathers, while more than four million people remained enslaved.

Both the abolition movement and the women's rights movement emerged as small groups of men and women argued for dismantling the hierarchies that bound enslaved people and women. But neither John nor Juliette advocated extending full and equal rights to all individuals. Their continued commitment to the traditional household based in responsibilities can be seen not only in their politics, but in the training they provided their daughter, Nellie. Her courtship and marriage played out amid the tumultuous political and economic debates of the 1850s.

Educating Nellie

The decisions Juliette and John made about their only daughter's education offer glimpses of their attitudes toward women and their place in the world. For a time Nellie attended public school with her brothers, but most of her education took place in a series of girls' schools operated by widows or single women. Her favorite, just a block north of home, was run by four sisters who "were thoroughly competent gentlewomen." As a teenager, Nellie entered an all-female academy on the South Side of Chicago where she studied geography, writing, physiology, arithmetic, German, and Latin. She "loved this school and the teachers and made many of the warmest friends." After two years she continued her classical studies, learning Latin "in a class of young men."[2]

Up to this point Nellie received a preparatory education that equaled (or even exceeded) that of her brothers. Although there were a few colleges that admitted women, including Oberlin in Ohio, this was not an option her parents considered. Oberlin was not an Episcopalian institution, and it had a reputation as a center for abolitionism. Neither of these qualities would help make Nellie a better wife and mother. While there was real uncertainty over the best training for the Kinzie sons, John and Juliette educated their daughter so that she could make a good marriage and be prepared to run a household.

In 1852 eighteen-year-old Nellie enrolled in a finishing school in New York City run by a couple who had spent years in Chicago. Madame Canda's French School was decidedly less academic than Emma Willard's Troy Female Seminary where Juliette had studied. At the school, known "for being one of the best and most fashionable institutions of its kind," Nellie studied French, literature, music, and art and took part in music recitals and theatricals.[3] This school in lower Manhattan was attractive because both John and Juliette had extended family in the area. Nellie did not remember "a moment of homesickness," largely because she was often in the homes of relatives she knew well. Two of the cousins who had lived for many years in the Michigan Street house now lived in New York: Henry Wolcott and Mrs. Joseph Balestier (Caroline Wolcott).[4] Also, Nellie's cousin Posey (Maria), daughter of Robert and Gwinthlean Kinzie, attended another school in New York City during these years.

Posey was especially close to the girls' uncle and aunt Lieutenant David Hunter and his wife, Maria, who were also living in New York City. Maria Hunter was delighted when her husband was assigned there, enjoying the social scene after years of isolated western postings. The couple rented a cottage near West Point and invited Posey, Nellie, and their friends to spend weekends with them. While there, the girls attended social events at West Point, much as Juliette had done decades before.

The cousins frequently brought classmates to the West Point retreat, including Nellie's closest school friend, Eliza Gordon of Savannah. Sometimes Eliza's brother, William (Willie), then a student at Yale, joined the group. Nellie's first impression of him was rather dismissive; she thought he "looked like a Methodist minister." But fairly soon Nellie was joining Eliza on trips to New Haven and the pair became better acquainted, enjoying lively conversations during weekend gatherings. The couple declared their love for each other in Yale's library in 1854 and began what became a long courtship.[5]

A Sectional Courtship

This match was not what Juliette and John had envisioned. When Nellie returned to Chicago, she was nearly twenty, and many of her friends were engaged or already married. Her parents still held out hope that Nellie would find a Chicago beau, ideally within the St. James congregation. Instead she began a long-distance courtship with William Gordon, who had returned to Savannah after graduating from Yale. Like her mother, Nellie was a skilled letter writer. Willie described their correspondence as like having "a little chat with you." He often referred to Nellie as "wife" during their courtship, while Nellie sometimes called herself "wifey," her father's pet name for Juliette.[6]

In September 1855, over a year after Nellie returned to Chicago, Willie came for an extended visit and the couple became engaged. Nellie showed Willie around Chicago and introduced him to her family and friends. Juliette's wealthy brother Julian hosted a large party in their honor. They hoped to persuade Willie to relocate to Chicago, but he remained adamant about staying in Georgia. So, late in the fall of 1855, Nellie traveled to Savannah, accompanied by her parents. She stayed into the spring of 1856, but wedding plans stalled.[7]

The delay in setting a date was tied to the contentious sectional politics that gripped the nation. In 1854 Democratic senator Stephen A. Douglas sponsored the Kansas-Nebraska Act, overturning the 1820 Missouri Compromise that had set the dividing line between potential free and slave states at 36°30′. Under the new law, residents of the Kansas and Nebraska Territories would decide for themselves whether to prohibit or allow the institution of slavery. For those opposed to the expansion of slavery, this legislation meant that slavery would no longer be restricted in the west. Within a matter of months, opponents and proponents of the extension of slavery poured into Kansas, beginning a guerrilla war that would eventually become the Civil War. Lieutenant David Hunter was reassigned to Fort Leavenworth in Kansas as the federal government added army units to tamp down the violence in the territory. Hunter was to come back from Kansas a committed abolitionist.

Although the Kinzie family knew Stephen Douglas, who had substantial real estate investments on Chicago's South Side, they opposed the senator and his legislation. John Kinzie was one of the disaffected Whigs who joined with Free Soil Democrats in Illinois to create the new Republican Party that opposed the expansion of slavery in the west. Over time, most Free Soil Democrats in Illinois, including William B. Ogden, would become members of the Republican Party. From the start, Juliette and Nellie joined John in staunch support of the new party. This made for unanimity within the Michigan Street house but for discord between Nellie and Willie.

Willie was a Southern Democrat who affirmed "slavery in its glory." Such a stand did not endear him either to Nellie or to her family, even though none of them were abolitionists. Willie wrote that while he "deplored the Kanzas [sic] and Nebraska Act for the agitation it roused," he found the principle on which it stood just and those who opposed to it guilty of "treason." Nellie rejected the notion that her family's views were treasonous. William suggested that Nellie had to change her opinions to match "the community in which she [was] to live" upon marriage. Instead, the wedding plans foundered.[8]

For Willie, and for much of the country, Chicago became a symbol of antislavery sentiment as new Republicans like Abraham Lincoln made impassioned speeches against the Kansas-Nebraska Act. In 1856 Senator Charles Sumner from Massachusetts was caned nearly to death by South Carolina representative Preston Brooks in the Senate chamber, marking a new low of incivility in the US Capitol. The young couple embodied a sectional crisis that was becoming white-hot; they barely corresponded during this time.

When Willie did write, he declared, "I would never care to step on Northern ground again."[9]

Still, the couple's attachment was not sundered; they restored their relationship in a series of letters. Yet slavery was not their only point of conflict. Willie was raised a Presbyterian, but Nellie wanted to be married in St. James Episcopal Church, where she had "been baptized, confirmed and catechized."[10] Willie did not want to get married in the Episcopal Church. Nellie prevailed on this issue, although she agreed to move to Savannah and tempered her expression of political views.

The wedding was delayed into 1857. Willie became ill and his mother tried to quash wedding plans. Mrs. Gordon wanted her son to launch his career firmly before marriage; she also was dismayed by Nellie's religion, region, politics, and lack of fortune. Juliette cringed at the gossip within their Chicago circle over the postponements. Nellie endured countless "misunderstandings and suspicions." In April 1857 she wrote to Willie that since they had not been together in over a year, "when we meet again we shall have to commence our courtship over again."[11]

During much of this time, Juliette had been ailing, and Nellie had been pressed into nursing her. To give her a break from sickroom duty and idle Chicago gossip, her parents encouraged her to travel east to visit relatives. Nellie spent the summer in Manchester, Vermont, with her cousin Lizzie Skinner, then returned to the New York home of Caroline Balestier. There she met William's mother, who also was visiting New York City. The encounter must have gone well, since the couple renewed plans for a fall wedding.[12]

By late 1857, though, there were just weeks left when they could be married in the old brick St. James Church across the street from the Kinzie house. After the first of the year, the congregation would be moving to their new grander building. After years of waiting, there was only a short time to execute plans; Juliette alluded to "the hurry of everything crowded into two days." Invitation cards were delivered to a small group of family and friends invited to the wedding on December 21, 1857. The marriage was solemnized by Dr. Clarkson.

A reception for more than fifty guests was held at the Kinzie home. Though it was late December, the house was filled with flowers provided by wealthy friends with greenhouses. This was one of the few moments when Juliette displayed no envy of such neighbors. The simple reception included cake and other refreshments as well as a display of wedding gifts.[13]

Noticeably absent was Willie's family; none of his Southern relatives accompanied him. Even his mother refused to travel to Chicago. A Gordon family member explained that "it is against our principles to spend our money and countenance by our presence a city so given unto fanaticism." While Willie acknowledged that Nellie and her family might "think this absurd," he maintained that "it is at any rate an honest absurdity and a conscientious one."[14]

Afterward, Nellie's brothers delivered cake and cards to those who had not been able to attend. The newly married couple had already left for New York City, spending Christmas Day with friends and relatives there and then boarding a steamer for Savannah. Both Nellie and her parents would make this trip many times. Members of the Gordon family would not.

Marriage

Nellie's marriage marked a major change in the Kinzie household. For more than two decades, their home had centered on family—raising children and offering a haven to relatives and friends. Juliette acknowledged her attachment to the place where "our own sons and daughters gr[e]w up around us." With Nellie's departure that home was diminished. John lamented to his wife that "we've got no daughter anymore."[15] While Juliette keenly felt Nellie's absence, she found great solace in letter writing. The letters they shared several times a week became their parlor conversations.

Nellie related the troubles she had in becoming a married

Fig. 18 This federal-style house built in 1821 at the corner of Bull and South Broad (now Oglethorpe Avenue) in Savannah was purchased by the Gordon family in 1831. Juliette Kinzie's daughter, Nellie, came here in late 1857 as the bride of William Gordon. They raised a large family, including Juliette Gordon Low, founder of the Girl Scouts of the USA. The house is maintained today as the Juliette Gordon Low Birthplace by the Girl Scouts of the USA. Image from the Collection of the Girl Scouts of the USA. Used by permission.

woman. She did not feel at home in Savannah and missed her parents' doting attention. She bristled when her new husband made decisions for her that were often at odds with what she would have chosen. She had no space she could call her own in a household run by her mother-in-law, supported by her husband. Nellie was learning that as individuals married women had little legal power.

Nellie may not have understood these stark realties because within the Kinzie household Juliette's opinions mattered and she made many decisions. Still, even this congenial household was not based in equality. John was the head and was recognized as such in the formal economy. Married woman were *feme covert* (literally, "woman covered"); they had no formal political status apart from their husbands. In a companionable marriage like that of John and

Juliette, this lack of status had little meaning, "but in a poor one the consequences could be serious."[16]

Juliette accepted her subordinate place in part because she experienced "wedded happiness . . . in spite of some sickness and sorrow with which we have occasionally been visited." She wanted her daughter to have a similar experience. But Nellie longed for the household that had been the anchor all her life. Juliette noted that, on marrying, women "choose a new home and then we find out that the old one was not so bad after all." Juliette acknowledged Nellie's homesickness, but her daughter had made a permanent choice. Juliette candidly reminded her that "you cannot run back to mother."[17]

Juliette thought a great deal about courtship and marriage as her daughter negotiated them both. During this time she wrote and revised her first full-length novel, *Walter Ogilby*, with these topics at its center. She watched as Nellie embraced the notions of romantic love then present in so many novels. Her daughter's courtship, while fraught, definitely met these expectations as Willie again and again expressed his undying love and devotion to his betrothed. But the novels seldom focused on life after the wedding, and here Nellie confronted a different reality. The romance of courtship glossed over the fundamental inequality of marriage, where "the wife's legal subordination persisted."[18]

Juliette reminded Nellie that even had she remained in Chicago, "surrounded by the kindest and best of friends," she still would have had to negotiate the separation from her parents in order to establish a new household. She encouraged her daughter to make a home with her husband. This was difficult, since Nellie became part of her mother-in-law's household yet did not feel like family. Juliette gently encouraged her daughter to accept the situation: Willie was "bound" to provide his wife with a "pleasant and happy home," but the particulars were his choice. Juliette wanted Nellie to understand a cold, hard truth: "You belong to him. . . . You must remember that as an individual you have ceased to exist, being only part and parcel of Mr. William Gordon."[19]

Even before their marriage Willie felt that Nellie belonged to him. For instance, he took a proprietary interest in the portrait of her painted by George Peter Healy, writing that he was "willing that your parents should keep the portrait." Nellie's image belonged to him, just based on their engagement. More troubling, Willie denied Nellie's requests to travel to Chicago to visit her parents on several occasions after their marriage. He saw Chicago as enemy territory even before the outbreak of the Civil War. Nellie again learned the limits of her authority.[20]

While Juliette was disappointed that she did not see her daughter, she supported Willie's views. The subordination of all members of a household to its head was the foundation of the civic society she embraced. Every person had a place within a household, and rights were subordinated to responsibilities. Her daughter's role was to fulfill her obligations as a good wife and mother. Nellie had a complaint only if Willie was not fulfilling his obligation to provide a "pleasant and happy home."[21]

Nellie's husband adhered to this traditional view. Indeed, a rigid hierarchy within households was more pronounced in the South, where enslaved people held no rights. While Nellie's place was "clearly subordinate in fundamental ways" to her husband, she in turn dominated the enslaved people in her household. This was a hierarchy that Juliette recollected from her youth but that was increasingly rare in Chicago, where servants regularly upset the established order by making their own decisions like getting married or taking another position.[22]

Yet Nellie was representative of the tension of her times in another way too. A growing cadre of women's rights proponents argued that married women—indeed, all women—had basic rights that needed to be recognized and protected. Juliette and Nellie were aware of this movement, and they knew and respected women who worked for change. Juliette encouraged Kate Newell Doggett, a leading local women's rights advocate, when she arrived in Chicago.[23] When Lucy Stone, a strong abolitionist as well as an advocate for women's rights, spent the winter of 1859 in Chicago, Juliette welcomed her into her home. She encouraged and entertained these women but counseled a different course for herself and her daughter.

Both Juliette and Nellie saw a clear connection between women's rights and the abolition of slavery. When sparring with a Chicago abolitionist, Juliette likened her position as a wife to that of an enslaved person. She opined that wives, like those enslaved, did not have "their own will and way." Both were subordinate to their masters' or husbands' will: "In that respect they stood upon the same platform with myself and his wife . . . who never thought of stirring a step without the consent of our lord and masters." Juliette added that she knew many wives "whose health and hearts were broken by cold tyrannical unsympathizing treatment from husbands," just as the lives of some enslaved people were broken by heartless masters.[24]

Although Juliette was explicit in comparing marriage to the bondage of slavery, she also understood her superior position as a free white woman. She placed herself higher than African Americans, free or enslaved, as well as immigrants like the Irish. But with her superior position came more responsibility. When Nellie became angry with being a wife (and then a mother), Juliette was quick to reproach her, instructing her to accept her place, especially since she was "surrounded with every comfort and indulgence."[25]

Juliette was neither an ideologue nor a reformer. Toughened by death and economic challenges, she clung to her position in America's social, political, and economic hierarchy. She accepted her place as wife and mother as she had been trained to do at home and at the Willard school. She sought solace for her lot in religion and in her family. She expected others to accept their places as well, none more so than her daughter.

Despite all this, Juliette and John still entertained hopes of persuading their son-in-law to move to Chicago. They offered the newlyweds a home and employment in the city. John even offered

Willie his own position as canal toll collector. Juliette wrote, "William would like Chicago—he would like the people—he would like the prosperity and the animation of the place."[26]

Not surprisingly, the Gordons stayed in Savannah, and John and Juliette journeyed there in December 1858 for the birth of their first granddaughter (named Eleanor but known as Blossom). Juliette encouraged her daughter to accept her responsibilities as wife and mother with grace: "You must put aside consideration of self, of your convenience, of your own preference."[27] Taking her mother's hard advice, Nellie began to build a home in Savannah. She asked her mother to send seeds from their garden. She sought her advice about remedies for childhood illnesses and complaints and requested recipes. In this way Juliette and Nellie remained close despite long periods apart. And over time Nellie grew fonder of Mrs. Gordon, whom she began to call Mother.[28] Unfortunately for Juliette and her daughter, developments outside their households were not so peaceable.

Sectional Politics

Juliette filled her letters to Nellie across 1859 and into 1860 with family and local news. John, her oldest son, worked jobs that took him away from home on steamboats and railroads. Arthur was at Kenyon, and George was still in public school. Both of the younger sons played baseball at a field near Union Park on the Near West Side. The new sport's rules and traditions were just being worked out, but it captured the imagination of both young men as much as steam engines engaged their older brother. While this was not the sort of outing Juliette would have chosen for herself, she attended one of their games to support her sons. She thought it "beautifully played" and noted that she had "never looked upon anything with so much interest."[29] It was a manifestation of civic culture unlike any she had envisioned in the 1830s, but she understood that her sons' world would be very different.

John also tried to enter into the changing world around him, particularly for the sake of his sons. In 1859 he made a sizable investment in a Vermont pottery works, hoping it would yield a profit and provide a career for at least one of their sons. Juliette believed her husband should be afforded this success, "for he has been suffering the flows of fortune for more than twenty years."[30] Juliette's optimism was misplaced, as it often was regarding her husband's business ventures. While John was distracted by negotiating the pottery partnership and while his sister Ellen was dying in Detroit, his clerk at the canal office stole $5,000. Although the clerk was indicted for the crime, John was forced to reimburse the canal commission—which meant mortgaging the Michigan Street gardens. Juliette blamed her husband's trusting nature: "Of course, your father suspected nothing." But she also complained of the tribalism of the clerk, who was supported by other Irish immigrants and by the Democratic *Chicago Times*. The family endured newspaper accounts "assailing your father's character."[31] This was too much for Juliette, who knew her husband to be beyond any kind of thievery. Fortunately, others agreed with Juliette's assessment and John was at least able to keep his post.

Beyond family news, politics took up more and more space in Juliette's letters. The rise of Abraham Lincoln was of considerable interest, since Juliette and John had known him for many years. Together they had campaigned in 1840 for William Henry Harrison. They had met again in 1847 when Chicago hosted the River and Harbor Convention, where Lincoln gave a short speech in favor of federal funding of infrastructure improvements. Lincoln later reminisced with Juliette about their travels "together down through the country long years ago."[32]

Juliette also admired Mary Lincoln, who evinced a "cordial wish that all around her should enjoy themselves."[33] Juliette understood what drew Mary Lincoln to her husband, "a self-made man with a high order of natural abilities improved by unswerving study and constant exercise of a natural gift of eloquence." She thought Lincoln a better man because he had been "more than twenty years the husband of a lady of education and refinement."[34]

Critical to the Republican vision of the west was an egalitarianism emerging from the Declaration of Independence. But in a society based not on individuals but on households, "all men are created equal" meant that fathers, husbands, and brothers—not women—represented their households within the wider public sphere. And yet everyone within a household—man or woman, bound or free servant, adult or child—was responsible for its smooth operation. This "republican liberalism" was at the core of what became the Republican ideology. It was the basis on which John and Juliette had promoted the development of a civic culture at Chicago and was central to Abraham Lincoln's vision of the public duty to foster opportunities for education, access to credit, and transportation improvements.[35]

The world was changing quickly in ways that families like the Lincolns or the Kinzies could not have imagined in the 1830s. Modernization, and especially industrialization, had overturned their world. Lincoln was especially fascinated with new inventions like steam power, telegraphs, steel plows, and railroads. He once suggested to Juliette that the cheap "little Lucifer match" was the most important invention in their lifetimes—a rather curious choice over the steam engine and telegraph.[36]

While Lincoln embraced the changes that came with these inventions, Juliette was less sanguine about their effects. She knew that, outside her front door, industrialization and modernization challenged robust traditional households as the building blocks of a civic society. Capitalism peeled labor and production away from households and shifted the focus to individual laborers and consumers in a growing formal economy. Industrial workers did not fit neatly into a household world. Wage workers, whether men or women, could more easily operate as independent individuals. As industrialization took hold, free labor came to mean long hours, inadequate pay, poor working conditions, and the absence of employers' responsibility for the well-being of their workers. But this is not what Lincoln had in mind when he extolled free labor. For him free labor meant an opportunity for men to rise based on their efforts, a little luck, and help from the state in the form of a stable financial system, good transportation, and public education.[37]

Juliette's worldview was becoming anachronistic in large cities. Decision making was moving from home parlors and dining rooms to the boardrooms of corporations and cultural institutions. The expansive informal public sphere that had been prevalent in western cities like Chicago was fast disappearing, and with it Juliette's civic vision. Households would remain organizing units for society, but they would never again wield the influence they had during Juliette's early decades in Chicago.[38]

Ironically, as industrialization was valorizing wage labor, the supporters of slavery became even more entrenched. For Juliette, the subordination of most people was of a piece with her acceptance of a household world where race, ethnicity, and gender prescribed roles. Slavery was a central part of her experience, from the profits Middletown merchants made on it to the African Americans enslaved by US Army officers across the northwest in the 1830s to older servants in her 1840s household who had once been enslaved. Juliette held deep and unmoving prejudices. She did not support equal rights for African Americans or even most immigrants, but neither did she claim equal rights for herself. She accepted her place. She did not believe, as we putatively believe today, that equal rights were meant for everyone.[39]

Juliette acceptance of patriarchy meant, in fact, that she believed ending slavery would not "add to the happiness and well-being of the blacks." She gave no evidence for this assertion but noted, perhaps more honestly, that abolition would threaten her own happiness by having "a horde of free negroes let loose among us."[40] She disliked slavery, but she disliked the notion of independence for African Americans even more. In the same way that she viewed William Gordon's obligations, Juliette focused her criticism on slaveholders who did not fulfill theirs. She decried Virginia as a "negro-breeding state . . . where mothers are kept to give birth to children who at a certain age are to be taken from them and carried away to a southern market." But she accepted slavery in well-managed households. Juliette considered abolition "a breach of loyalty and patriotism" that undermined civil society.[41] She viewed abolitionists not as radical reformers so much as advocates of social upheaval.

Juliette rejected the views of a small but important group of abolitionists in Chicago who supported the *Western Citizen*, a newspaper edited by Zebina Eastman and backed by families like John and Mary Jones. She had nothing but disdain for Harriet Beecher Stowe, especially after the 1852 publication of *Uncle Tom's Cabin*. To her mind Stowe simply fomented turmoil and unrest. Juliette feared that the enslaved people in Nellie's household would one day attack the Gordon family.[42]

Juliette knew that abolitionists were in a small minority across the west; she was particularly incensed with those who aided runaway slaves because of their "mistaken views of duty and philanthropy." She advocated severe punishment for breaking the fugitive slave law, since "when people make up their minds to meddle with what does not concern them, it is to be supposed they have weighed the consequences and are ready to meet them." Juliette was particularly intolerant of male abolitionists in their circle of acquaintances who were not also supporters of women's rights. From her perspective, these men were tinkering with a hierarchy that would keep her bound even if it managed to set African Americans free.[43]

Election of Abraham Lincoln

In May 1860 Chicago hosted the Republican presidential convention. John and Juliette Kinzie were both members of the local arrangements committee. For months they planned how best to spotlight Chicago and their candidate, Abraham Lincoln. Most important, the committee financed and supervised the construction of the Wigwam, at the corner of Lake and Market Streets, to house the convention. The name Wigwam was appropriated from a Native American term for a temporary structure, but it had particular resonance as Chicagoans proudly displayed all they had accomplished in the less than thirty years since the removal of the Potawatomi. Built in only five weeks, the frame structure was large enough for more than a thousand delegates on the floor level and at least that many spectators in balconies. A long stage along one side of the space held dignitaries and members of the press.[44] Juliette, with other members of the local arrangements committee, decorated the interior of the Wigwam with paintings, wreaths, flowers, and banners. In many ways they made it into a domestic space, modeled on the fairs and fund-raisers they had organized for decades using temporary ornaments often borrowed from their own homes.[45]

Because thousands more delegates, reporters, and spectators were expected than could be accommodated in hotels, the committee recruited dozens and dozens of host families. Juliette and other Republican women opened their homes to these visitors. After a thorough cleaning of her house, Juliette offered delegates "three nice beds in the attic and two spare rooms on the second floor." She invited many more for meals and visits.[46] Juliette and John enjoyed themselves immensely during the convention, attending several evening receptions at the homes of leading Republicans. They delighted in comments like that of one delegate who told Juliette that "it takes Chicago to do up a thing splendidly."[47]

The local arrangements committee, including John and Juliette, sat on the speakers' platform at the opening festivities. Once the official business began, Juliette moved to the balcony, since the floor and platform were almost exclusively reserved for men. She stood for three and a half hours "jammed in at one corner. . . . Below us in the pit was a mass of heads . . . [but with] everyone dressed in their best and pursuing the most perfect propriety of demeanor." Lincoln's nomination gave "great satisfaction to all parties concerned." Even the New York delegation, who backed favorite son Senator William Henry Seward, committed to working "heart and hand for Lincoln—honest old Abe."[48]

Juliette told Nellie all this in long, newsy missives. For a time she seemed to enjoy describing events that were sure to enrage her son-in-law. John sent Nellie several issues of the Republican *Chicago Tribune*, jokingly suggesting that they would "bring the suspicions of the public authorities upon you and they will deliberate about banishing you from the city." Indeed, John hoped for this, so that she would "be returned to us without delay." But by the fall of 1860, they realized how precarious the situation had become. Juliette cautioned her daughter that her letters might "best be for her eyes only—it might upset the southerners."[49]

The presidential election heightened the animosity Nellie's husband had for the North. That Chicago was the site of the 1860 Republican convention precluded Nellie's venturing north that year while making Savannah an inhospitable place for John and Juliette to visit. Nellie was pregnant again, so when their second granddaughter, Juliette (Daisy), was born, they got the news by telegram.[50]

With Lincoln's election, Juliette hoped to allay Willie's fears. She placed Lincoln within the company of a "great many wise conservative men" who would guide the country safely through the political turmoil.[51] She wrote passionately, "Mr. Lincoln is not an abolitionist as the whole country will find out when the time comes. He is a calm, cool, dignified man of just and comprehensive views, who will never be the tool of a party." Juliette reminded her daughter that she had "stood more than five hours listening to the debates preceding the nomination of Lincoln; if Mr. William Gordon had been next to me, he would not have heard anything that he would have objected to."[52]

Juliette, who had for so long considered herself a westerner, bridled at her son-in-law's characterizing her as a Northerner. She was an easterner by birth, a westerner by choice, but a Northerner because Southerners categorized her as such. She continued to present Lincoln (and Chicago Republicans) as westerners. Juliette asked only that her daughter and son-in-law judge Lincoln by his actions, "a privilege that we, at the west, accord the humblest of our citizens." She argued that none of the Republicans of Illinois would interfere with the South's domestic institutions.[53] But she could not counter the growing sentiment in the Gordon household that Lincoln was a radical intent on destroying slavery.

Nellie found many Savannah residents who believed that Abraham Lincoln would abolish slavery on his inauguration. While Juliette agreed that there "very strong sentiment against slavery in the Republican Party," she did not think that Lincoln would abolish it. Juliette urged moderation and caution: "All our brains are addled I think. God grant we may all be straight again ere long!!"[54]

Juliette's son-in-law and many other Southerners did not see Lincoln as a moderate. In January 1861, William Gordon supported Georgia's secession from the Union. He joined the Georgia Hussars, a militia unit long supported by his family, and began training for war. Nellie Gordon also responded quickly; she protested Georgia's secession by "extinguishing all the lights in the family residence." This dramatic move "mortified" her husband, who "ordered them turned back on."[55]

After this passionate public protest, Nellie and Willie kept their disagreement inside their home. Nellie wrestled with her own allegiances as well as her husband's. She had disagreed with him about politics through their long courtship, but ultimately she had married him and left her home for his. Now she confronted a more profound break from Chicago. She faced a choice: accept her husband's views or return home to her parents.[56]

Nellie was not alone in having to make this choice. Her cousin Posey faced a similar dilemma. She had married a young officer, Colonel George H. Stuart from Baltimore. After the organization of the Confederate States of America in February 1861, Colonel Stuart left the US Army. However, Posey publicly countered that "she for one is never going out of the United States." Indeed, when war broke out and her husband was commissioned into the Confederate army, Posey went to Washington, DC, rather than follow him into Virginia.[57]

In contrast, Nellie stayed in Savannah, following her mother's earlier dictum that wives "belonged to their husbands." The loyalty Juliette had so vehemently preached in the previous few years now made it difficult for her not to support her daughter's decision. She understood that Nellie would "not quit her husband."[58] Juliette agreed that a wife should "espouse [her] husband's views and those of his friends," but she also made it clear that Nellie's family in Chicago felt "that Jeff Davis [was] an ambitious traitor who has led his fellow citizens into rebellion and treason."[59]

Juliette wrote to Nellie describing her as "my little rebel daughter." Her phrase must have hurt the quick-tempered Nellie, since it diminished her by calling her "little." And "rebel" was a dangerous word in these contentious months as Nellie and her husband hardened their allegiances. When Nellie sent a drawing of the new flag for Confederate Georgia, Juliette did not remark on it. When Nellie pressed for a response, Juliette acknowledged that she had indeed gotten the drawing but made "no comment because I could say nothing in regard to that subject that would not perhaps pain you."[60]

The political crisis was dividing their family even as it eliminated the line between the public and private spheres. It shattered the fragile home life that Juliette and Nellie had constructed through their letters. The protection of a household had now been breached. Politics moved to center stage in both their homes and their communities.

7

....

A Divided House

i

The story of the Civil War is often told in terms of battles and political debates. Fort Sumter, the Emancipation Proclamation, Vicksburg, Gettysburg, and the Thirteenth Amendment are among the markers in a public chronology of the war. But these events also drove deep into the private realm of kin and personal networks, fundamentally altering the lives of virtually all Americans. Individual men and women found their private lives and homes disrupted by death and destruction.[1]

Beyond the immediate horrors, the conflict threatened extended families like Juliette's. The Kinzies were not alone—thousands of American families suffered the estrangement of war. President Abraham Lincoln understood this situation well; his wife's family fought on both sides of the war. He thought of civil war as a conflict between family members. In his 1856 "House Divided" speech, Lincoln compared the roiling political debate about slavery to a household, making it clear that "a house divided against itself cannot stand." Again in his March 1861 inaugural address, President Lincoln likened the devastating impact of a potential civil war to a family broken by divorce. Implicit in these comparisons was an understanding that the country rested not just on formal public institutions but also on extensive kin and personal networks that would be disrupted by war.[2]

Nellie Gordon and Mary Lincoln were among those who found themselves in "intersectional marriages," pressured to declare their political allegiance in a world where they had few political rights.[3] This was particularly trying for women, who had no formal voice in the political process that had devolved into war. Even so, at the outset of the conflict women like Juliette stepped up with little hesitation to support their communities and nation.

All through the 1850s, Juliette had been aligned with her husband, President Lincoln, and the Republican Party in their efforts to halt the expansion of slavery. None of them had been in favor of abolition, but Lincoln's views evolved. As the war went on, the issue of slavery challenged the standing social and economic order. Lincoln moved from reassuring the South in his 1861 inaugural address that he would protect slavery where it existed, to ending slavery across the Confederacy in 1863, to embracing the complete outlawing of slavery with an 1865 constitutional amendment. In the course of this shift, he also moved away from advocating colonizing freedmen and freedwomen to extending equal rights to freedmen. Lincoln understood as well as anyone that an end to slavery signaled a fundamental change in American public life. By the time of his 1865 inaugural address, Lincoln intimated that the war itself might be a punishment for slavery and might last "until all the wealth piled by the bond-man's two hundred and fifty years of unrequited toil shall be sunk and until every drop of blood drawn with the lash, shall be paid by another drawn with the sword."[4]

Many of Lincoln's supporters, especially those who had come from the Democratic Party, did not support the president's evolving stand on slavery. For instance, William Ogden, a latecomer to the Republican Party, found slavery morally bankrupt but did not support abolition without colonization. He did not approve of the 1863 Emancipation Proclamation and broke with Lincoln as well as with "many of his old personal and political friends in Chicago."[5] Although John and Juliette did not break with President Lincoln, they did not wholeheartedly endorse his evolving policy on slavery. Juliette accepted the responsibility of all citizens, including members of her family, to serve and defend their "country in her hour of need." But from the outset she rejected the idea that the war was a punishment for slavery. Juliette wrote, "If my son died in the defense of the honor and existence of his country I should feel that he was a martyr in a righteous cause but not an object of vengeance for another man's sins."[6]

Her discomfiture can best be understood within her worldview. Juliette embraced households as the base for American society. They were hierarchical, not egalitarian. Juliette decried the excessive violence and mistreatment of enslaved people, but she did not reject the institution of slavery. Indeed, she seems to have seen it as an "organic part" of households, with enslaved people having their own prescribed places and obligations.[7]

Yet as Lincoln and others pressed for abolition, individual rights took precedence. The war joined the individualism fostered by industrial capitalism in places like Chicago in shifting the basic orientation of American society. Individuals, not households, augured the future of public life. Juliette was unwilling to change and would grow out of step with men and women who came to see abolition as essential to the survival of the nation.

The War Begins

At the beginning of the Civil War, John and Juliette were dismayed to find men they knew well taking opposing sides. Their old friend from Wisconsin General David Twiggs left the Union army and enlisted in the Confederacy, while their brother-in-law soon-to-be General David Hunter worked closely with President Lincoln. When Jefferson Davis was elected the Confederate president in February 1861, Juliette recalled her acquaintance with him in the early days of her marriage when he had served in the US Army across Wisconsin and Illinois. Juliette was critical of the secessionist Davis, sniping that "he meant to be president of the United States and seeing no prospect of that, he rushed that portion of it that he could control into ruin, to gratify, to satisfy his insatiable ambition."[8] Even in Chicago, where Stephen A. Douglas championed the Union and supported President Lincoln, other Democrats were openly sympathetic to the South.

Lincoln's inauguration on March 4, 1861, marked a moment of relief after months of uncertainty. In the days afterward, Juliette wrote to her daughter that they were "enjoying the satisfactory knowledge that Mr. Lincoln is inaugurated . . . despite conspiracies to stop his inauguration." She reassured Nellie that "there is no danger of Mr. Lincoln resorting to coercion—if there is to be bloodshed, it will be the south who invokes it." Juliette's college-age son, Arthur, even sent his sister a playful letter suggesting among other preposterous events the arrival of Confederate emissaries trying to buy canal boats at Chicago, Jeff Davis's plan to address the residents of Bridgeport, and the Republican candidacy for mayor of a "younger brother of Fred Douglass."[9]

But just a few weeks changed the tone dramatically. In late March Juliette received the news she had feared: fighting had begun. Her thoughts flew to her daughter, whose home had become "a foreign and hostile one!" Juliette regretted having "yielded a reluctant consent to give up my daughter to a distant home."[10] While Juliette understood her daughter's decision to stay in the South and support her husband, Nellie's younger brothers were heartbroken. Arthur was dumbfounded by her decision to side against her family, her home city, and her home region: "I should never have thought it of Nellie!!"[11] Juliette tried to explain that Nellie was no longer just their sister, and that wives were expected to adhere to their husbands' public positions. But Arthur could not imagine his sister not taking the Northern side in the war.

Arthur was not entirely wrong; it would be difficult to describe Nellie as simply loyal to the Confederacy. Her allegiance was to her husband, not to the South. Juliette worried that her daughter would do something reckless, as she had on Georgia's secession. She implored Nellie to "add no word to encourage this wrong feeling of one part of our country against another. Women have alas, had much to do in rousing up and aggravating feelings of animosity and hatred in those who should have been brethren."[12]

Still, Juliette never stopped encouraging her daughter to come to Chicago with her children. She began her invitations when Willie left Savannah to train with the Georgia Hussars and continued as he traveled north to Virginia, where he spent the first years of the war. Juliette developed scheme after scheme for Nellie to travel home, arguing that her husband had a duty to send his family beyond the fighting. She offered an endless number of alternatives, including meeting in Canada or Cuba, but these trips never got beyond consideration.[13]

Juliette assured Nellie that she did not want her to leave Willie but just wanted her safe in Chicago. Nellie remained steadfast in her support of her husband, but at the same time she never wholly rejected her birth family, Chicago, or the northwest. Whereas Willie identified Chicago as one part of the enemy North, she saw a network of family and friends that overlay both regions. For Willie, allowing Nellie to travel to the North would be an affront to him, his family, and their neighbors. Nor were Juliette and other members of the Kinzie family welcome in Savannah. Even when Nellie gave birth to her third daughter, Alice, in the summer of 1863, Juliette was unable to make the trip.[14]

Although the war split the nation in two, family and friends maintained loyalties that transcended the sectional divide. When Willie worried about Union troops capturing his family, Nellie noted, "this fate did not appear to me so very terrible." Her plan was simply "to report to the Yankee commanding officer, explain who I was, and telegraph to Chicago to my father; or still better, request to be sent to Washington to my Uncle General David Hunter." To Nellie the Union was not really the enemy but represented friends and family who could be relied on even in wartime. She shared this view with her mother but "wisely kept" it from her husband.[15] Her outlook may seem profoundly naive, but Nellie knew many Union officers from Chicago or West Point. Like Juliette, she believed personal loyalties were more important than national ones.

With the start of the war, Chicago and other Northern communities went into frenzied activity. Women like Juliette took prominent roles, following the well-worn organizational paths they had developed over the preceding decades. Neighbors raised troops and supplies. Juliette boasted of the "enthusiasm and the deep devotion that reign here." She noted that some leading Chicago businessmen were offering to outfit units, while others agreed to continue to pay the salaries of employees who enlisted and still others volunteered to support families left behind. Regiments became "extensions of the community, closely watched and worried over."[16]

Raising troops once again extended the reach of the public sphere into Juliette's home. In April 1861 her twenty-year-old son Arthur, about to finish his senior year at Kenyon College, responded to President Lincoln's call for 100,000 loyal troops. He enlisted in a light artillery company composed of his neighbors and classmates, including his pastor's son. They were among the first troops to leave Chicago, taking a train to Cairo, Illinois. Juliette and John braved the crowds to see Arthur off: "In every direction were throngs and crowds of people. From every roof, door, streetcar, and from all the shipping the U.S. flag flying." Juliette proudly noted, "I give him freely to my country, as I would the two others and my own life if necessary." Arthur would later join the staff of his uncle General David Hunter.[17]

Juliette's oldest son, John, did not immediately enlist. He was focused on launching a career in building and maintaining railroad steam engines, work that took him around the Midwest. Just a few weeks after Arthur enlisted, John had married his Racine sweetheart, Ellie Janes. Though he had kept his courtship hidden from his parents—though not from hers—the surprised family welcomed Ellie as a daughter. At the end of 1861, when John enlisted in the US Navy to work on steamships along the Mississippi River, Ellie often remained with Juliette in Chicago, especially after the 1862 birth of her daughter Laura. Juliette's youngest son, George, remained at home in high school at the start of the war, later attending the new University of Chicago.

Juliette's husband also wanted to do something for the war effort, and in June 1861 he journeyed to Washington, DC. President Lincoln was well acquainted with him and had referred to him as so long a resident of Chicago that "he is common law [t]here; as one who dates back to the time whereof the memory of many runneth not to the contrary." When Lincoln found that John had come east, he asked him "to call on him as soon as he arrived." John and his brother Robert were both appointed paymasters for the US Army with the rank of major (John was later promoted to lieutenant colonel). John was headquartered at Chicago for much of the war, but he traveled frequently to pay soldiers.[18]

John Kinzie was part of a larger group of politically connected Chicago men. Juliette's brother-in-law Lieutenant David Hunter traveled with Lincoln from Springfield to Washington, DC, and was part of the initial military contingent that protected the White House. After Fort Sumter, Hunter was promoted to colonel, but he quickly received political promotions that raised his rank to major general in August 1861. St. James congregant Isaac Arnold served the Republican congressman from Chicago during Lincoln's presidency. William Ogden, who had hired Lincoln for several Chicago real estate cases, came to Washington to advise the president on the proposed transcontinental railroad.[19]

Although Juliette did not leave home, her responsibilities and daily life were much changed by the outbreak of war. Just after Arthur enlisted, she volunteered to send more supplies and food as well as Sunday dinners to him and his company, and even went to Cairo to deliver "a good dinner." When the traditional women's groups came together at Bryan Hall to strategize about nursing care for the wounded, Juliette attended with the mothers of many of the young men in Arthur's regiment drawn from St. James Church.[20] The hall, one of the largest in the city, was "filled to overflowing . . . crowded with those who could not get seats." Three women from each congregation were chosen to serve on a coordinating committee that evolved into the Northwest Sanitary Commission.[21] But this time Juliette, now fifty-five years old, did not take a lead. A younger generation of female leaders—including Mary Livermore, Jane Hoge, and Kate Doggett—would head Chicago women's relief efforts. They would link their support for the war with support for abolition and women's rights. In contrast, Juliette remained focused on St. James and her immediate family.

This approach was due in part to Juliette's traditional worldview, but also to her age and health issues. She continued to suffer from asthma and rheumatism, and both incapacitated her for days at a time. As she grew older, she relied more on the doctors who made regular calls at the Kinzie house and prescribed their own medicines. In addition to her home remedies, Juliette was able to purchase specially made compounds as well as patent medicines at the first pharmacies in Chicago. There was little regulation of these potent tonics, which often contained laudanum (tincture of opium). She took various forms of this powerful opioid, which reduced pain and discomfort, but her growing dependency on these powerful narcotics restricted her activities.[22]

Despite this, Juliette took on greater responsibilities. Just months after the beginning of the war, she told Nellie that she had become the "chief man of business in your father's absence." Juliette operated as her husband's clerk and assistant—something she was comfortable doing. She supervised the training of a new canal collector after John became an army paymaster. Despite this work, Juliette never suggested that she was earning an income; she was only protecting household interests. The relative ease with which women like Juliette stepped up suggests that they had been active observers of, if not actual participants in, these functions before the war.[23]

From time to time, Juliette found herself "all alone in the house with my servants." This was an entirely new occurrence for her, since she had always been surrounded by family. Her servants became vital to maintaining her household, especially an "outside man" to take care of the horses and other animals. When her Irish servant joined the army months into the war, Juliette unsuccessfully tried to persuade him to stay.[24] Unable to replace him and now alone, Juliette rented the Michigan Street house to Mrs. Johnson, a neighborhood woman who established a boardinghouse there. Juliette sold the woman carpets, mattresses, chairs, and "such things as would be injured by boarders." Then Juliette and John, when he was in Chicago, became boarders in their own home. This incongruous scenario was in fact an ingenious solution to Juliette's difficulties with running a large house alone. She noted that the "table is super-excellent" and that Mrs. Johnson was a "kind affectionate lady." She also enjoyed the company of other old neighbors and friends during the long winter that followed.[25]

Letters

Even as her household circle dissipated, Juliette worked hard to support her husband and children. During the war she and Nellie wrote more often to each other than to their husbands. Photographs, drawings, and other small keepsakes were included in envelopes to treasure and share, providing a tether between their homes.[26]

In the early days of the war, Juliette worried about losing contact with her daughter. In deep despair she wrote, "Oh my children! My children! Am I indeed to be cut off from them?" She was concerned that Nellie's only link to her "beloved home" would be broken if she could not get letters through.[27] Juliette decided to continue to write to her daughter in Savannah despite the uncertainties. When letters quickly went missing, Juliette blamed secessionists in Baltimore for "obstructing troops, supplies and the mail." But Nellie blamed President Lincoln and an unscrupulous Chicago post office for the interruptions.[28]

Despite President Lincoln's assurances in his first inaugural address that mail delivery would continue across the country, after Fort Sumter the federal government halted mail service to the seceded states. The Confederate post began delivery within the South

Fassett,   Chicago.

Fig. 19 Juliette Kinzie and other members of her family had photographs taken in 1861 at the start of the Civil War. Juliette sent this image of herself to her daughter, Nellie Kinzie Gordon. Courtesy Georgia Historical Society, MS 318-41-455-5814.

in June, but there was no provision to move mail from North to South. Eventually an official mail exchange was set up at Fort Monroe, but letters had to be unsealed and accompanied by Confederate postage that was affixed after censors reviewed the contents. This process was neither easy nor reliable.[29]

Thus Juliette turned to her deep informal kin and personal network. She devised a number of ways to get letters into the South, where they could be mailed in the Confederate system. For instance, her husband regularly traveled to Cairo, Illinois, where Juliette found a friend willing to forward mail into the Confederacy. She used contacts made by her son John to send mail through Jackson, Tennessee, and Columbus, Kentucky. And Juliette could send letters to Arthur, who sent them into Savannah under flags of truce.[30]

Juliette also relied on more distant relations and Chicago friends. Magill Robinson, a cousin in Louisville, Kentucky, forwarded letters through a private border-crossing operation, the "Adams express." Robinson also sent letters privately to Nashville, where they were put in the Confederate post. Nellie took advantage of her cousin Posey's in-laws, Confederate supporters in Baltimore, who also helped exchange letters. Several longtime congregants at St. James were especially helpful in passing letters. An old Chicago neighbor, Colonel Henry Fitch, posted in Memphis, forwarded letters across enemy lines. Juliette sought out anyone in Chicago who was traveling to or near Savannah; she did not scruple about whether the traveler was a Union or a Confederate sympathizer.[31] John and Juliette also sought out news from anyone who had been to Savannah. In 1864 her sister-in-law Delia Magill managed to visit Nellie by traveling first from New Orleans to Havana and going through Montreal on her return. The couple savored descriptions of their daughter and her "chicks and the details of your welfare all the day long."[32]

Juliette also mailed letters to contacts outside the United States, who could then forward them to the Confederate postal service. Over the course of the war, she sent letters via Canada, London, Bermuda, and Havana. When Juliette's brother Julian and his wife,

Laura, traveled to Europe, they became another contact for Nellie and Juliette. At one point John Kinzie noted all his wife's scheming about routes, suggesting tongue in cheek, "I expect she will try the China route next."[33]

Perhaps the most surprising method Juliette used to remain in contact with her daughter was through prisoners of war. Juliette successfully sent a letter to Nellie through a neighbor whose husband was a prisoner of war at Richmond. The imprisoned man was able to send mail on to Nellie. When Juliette's sons were held as prisoners of war in Alabama, she got news from letters Nellie wrote to her brothers.[34]

Some people forwarded letters as a favor to Juliette or other members of her family; others expected payment for their service. Many—perhaps most—of Juliette's letters to her daughter did not reach Savannah. Juliette's frustration mounted to a point where she wondered if it was worth to effort to write to Nellie. In one particularly trying stretch, from September 1862 into January 1863, Juliette sent eighteen letters to Savannah that were never delivered. Juliette laid the blame squarely on the shoulders of the "the functionaries in your Savannah P.O. who do not want you to have any northern comfort."[35]

At the start of the war, the letters between Juliette and her daughter were much as they had been before—full of family and community news—but the feverish discussions of political speeches and public issues all but disappeared. Juliette realized the growing futility of arguing politics and instead wrote only good news and stories. Juliette did not want to harp on their differences to the point of losing her daughter, so she filled her letters mostly with the comings and goings of family and friends as well as updates from Chicago.[36]

The shifting content also came in recognition that their letters would have to cross enemy lines and so were open to censorship and seizure. Juliette tried to avoid giving any details on the movements of family members in the military. Beyond official censors, the pair understood that their letters to each other were going to be read by family and friends. Sometimes Juliette reminded Nellie to acknowledge gifts or information in a reply so that she could share the letter with family and neighbors.[37]

Juliette encouraged her daughter to "keep a faithful journal" that could take the place of letters. She did not want to miss anything. She implored Nellie to "write down every event and all that you feel and everything our precious, precious children say and do."[38] Nellie did not mail the journal to her mother; she entrusted it to someone traveling north. On one occasion Nellie gave her journal to a visitor who turned out to be a Confederate spy. When Union soldiers captured the spy, they confiscated the journal and sent it on to Juliette in Chicago. In contrast to their letters, which were written with the understanding that they would be shared with other family members, Nellie's journal offered an opportunity for more honest reflection on her feelings and experiences. Juliette understood this, and when it came into her hands, she read only parts of it aloud to her husband: "There are some things recorded there . . . that I will not tell him."[39]

Throughout the war, Juliette and John worked to get money, packages, and a few trunks to their daughter. Before the war, the couple had sent her rents collected on properties in Chicago, which were wedding gifts from close family, as well as cash gifts when they were able. From the moment of secession, it became very difficult to send money, since the express office would not handle the transaction.[40] The Kinzies sent silver and gold coins or paper money through their most trusted contacts. Eventually, they were able to set up a line of credit in London that Nellie drew on.

On several occasions Juliette sent her daughter and granddaughters trunks. Juliette's daughter-in-law, Ellie, and sister-in-law Laura Magill helped to fill them with food, clothing, and other supplies. They tried to supply Nellie's requests as well as to include surprises for the children. All the trunks Juliette sent were inspected to be sure they contained no contraband. She used all the means at her disposal to get them to Savannah. Juliette wrote her daughter, "You will laugh someday when you hear of the all the schemes I have to get necessaries to you."[41] In 1862 Juliette's son Arthur carried the first trunks himself, using a flag of truce, from Port Royal to Fort Pulaski, just outside Savannah, where he met Nellie. In November 1863, months after the birth of Nellie's third daughter, Juliette wrote directly to President Lincoln for permission to send another trunk to Savannah. Juliette described her daughter as a "poor little prisoner of war" who was "a citizen of Chicago . . . who loves her home and the old flag." She closed her letter "very truly and respectfully your friend, Juliette A. Kinzie." Sometime in early 1864, a trunk was sent through to Nellie with President Lincoln's approval.[42]

These trunks presented a dilemma for Nellie. She welcomed the supplies, but she worried that the "indulgences" would cause more harm than good among her Savannah relations. After Juliette spent considerable time and expense finding clothing for her granddaughters, Nellie returned a box of shoes that were not quite right for them. Juliette despaired. She did not entirely understand the distress her heroic efforts caused, but Julian gently suggested that the Northern boxes only increased "the bitterness of those who now make it hard" for Nellie.[43] For Nellie, caught between Gordon and Kinzie relatives, family matters had become public displays of loyalty.

Family Loyalties

Both Nellie and her mother remained committed to traditional notions of loyalty within marriage. This was easier for Juliette, since she and John both supported the Union. Nellie wrestled with her divided sympathies. In contrast, her cousin Posey, though married to a Confederate officer, declared her allegiance to the Union. She often stayed with her uncle General Hunter and his wife, Maria, behind Union lines, but when her husband was injured, she crossed back into the Confederacy. Posey nursed him back to health, giving birth to another child after their time together.[44]

Posey was the only member of the Kinzie family welcome in

the Gordon household, and she spent over six months with Nellie in Savannah. Juliette was grateful that the cousins were together. But the Gordon family couldn't "help themselves" from expressing their displeasure with Posey's defiant support of the Union, nor could their neighbors. One night, when the cousins returned to the Gordon home, they found the contents of a privy had been thrown over the steps and the front door.[45]

This tense situation was exacerbated after April 1862 when Union forces camped eighteen miles east of Savannah. General Hunter, accompanied by Nellie's brother Arthur, headed the Union campaign to retake the region. Nellie and her cousin found themselves targeted specifically "because we were the nieces of General Hunter!!!" Their distress was even more acute when Hunter proclaimed an end to slavery in the district under his command. On his uncle's order, Arthur began organizing and training a regiment of African American men. President Lincoln, who had not yet moved forward with plans for emancipation or for enlisting black troops, summarily renounced Hunter's proclamation and Arthur's efforts. But Hunter's actions created even more uproar in Savannah, where white elites were already fearful of uprisings by enslaved residents.[46]

Although Nellie defended her uncle and brother in the face of Gordon criticism, privately she railed against their actions. She was even more conflicted because she wanted an end to slavery even as she "hated all negroes and didn't care what became of them." Like her mother, Nellie was weary of slavery but maintained a real antipathy toward African Americans. They more easily blamed the war on enslaved people than on slaveholders like Willie Gordon.[47]

While stationed with General Hunter, Arthur desperately wanted to visit his sister and her children. He did not understand how she could be more loyal to a Confederate husband than to her Chicago family. Arthur knew his uncle would smooth the way for the visit, but Nellie felt she could not afford to meet him. She did not understand how her family could be "so blind!" to the threat posed by her brother and uncle. In her journal Nellie wrote, "I love Arth dearly, but to meet him under such circumstances would only give me pain, not pleasure."[48]

Despite her protestations, Nellie relented and met Arthur not in her home but near Savannah. Arthur embraced his sister and spent hours with her and her "little chicks." Both wrote to their mother with details. Juliette was delighted: "I cannot tell you what a jubilee there was when the news came that Arthur had seen you and the children. . . . [N]ews spread like wildfire."[49] Arthur shared worries about their mother's bouts of asthma and rheumatism because Juliette had not written about them. Arthur hoped this would give his sister an incentive to come "to us for a visit." When Juliette learned that Arthur had told his sister about her health problems, she gently chided him: "My dear boy! How could you worry our darling in that manner?"[50]

Nellie had agreed to meet Arthur, and her brother had pressed her to come north, at least in part because of the recent death of their older brother. John had been assigned to the *Mound City*, a steam gunboat on the Mississippi River that he had helped to build. After seeing action at Memphis, his ship was hit by Confederate fire on June 17, 1862. The shot that penetrated the steam engine killed most of her crew, including John Kinzie.[51]

Juliette was in New York City when her son was killed. She was staying with her cousin Henry Wolcott while Arthur was with her on a short furlough from his Georgia posting. Juliette read a newspaper report of an attack on the *Mound City* and found her son's name on the casualty list. Juliette and Arthur hurried back to Chicago while her brother Julian went to claim John's body. The funeral was held at St. James Church, and he was buried "in a coffin draped with the flag of his country and covered with beautiful wreaths of white flowers."[52]

Like her mother, Nellie first read about the firing on the *Mound City* in a newspaper, but she decided it was a mistake. Willie soon confirmed John's death. In her journal Nellie wrote, "Poor Johnny, poor dear boy! I cannot believe it." She lamented, "Home! Home! Shall I ever see it again? Oh, *how* I long for it!" She broke down and asked her husband if she might travel across enemy lines. She found his refusal "unkind," and she remained in a "state of utmost distress."[53]

Although the family did not lose another soldier to the war, there were more hardships. In May 1864 George, not yet eighteen, wanted to enlist with the Union army as a military guard. He needed his parents' permission; Juliette was not moved by his "crowning" argument "of how would he tell his grandchildren that he had not fought for his country?" In the end Juliette relented because so many of George's schoolmates were going to serve in this limited capacity.[54] He joined the unit with a group of his friends from the University of Chicago, and they were posted to Kentucky.

A few months later George received a leave and traveled to Memphis, where Arthur then served as an aide to General C. C. Washburn. Unfortunately both were captured when Confederate general Nathan Bedford Forrest raided the Union headquarters. The brothers were sent to a prison at Cahaba, Alabama, ten miles south of Selma and one of the "most overcrowded of all such Civil War camps."[55]

Juliette and John knew the whereabouts of their imprisoned sons only from newspaper reports. For many weeks they had "no further news of our dear boys." They feared their sons would be sent to Andersonville Prison, where more than ten thousand Union soldiers died from scurvy, dysentery, and diarrhea in the final year of the war. But with the Union's General William T. Sherman leading troops against Atlanta, just over one hundred miles north of Andersonville, this seemed unlikely. Juliette reassured herself that "everyone who talks with us on the subject tells us that there is no probability of their being sent to Georgia." Still, Juliette began putting together a box of clothing and supplies for them. She intended to use the networks she had honed getting letters and trunks to Nellie for their benefit.[56]

General Washburn worked for the return of his staff members, despite the Union prohibition against prisoner exchanges. Negotiations moved slowly, with Union prisoners of war serving as couriers. Arthur himself carried messages at least once between Cahaba and Memphis on a Mississippi riverboat.[57] At the same time, the family contacted friends and acquaintances who might be able to help get the young men released through informal channels. Nellie wrote directly to Jefferson Davis. She appealed to his old association with her parents as well as her connections through the Gordon family. Although it had been thirty years since his days at Fort Winnebago, Davis ordered the release of Nellie's brothers as a favor to the Kinzie family—especially John, "whose moral character was above reproach."[58]

After Nellie wrote to Davis, she traveled alone across Georgia and into Alabama, where her brothers were held. She moved west as General Sherman's troops were moving east, a most dangerous journey. Nellie arrived at Selma only to find "that [her] brothers had left the day before." While certainly relieved that her personal appeal had been successful, she could not help being disappointed that she didn't see her brothers.[59]

Throughout her travels, Nellie also worried about her husband, who was standing against Sherman's forces at Decatur, Georgia. The fighting was fierce, and he was listed on initial casualty lists. Although Nellie quickly found he had survived, Juliette and John received the inaccurate accounts of Willie's death. Juliette wrote to her daughter that "we had been mourning over you as widowed and broken hearted." They urged Nellie to come to Chicago as soon as possible. When John and Juliette realized their son-in-law lived, they quickly wrote reassuring her that they did not want her to abandon her husband.[60]

War's End

Over the course of the war, Juliette worked to keep her family close and her household strong, but the romantic vision of stoking the home fires faced the stark reality of separation, loss, and death. Indeed, the war made it difficult for her to remain at home. Her husband's work as a Union army paymaster often took him away from Chicago. Early in the war, Juliette rented out their house and became a boarder in her own home. When John was reassigned to Detroit, Juliette accompanied her husband. She heard about her sons' capture while in Detroit.

When she learned that Arthur and George were Confederate prisoners, Juliette returned to Chicago and took a room in a neighbor's house, glad to be "back in dear old Chicago!" She did not want to miss her sons if they were released. Fortunately Juliette and John were able to move back into their longtime home in time to welcome George and Arthur back from Cahaba prison. Juliette noted that "our friends rejoiced to have us back again." By mid-October she had her daughter-in-law, a granddaughter, surviving sons, and husband under one roof.[61]

The reelection of President Abraham Lincoln in early November 1864 served as a plebiscite on the war and the abolition of slavery. Lincoln worked toward the passage of the Thirteenth Amendment to end slavery while General Sherman moved eastward across Georgia to Savannah. Anxiously awaiting news of the Union occupation of Savannah, Juliette tried to smooth the way for Nellie and her family. She wrote to a friend who was one of Sherman's officers that her daughter might need "your kind efforts to assist her." Not surprisingly, she also asked him to deliver letters to her.[62]

Just before Christmas, Union forces marched outside the Gordon residence. Juliette's granddaughters peeked through shutters "tightly closed" against the Yankees. They wondered out loud which was "OLD SHERMAN." A few days later Sherman came to Nellie's house, accompanied by Juliette's friend. Nellie received the Union commander courteously, remembering later that "she was truly glad of the visit and the home letters that he had brought around in person."[63]

Early in 1865 the families of Confederate officers were ordered out of Savannah. Nellie gratefully accepted special arrangements General Sherman made to send her with her daughters to Chicago. Arthur and George met them at New York, and together they made their way to Chicago by rail during a terrible snowstorm. The family enjoyed a joyful reunion at what Nellie described as "home sweet home." John and Juliette spoiled their granddaughters with special treats and large meals. Because of wartime shortages, the girls had never tasted some common foods, including chicken. When one of the girls asked for that little "beefsteak with legs," her Northern family erupted in joyous laughter and delighted in retelling the story.[64]

Though Nellie was happy to be in Chicago, she contended with an angry husband. Faced with an imminent Confederate defeat, he lashed out at what he saw as her betrayal in entertaining General Sherman in their home: "What really galls me is that you should associate with my enemies upon any other terms than those politeness demands." He was furious that Nellie had gone to Chicago, a place that for him remained beyond the pale.[65] Nellie was not repentant. She wrote in response, "I have felt hurt at your letters." She was not ashamed that federal officers had been kind to her because of her father and brothers, and she pointed out that it was his own relatives who benefited most from the favors. She wrote that she never asked the Union officers for anything except to "be allowed to stay at Savannah which was refused."[66]

Nellie used her influence in one substantial way that would be vital to her husband after the war. She had defied a Confederate order to burn all cotton in Savannah by storing thirteen bales in her home. On the advice of friendly Union officers, she marked them with her father's name instead of her husband's. The Union army shipped the cotton north to New York City in what was truly special treatment. It required Nellie to align with her father, not her husband, which infuriated Willie even though it would be a financial boon to him.[67]

From Chicago, Nellie worked with her family to get those cotton bales. She presented herself as a loyal Northerner who needed to sell them for the sole benefit of "herself and children." When the cotton was not immediately released, John Kinzie wrote directly to President Lincoln. He described his daughter in Chicago "with her little family of three children." John requested that "her cotton" be released because it was all his daughter had "in the world for the maintenance of herself and children." There was no mention of her Confederate husband.[68]

President Lincoln had not yet responded when he was assassinated in April. Undaunted, Nellie left her children in Chicago and traveled to Washington, DC, to plead her case with the help of her uncle General Hunter. Her husband was furious, writing to Nellie: "If you have availed yourself of his [Hunter's] protection, or used his name to get pay for your miserable cotton or to procure any other favor from the Yankee Government, I shall never forgive you so help me God!" The couple appeared to have reached an irreconcilable moment, but Nellie traveled to Richmond, where her husband was. In person she was able to placate him, and they made plans for the future in Savannah.[69]

As Nellie and Willie reconciled, John and Juliette held out hope that their family would once again be together. John had been transferred back to Chicago, and the family was in their longtime home on Michigan Street. While the death of their oldest son, John, remained a sorrow, his widow and young daughter lived with them. Their granddaughters from Savannah temporarily added a lively presence to the household. Their surviving sons, Arthur and George, could return to school or launch their careers.

All through the war, the couple had dreamed of building a large new house outside the city in Jefferson Township, where they owned land along the north branch of the Chicago River. They called the property, on the riverbanks at Irving Park Boulevard, Northwood. To finance this dream, John and Juliette needed to sell the Michigan Street house and property. At various points during the war years, John had tried to negotiate a sale but was unsuccessful. Juliette dreamed of the "joyful day" when they would get a good price that would help the family members pay their debts and "have a little left to make a home at Northwood."[70]

While they waited for the sale of the Michigan Street house, John had some of the Northwood acreage put into farming, and he built a footbridge over the river. He and Juliette walked about the

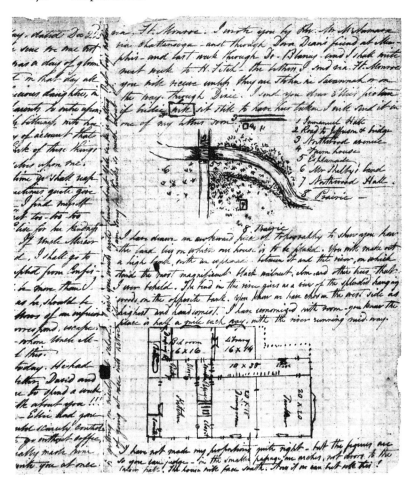

Fig. 20 From the late 1850s, Juliette and John Kinzie planned to build a new home on a piece of property they owned at Irving Park and the north branch of the Chicago River. Juliette sketched the house she hoped to build, calling it Northwood. Juliette Kinzie to Nellie Gordon, January 27, 1864, Gordon Family Papers, University of North Carolina Archives.

property to find the best location for their new house. The couple chose a high spot on the west side of the river. Juliette envisioned that "the eastern windows of the house will look over this lower [magnificent] ground to the river."[71] Juliette planned for a home filled with husband, children, and grandchildren, all "as happy as the day is long." There would be a children's room large enough for rainy-day play. George wanted a boat, but Juliette reassured Nellie that there would be a "big fence to keep little folks in and not let them go near the river by themselves." It was indeed a magical place that Juliette and John envisioned.[72]

Death of John Kinzie

The happiness the family felt at the end of the war was tempered by Colonel John Kinzie's health problems and new business troubles. Much like the embezzlement case at the Canal Office in 1861, it appeared that bank clerks had skimmed money from accounts he supervised as army paymaster. An investigation was under way.[73] Worse, in the closing months of the war, John suffered from a "terrible oppression of the chest" for days at a time. He who had so long tended Juliette in her illnesses was now the patient. She called in doctors, who tried acupuncture and draining "bile from his system." Besides his chest pain, John's legs and ankles swelled, making it difficult for him to walk. Still unwell in late summer 1865, John received a furlough from the army to accompany Juliette and their three granddaughters to rejoin Nellie in Savannah.[74]

The Kinzie party boarded a railcar headed east on July 20, 1865. Just a few miles shy of Pittsburgh, John had a massive heart attack and died before he could be taken from the train. Juliette returned with her granddaughters to Chicago, where Nellie and her husband soon joined them for the funeral at St. James Church. The Chicago newspapers marked the passing of one of Chicago's oldest American settlers. In a front-page obituary, the *Tribune* noted that his death "surrenders the last survivorship of those who looked out upon prairie and woodland before it was Chicago." The article declared that "his history is the whole history of this city."[75]

From St. James Church, the funeral procession made its way north to Irving Park Boulevard. John and Juliette had happily made this same trip many times in recent years on their way to Northwood. But instead of journeying west to the Chicago River, the mourners turned in to the recently opened Graceland Cemetery, where son John was already buried. After the funeral, other deceased members of the family who had been interred at the City Cemetery were reburied in the new family plot. By the spring of 1866 Juliette had a low stone wall constructed around the entire plot, "with broad steps at one corner and Kinzie in relief." But she could not immediately afford to put up the "handsome monument" that she wanted to honor her husband's memory.[76]

Among the mourners at John's funeral was his son-in-law, William Gordon, who had not been in Chicago since his 1857 wedding. He took the opportunity to benefit from his in-laws' business connections. Despite all his bluster about not accepting the aid or protection of "Yankees," Willie and Nellie took advantage of her family's good standing to obtain a loan to rebuild his cotton brokerage firm. In July 1865 the couple received a $7,000 mortgage from a Chicago banker that allowed Nellie's husband "to make a start again."[77] To get this financing, William Gordon did something that seemed anathema to him: he presented himself as "of the City of Chicago." The husband who had so recently ranted about his wife's accepting aid and comfort from the North now took advantage of the Kinzie name in Chicago. It is unlikely that the banker who made the loan was unaware this ruse, but he made it anyway out of respect for the Kinzie family and because Nellie's Chicago lots were posted as collateral.

8

....

Losses

Juliette described her marriage as one that had provided "companionship that was my solace for thirty five years."[1] Her husband had been quick to aid friends and family. He was regarded as a good and caring man who tempered the edge of Juliette's sharper personality. Following his death, Juliette missed many things he had done, like bringing the morning papers to her bedside or relating the latest news when he came home for dinner. On the anniversary of the birth of their first son, she noted that her husband "always remembered and kept this day! We never made or received visits on it."[2]

Juliette particularly missed the help and comfort that John had offered during her periods of ill health. She had in many ways been "an invalid for years." After months of nursing her husband during what proved to be his final illness, Juliette succumbed to a serious bout of asthma, followed almost immediately by an attack of rheumatism that had her family scrambling to light fires in rooms that only weeks before had been overheated.[3]

Beyond her uncertain health, at the end of the Civil War Juliette faced particular challenges as a widow. The country was undergoing a great transformation with an explosion of industrial work, the abolition of slavery, and the extension of equal rights to all men. Male wage workers and formerly enslaved men gained recognition of their individual rights. Chicago workers organized the General Trades Assembly, which successfully pressed the Illinois state legislature for an eight-hour workday, seeking broad equal rights for workers as well as workplace protections. The group's massive May 1867 march passed just a block or so from Juliette's front door. After the passage of the Thirteenth Amendment outlawing slavery, many local abolitionists pressed for extending full equal rights to African Americans. Frederick Douglass drew large Chicago crowds when he spoke on "behalf of the rights of colored American citizens."[4]

Some Chicago abolitionists argued that women also should have full and equal rights in American society. Reformers Juliette knew—such as Kate Doggett, Myra Bradwell, and Mary Livermore—helped organize the Chicago Sorosis Club for women's rights and the city's first woman suffrage convention in February 1869.[5] Their focus was not simply on gaining the vote, but on overturning myriad laws that discriminated against women. The final resolution of the convention forcefully argued "that all facilities for education, and all the avenues of remunerative industry should be open to women; and no legal impediments should be placed in the[ir] way." Myra Bradwell spearheaded efforts to reform married women's property laws and establish custody rights for mothers. She had trained as a lawyer but was refused admission to the Illinois State Bar because as a married woman she could not legally operate independently of her husband.[6]

Juliette did not join with abolitionists and women's rights advocates in seeking to upend a world of households where women held subservient roles. She still expected others to do as she had done: accept the status quo and operate within it. But Juliette could not stop change from coming into her world. Her servants disappeared for days at a time and often walked away from their positions. Against her wishes, they used their wages in saloons and on gambling and sought other employment. When her daughter complained about the new freedmen and freedwomen in Savannah, Juliette wrote angrily to her that the Gordon family had no responsibility for those "worthless negroes," whom she felt had no claim on their former masters.[7]

Juliette was deeply uncomfortable as her hierarchical household world was increasingly challenged. While Myra Bradwell wanted to eliminate special treatment of widows, Juliette opposed this expansion of women's rights. Across her life Juliette had shown great pride in her roles as a daughter, wife, and mother, accepting her responsibilities without complaint. Even as a widow, she did not reject these traditional roles. She accepted that women, particularly widows, "continued to be defined as parts of a household," not as individuals. Although in a low moment Juliette wistfully considered how different her life would be if she "were a man," she never wavered in her acceptance of women's subordinate place within households.[8]

Probate

While Juliette contended with the loss of her husband, she also confronted the legal repercussions of widowhood. A few weeks after John's funeral, his estate was submitted to the Probate Division of Cook County Court without a will. Juliette was accepted as the estate administrator before Judge James Bradwell, the husband of Myra Bradwell. The probate of John's estate was complicated by the fact that their youngest son, George, was only nineteen, while granddaughter Laura would not attain her majority for more than fifteen years. In cases like this, the probate court weighed in as representative of the minor heirs, to make sure their inheritance was in no way imperiled by the widow's actions.[9]

A court-appointed appraiser took an inventory of the Kinzie household. Among the categories assessed were household and kitchen furniture, stoves, cooking equipment, beds, bedsteads, and bedding, books, pictures, wearing apparel (for the widow and minor children), jewels, ornaments, gardening tools, equipment for animal husbandry (carriages, wagons, harness, saddles and bridles), and any farm animals (often a milk cow, sheep, and horses). Also included were items like dining room tables and chairs, sideboards, carpets, clocks, parlor tables, crockery, knives and forks, lamps, and bedroom furniture. The assessor valued the house and the property it stood on (the "homestead") and made an estimate of the funds needed by the widow and minor children for the coming year (including food, fuel, and other provisions).[10]

The court decided how much money Juliette needed to run her household during the probate period. If she needed more, she had to petition the court. Juliette had long handled her household's budget and knew to a penny the state of her accounts. She hired and fired servants, purchased food, and maintained accounts with local stores. She supervised all the clothing, meals, and furnishings for her family. She managed rental properties owned by her family—advertising for and interviewing tenants, collecting rents, and dealing with the frequent aftermath of bad tenants. It exasperated Juliette to spend days in court wrangling over private household matters that she had long overseen.

But the biggest challenge for Juliette, as administrator of the estate, was debt. A central concern of the probate court was settlement of outstanding claims against the estate. A widow was not shielded from the harsh settlement of debts; she was forced to dissolve her household if debts could not be repaid. In contrast, a widower avoided this whole process, since his spouse neither owned assets nor carried debt. He did not have to settle outstanding claims under the supervision of probate court. Only widows suffered this indignity.

Widows, despite not having full individual rights, were responsible for steering their households through the troubled waters of debt settlement. Household debt grew over the 1850s and 1860s when credit was extended by a wide variety of retailers, banks, and other institutions, especially to the urban middle class. The ups and downs of the business cycle made it difficult for many households to stay on an even keel. Often, just as one set of debts was paid off, a business depression would set up the need for another round. The extension of credit ended, however, with the death of a household head, which "always brought a settlement and, indeed, provided the ultimate security for loans alongside a reckoning of family obligations."[11]

Juliette was no stranger to household debt. Her father had been charged with defalcation from the Second Bank of the United States. Her husband had been unable to pay his debts to Arthur Bronson in the early 1840s. And twice John's business accounts had proved out of order. Her husband did not leave his widow financially secure, and she was soon overwhelmed by those seeking repayment.

Judge Bradwell suggested that Juliette "get a lawyer who knows something" to help her sort through the household finances. But Juliette was unable to engage any of the prominent lawyers who were fellow congregants at St. James, including her cousin's husband Mark Skinner, because many of their clients had claims against the estate. Nor did she get much counsel from her son-in-law, William Gordon. Her wealthy brother Julian spent most of the probate period traveling in Europe. Her brother-in-law General David Hunter was initially unavailable as he headed the military commission that tried and convicted the conspirators in Lincoln's assassination. Only afterward did he turn his attention to his sister-in-law.[12]

So Juliette forged ahead on her own to identify their assets and debts. She worked for months "looking over old letters and papers" to identify all household property. Real estate was a crucial part of household wealth; fortunately Juliette had served as secretary for many transactions.[13] While most of their remaining property was on the North Side, there were also parcels in Thornton and along the canal in LaSalle County. Alexander Wolcott, a cousin who had been a city surveyor for decades, worked with son Arthur to help Juliette assemble the property list.

Juliette also had to seek out those to whom her husband owed money. As Illinois law required, notices were placed in Chicago newspapers "for claims and demands against the estate." This alerted potential debt holders to Kinzie's death and the open probate. Juliette was soon overwhelmed with claims.[14] Although probate was intended to protect widows from unscrupulous claimants, Juliette believed it did just the opposite: it took "advantage of a woman's general ignorance of business." If someone made a claim, it was up to the widow to "go and collect proof" that it was not valid. This infuriated Juliette, and she "resolved that no one shall cheat me if I can help it!"[15]

Some of the debts owed were to family members, whom Juliette was able to put off for a time, but others demanded immediate attention. William B. Ogden put in one of the first claims. Juliette had never warmed to Ogden, harboring resentments that went back to his 1837 mayoral victory over her husband. Ogden submitted a bill for $375 that Juliette thought her husband had paid the previous year. But if she could not find proof, the court would force her to pay him. She worked with Arthur to uncover documentation but fumed about a claim against a struggling widow from "a man who schedules his income at $300,000 and his property is rated at $10,000,000."[16]

Besides these debts, at his death John still owed money related to the 1860 canal office embezzlement case and was involved in an investigation of his wartime paymaster accounts. Questions of malfeasance were raised, although few believed he had deliberately taken the money. Juliette came to believe it was his clerks' "rascality" that left the estate under a cloud. And once again, lurking in the background was Ogden, who had posted the $20,000 bond for John's paymaster position. If malfeasance on John's part was found, Ogden would have to pay the bond to the US Army.[17]

Juliette found herself in a vulnerable position, and she was not alone in an anger sparked by the indignities of widowhood.[18] Women's rights activist Kate Newell Doggett, whom Juliette had welcomed to Chicago in 1855, had also been widowed, and like Juliette she found herself railing against the probate system. She, too, had been part of a loving, happy marriage that left her unprepared to face creditors who sued her husband's estate and made it difficult to access needed funds. Eventually Doggett would fight to reform this system, so that other widows did not endure what she faced.[19]

Like Kate Doggett and Juliette, Mary Lincoln became an angry widow. Her husband's assassination fueled an emotional response that was accompanied by a profound sense of loss of a partner and a household world. She had to vacate her home in the White House, found household finances out of her control, and even had to fight over her husband's burial site. Congress was not generous in providing her a pension, and private efforts to aid her family were thwarted not only by her husband's political enemies but also by many of his allies who sought to protect the martyred president's image at all costs. She was pilloried in the press, and eventually her son committed her to a sanatorium. But at least part of Mary Lincoln's supposed insanity can be explained by a probate system that left her vulnerable without the protection of a sympathetic husband but still unable to make decisions for herself. Like Juliette and Kate Doggett, Mary Lincoln was outraged by her treatment as a widow, in contrast to the insulation from the legal system that had been offered by a loving husband.[20]

Juliette realized that some of her husband's real estate would have to be sold to settle debts, but she quickly learned that the Michigan Street house was her "homestead," so that as long as she lived there, the probate court could not sell it for debts. Juliette petitioned Judge Bradwell to sell some other parcels privately but found that "the law is unfortunately explicit in its requirement that the property to be sold shall be put up at auction and bid upon." Bradwell explained that though he understood she might do better at private sale, he could give her "no liberty to fix a price." The property had to be sold at an outdoor public auction off the north door of the courthouse at a time set by the probate court. Although the process was instituted to protect minor heirs, it also let bidders collude to drive down sale prices.[21]

After months of delay caused by slow court proceedings, the

auction was scheduled for March 1866. Juliette worried that bad weather on the auction day might "keep people from the sale." Most of all she worried that the property would "be sold under appraised value,"[22] and she had no way to stop the sale if this happened. On the appointed day, as Juliette feared, no one bid the appraised value of the properties. Instead, speculators waited, hoping to gain the valuable real estate at a discount. Fortunately for Juliette, General David Hunter purchased six lots to protect her investments.[23] Yet the process fueled Juliette's distrust for and discontent with the probate court.

The auction did not lead to a quick court settlement. More real estate had to be sold, and on several occasions Juliette tried to do so without Judge Bradwell's permission. He threatened to have her jailed. Every time potential buyers learned that the transaction had to go through probate, the bidding price dropped, making it harder to settle the case. Juliette complained that "it is so trying to have one's hands tied and be at the mercy" of speculators.[24]

For nearly four years, Juliette was a fixture in Judge Bradwell's court dealing with one claim or another against the estate. Term after term, Bradwell put off closing the probate case. Not until 1869, after division of the Michigan Street property among the heirs and settlement with all remaining creditors, was the estate finally closed. Betraying the depths of her antipathy toward Ogden, he was the last one Juliette paid; she did so only because "the court ordered me to pay the debts and I had no choice."[25]

Juliette Kinzie had known Ogden virtually the entire time she had lived in Chicago. Ogden and her husband had engaged in the real estate market from the start. Both built substantial homes on the Near North Side and helped to build St. James Episcopal Church. Ogden, John, and Juliette were leaders in many civic enterprises. Ogden's nieces and nephews grew up alongside Juliette's children, and their large extended families attended the same parties and events. But Ogden also represented many things the Kinzies had sought and never attained. Beyond defeating John Kinzie in the 1837 mayoral race, Ogden became one of the wealthiest and most influential men in the United States. Representative of his growing dominance, Ogden had shepherded the relocation of St. James Church away from the Kinzie house.

Although John had maintained cordial relations with Ogden over the years, Juliette harbored considerable personal animosity toward him, which surfaced particularly after her husband's death. While Ogden's public persona was of a leader dedicated to the public good, Juliette was quick to point out what she saw as his personal failings. She charged that Ogden took advantage of two credulous women in their circle by persuading them to "sign away a valuable tract of land." She also questioned whether some of Ogden's manifest good works, which her husband had thought "wonderful," were done for some private gain. Juliette dreamed of forcing Ogden and his family "to disgorge all that they have got by fraud and swindling—I fear their incomes could not be scheduled at such a splendid amount as they now represent."[26]

Dower Claims

As part of probate, Juliette spent "days writing up and copying the particulars" of property transactions from her husband's correspondence and business papers. She had participated in many of the sales because of her dower rights.[27] Underlying dower rights was the notion that husbands operated in the real estate market not as individuals, but as heads of households. Although a wife lost control of property she owned before marriage, on the death of her husband she had dower rights to one-third of the household real estate. This dower portion was traditionally "reserved to his wife for her use during her widowhood" in order to maintain their household. To keep a husband from selling household real estate (and thus eliminating the dower portion), a wife had to freely sign an affidavit to accompany every property sale. In a traditional household world, where real property was only infrequently bought and sold, these transactions and interrogations were rare. But in Chicago real estate changed hands quickly and dower rights were often ignored.[28] It became more and more common for specu-lators to purchase property that did not have proper dower affida-vits. Also, reformers fought to eliminate the dower altogether so that married women themselves could own property. By the 1860s, state courts worked toward streamlining real estate transactions by eliminating dower.

Myra Bradwell, who believed "in the true equality of the sexes," was one of those fighting against dower rights in Illinois. She op-posed the dower, "designed to protect women from their own folly or ignorance, or from undue pressure by their husbands." Bradwell argued that a married woman should "feel that she is a person ca-pable of thinking and acting" and that dower rights were humiliat-ing and "an insult to the intelligence of every wife and the integrity of every husband."[29]

For those who sought individual rights, whether speculators or women's rights activists, dower portions were anachronistic. But Juliette had never been a proponent of individual rights. Her vision of society was rooted in the responsibilities that individuals bore within households and in a wider community. The dower was a way to support widows and their families. The push to eliminate it seemed anathema to Juliette, whose household was in a precarious position.

Juliette sued hundreds of individuals in Cook County Circuit Court between 1865 and her death in 1870. In each of these suits, she claimed that she had not waived her dower rights when her husband sold pieces of property across the North and South Sides of Chicago, with most transactions dating back to the 1830s. She was angry with leading businessmen who knew about her dower interest but kept quiet, hoping she would die before she could successfully press her claims. Juliette indignantly noted that "the property now belongs to rich, rich people who have made their for-tunes out of it—let them pay for it."[30]

Juliette was unable to hire any of the top lawyers in Chicago, including relatives like Mark Skinner, because she was suing their regular clients. But she remained confident: "I can manage most things that I undertake." She did not win all these cases, or even most of them, but legal victories and settlements began a slow trickle of money that eased her family's financial straits.[31]

Many of those Juliette sued had been friends and neighbors. She knew that "there is a furious long list of people whom I am warning off my lands." A string of lawyers she hired took a rather lax approach to these suits and were often out of town. By the fall of 1865, Juliette looked "impatiently at the *Law Record* every morning to see if any suit is yet decided or any new one begun." Juliette understood that she was being judged as a "litigious old dame" and was losing her genteel reputation. She found herself unwelcome in the homes of many she had long considered friends. She was particularly distressed when her niece Carrie Skinner began to snub the Kinzie family. Carrie had grown up in the Michigan Street house, but now she accused Juliette of having a "covetous disposition." The Skinners, as well as other leading families, "quit speaking to Arthur and George," who found their social circle shrunk by the dower suits.[32]

Juliette targeted William Ogden with particular vengeance, because he was "immensely rich." In 1835 Ogden had purchased nearly half of Kinzie's Addition. Much of his real estate fortune was based on that opportune purchase.[33] Her suit against Ogden and the Chicago Dock and Canal Company was one of the largest she pursued. A successful outcome would have provided thousands of dollars in annual payments to Juliette for as long as she lived. Filed in late 1865, it slowly wound its way through the court system. This leisurely pace worked in favor of Ogden and other landholders, since dower claims, if successful, had to be paid out only over the widow's lifetime. If Juliette should die (and she had been in ill health for years), the claims would be dismissed.

In Ogden Juliette found a shrewd and disciplined adversary who had used the court system to his advantage for years. His long involvement in real estate and railroads, "two of the most litigious businesses in the mid- to late nineteenth century, insured he would sue or be sued on a constant basis."[34] Despite this, in September

1867 Juliette initially won her dower case against Ogden's Canal and Dock Company. She was jubilant when the local papers opined that she would reap thousands upon thousands of dollars. Juliette looked forward to the money, but also to beating the businessmen who thought she would not stand up against them. She betrayed a long-standing antipathy, writing that "it will not hurt my feelings to come down on Mr. Ogden."[35]

Following Juliette's lead, other widows also filed suit against Ogden. While many of those dower claims were fraudulent, they were a drag on business. At one point Juliette giddily wrote to Nellie, "Poor Mr. O!! All old women jumping at him!" Walter Newberry, worth $3,000,000 in Chicago real estate, was so dismayed by the raft of dower claims against him and others that he rewrote his will. On his death in 1865, he offered his widow $10,000 a year if she did not make any dower claims. Julia Newberry, furious at her husband's attempts to control her even after death, successfully contested the will.[36]

Finding that dower claims were a "great hindrance to the purchase and sale of land," Ogden fought them vigorously. Rather than seeking to compromise with Juliette, he appealed the initial decision, which was overturned by the superior court in February 1868. The reversal reflected the unsettled nature of dower claims, since some judges were unwilling to enforce them, especially after an 1861 Illinois law allowed married women to own property. Juliette's public triumph had been reversed; while all was not lost, she no longer had confidence in a bright future. Nevertheless she challenged the ruling, pushing the case (and several others) to the Illinois Supreme Court.[37] Perhaps not surprisingly, Juliette ultimately settled for a fraction of what she claimed Ogden owed her.

Reluctant Capitalists

Above all, Juliette wanted enough money to build the family's dream home at Northwood and to help launch her sons' careers. Both young men were deeply affected by their experiences during the Civil War. Arthur suffered combat injuries to his back and eyes as well as having emotional difficulties because of the war. Periodically he was laid low with what Juliette described as "his <u>army</u> derangement," when all he could do was stay home and rest.[38] Although George did not see fighting during the war, he was exposed to what his mother saw as immoral behaviors like drinking and gambling. He returned home with "a tendency to extravagance."[39]

At first the young men wanted little more than to take up the amusements of their prewar lives, like riding, fishing, boating, ice-skating, and hunting. They devoted themselves to baseball and played in the city and across the region. While they mainly played for fun, boosters began paying their expenses and offered prize money.[40] Arthur and George also rekindled old friendships and cultivated new ones. Through school and church, their circle included the children of some of the city's wealthiest families. In the first year after the war, they attended parties at the Ogden, Rumsey, Skinner, Turner, and Dole family mansions. But as Juliette's dower suits became public, the young men were less welcome in those homes.

Juliette was anxious about careers for her sons because "half the missteps of young people [were] in consequence of having nothing to do."[41] The death of their father and older brother deprived them of mentors. While Juliette felt sure that Arthur "would make a good lawyer," he was not interested in the years of training that would be needed. General Hunter promised a government position, but nothing was forthcoming from him or from wealthy Uncle Julian, who lived in Europe during these years.[42]

Instead, Arthur tried unsuccessfully to establish a sash and blind factory with a fellow baseball player, using an empty distillery owned by the Kinzie family. Then, with a $1,200 loan from Juliette, he launched a storage and forwarding business. This also failed, causing Juliette "great anxiety." Adding to her concerns, Arthur had taken up with Caroline Gilbert Wilson. Juliette found her "pretty, sweet, and affectionate," but the couple married secretly in June 1867 because their parents demanded they wait until

Arthur made a "comfortable income." Despite this, Juliette welcomed the newlyweds into the Michigan Street house.[43]

Soon after the secret wedding, Arthur invested in a lumber mill in Michigan, even as Juliette worried about his making a good living in this complicated business. Indeed, one of the clerks embezzled from the mill's assets. Although the clerk was arrested, the theft dampened the outlook for profit. Juliette, who seldom criticized her sons, advised Arthur to quit this business that "he does not understand." She worried that her son was "like his dear father, inclined to put faith in all men until dire experience teaches him a bitter lesson for his credulity."[44]

In many ways Arthur's younger brother, just twenty, was even more at loose ends. The family encouraged George to return to college, but he showed little interest in that or in finding a regular job. He threw his energies into baseball and courting their longtime neighbor Tillie D'Wolf. Her family discouraged the match because George had no position nor any prospects. Under pressure from her parents, Tillie broke off with George and was soon engaged to a young man with a solid position. As George slipped into despair, William Gordon agreed to take him into his Savannah firm. Juliette only hoped that William would "make allowances for George's shortcomings by being inexperienced in business." Despite Nellie's best efforts, the former Confederate officer and the Union soldier did not work well together; George missed his mother and was deeply uncomfortable in a Southern city. After just a few months, Juliette had to ask her daughter to lend George the money to come home.[45]

After George returned to Chicago, he and Arthur launched a real estate business, Kinzie Brothers. They hoped to capitalize on their experience in settling their father's estate, but they found it hard going. With their mother and sister as key clients, they failed to pay taxes on numerous properties the family owned, including the Michigan Street house. George seemed unfazed, explaining to his sister that "I had no money as you well know dear Nell." He suggested that if his brother-in-law was dissatisfied, he could switch to another real estate firm. Indeed, that is exactly what William Gordon did, and Kinzie Brothers languished and died.[46]

George expressed the sentiments of the household when he confessed that he wished "we were rich!" Juliette wanted money enough to help her children, even as she sought to "leave it in God's hands." Although she professed to accept God's will, she pursued dower suits and fought debt claims with vigor. She also tried to make money from the writing that had so long sustained her.[47]

After her husband's death, Juliette devoted more and more of her time to writing. She revised *Walter Ogilby* as well as writing a novel set in 1827 Wisconsin, a story about Indians in the Revolutionary War period, and another about young women in a religious benevolent association. As she had done before the war, she shared her writing with her family and friends, especially Elizabeth De-Koven Dyer, who had moved back to Middletown, Connecticut. Despite their physical separation, they remained fast friends. When *Walter Ogilby* was finally published, Juliette dedicated the book to "Mrs. E. DeKoven Dyer, the friend whose words of encouragement first suggested [the volume] . . . and whose genial, sympathizing smile has beamed on its progress and completion."

Although Juliette finally arranged publication of *Walter Ogilby* in 1868 with J. B. Lippincott of Philadelphia, she did not earn any money from it. The publisher demanded that Juliette pay the plate costs in advance—more than $700. Only writers proven successful avoided this outlay, which put further pressure on family finances.[48] Juliette continued to write, and by 1870 she completed her second novel, *Mark Logan*, set in the Great Lakes Indian country. but at earning income she was no more successful than her sons.

Losing Place

In the first years after John Kinzie's death, the Michigan Street house remained a refuge for the family. As their homestead, it was shielded from claims on John's estate and was large enough to accommodate George, Arthur and his new bride, and also Juliette's widowed daughter-in-law and young granddaughter. But the neighborhood around the house was no longer filled with "pleasant places." Some of Chicago's poorest residents lived nearby, and rumors swirled that the Chicago and North Western Railroad intended to put a large new depot just south on Cass Street. More grain elevators and factories were attracted to the area, increasing the noise, dust, and commotion around the Kinzie house even more. As Juliette rather disingenuously noted, "Business is coming nearer to us."[49]

The changing neighborhood posed many threats. When cholera returned to Chicago in 1866, many of those taken ill came from the dense neighborhood around the Kinzie house. The following year a fire tore through the neighborhood. Their house was spared only because the wind took the flames in a different direction. Juliette wrote to Nellie, "I never saw anything so splendid yet so awful." She also worried about burglars and poachers among all the people she did not know. When the Unitarian Society considered purchasing lots along the north side of her garden, Juliette was relieved. Having their church there would protect her from "bad neighbors to my rear," and "heresy and schism are neither contagious or given to trespassing."[50]

Of course, the changing neighborhood also offered opportunities. Juliette exulted in any news about increasing property values and was buoyed by expectations of "how valuable this block will be," possibly worth as much as $60,000. With such profits she could finance the Northwood dream.[51] As her sons floundered in the postwar economy, Juliette saw farming on that property as a potential occupation for them. Her instinct to retreat into self-sufficiency had helped her family weather multiple business downturns, and she hoped it would do so again.

Several times a sale of their home and nearby lots seemed imminent only to fall through. Selling property through the probate court was difficult, but Juliette also worried because Michigan Street had "such a bad name." Eventually she concluded that no one wanted to buy their house to live in, calculating that the brick and woodwork could be sold for as much as $8,000. But there was no timely sale to relieve the family's financial difficulties, nor had there been a substantial settlement of dower claims or royalty checks from her novels. Still, Juliette wanted to continue providing a home for her sons, daughters-in-law, and grandchildren. In the spring of 1868, she found a modest house to rent not far from Graceland Cemetery, outside the city limits in the suburb of Lake View. She expected to live more cheaply there.[52]

Soon the family was busy taking down fences and sheds and moving shrubs, flowers, and other plantings from Michigan Street to the new property. Moving was wrenching and exhausting. Because they had rented a smaller space, Juliette planned to take only what would be useful to them there, but her sons pressed to keep old schoolbooks and muster rolls. Juliette obliged because she understood they did not want to totally dismantle their life. She could not part with the piano she had brought west in 1830, even though special movers were needed for it.[53]

After weeks of work, the Michigan Street house was empty save the pictures hanging on the walls. Juliette mourned leaving her "nice house and garden" where she had been "so happy." She sadly wrote to her Savannah granddaughters that they would not be able to play where their mother had played as a child. As in the past, in giving up her house Juliette took comfort from her faith: "We cannot hold fast to anything in this world." Once they had moved, Juliette strove to make a new home. With the help of servants, she scoured the house and filled her first-floor bedroom with furnishings from their Michigan Street parlor.[54]

But there were challenges, not least her rheumatism. For the first time in over thirty years, Juliette had no fireplace in her bedroom, and she suffered terribly. The whole house was cold except during the summer, so her daughters-in-law sought respite with relatives who could keep them warm. Without a carriage Juliette was isolated, for it was a long walk from the train stop to their house.

And they found themselves too close to the Lake View House, a suburban hotel that drew many strangers, making it unsafe for "a woman to come alone down the lane after dark."[55]

So Juliette was housebound and often alone, especially in winter, when that long lane to the train station became impassable after a heavy snow. She tried not to complain about the cold, instead reminiscing about happy childhood days playing in the snow. Her letters to Nellie became even more important as her daughter became her primary comfort and confidante. But during lonely stretches, Juliette began to question whether she was "as agreeable a companion to myself as I have all my life seemed to be." She found herself wishing someone else was there, noting, "I do not remember having much of that feeling before." She wallowed in self-pity for just a bit before setting herself tasks that might help her family. She practiced the piano and her drawing and painting, hoping she could teach her granddaughters these skills. She also devoted considerable time to her writing, which remained a primary occupation even though it was hard to find publishers.[56]

The move to Lake View also challenged Juliette's long relationship with St. James Episcopal Church. She was no longer an active participant, relying on family and neighbors to bring her to services, a trip of almost five miles. But her distancing from the congregation had begun even before this time, starting perhaps in 1866 with the departure of longtime pastor Robert H. Clarkson. In the aftermath, "Low Church" supporters installed a new pastor, to Juliette's disappointment. She was also dismayed with the rise of new congregational leaders like Mrs. Walter Newberry. Juliette, who had once been "the ruling spirit" of the congregation, now found that Julia Newberry styled herself "a combination of the Virgin Mary and Queen Victoria."[57]

Still, Juliette continued to pay for a family pew at St. James even after she moved to Lake View. It became the "last tie to [her] former life at Chicago." Juliette found her congregation had "grown so selfish—so money loving that they seem not to care about anybody who is not rich and fashionable."[58] Juliette understood the sources of her growing isolation, but her disillusion with Chicago society was profound. Industrialization and modernization had shifted conditions and attitudes in ways that no longer allowed her access to power and influence. More and more, she retreated from any public role or even affiliation with Chicago.

There were deep changes in her household as well. Her home had long been the center of a dense web of family and friends. Now her family gravitated instead to the Near North Side home of her brother-in-law Robert Kinzie and his wife, Gwinthlean. Returning to Chicago after decades away, they rented a large house near Michigan Street that became the center for family life not only for their own children but for Juliette's children as well. Juliette was envious. When Robert and Gwinney's son Hunter began courting Ellie Kinzie, Juliette's widowed daughter-in-law, Juliette found it "a terrible grief." She deeply resented Ellie's growing friendship with her sister-in-law.[59]

Juliette's Leave-Taking

During these years Juliette lost her home, her neighborhood, her church, and in many ways her city. Where once she and her husband could offer their children support, now she had little to share. In the late spring of 1870, Juliette moved out of her rented house in Lake View. She no longer harbored hopes of building at Northwood or even continuing with housekeeping. Arthur, Carrie, and their three children (son John, born in 1868, and twin daughters, Eleanor and Juliette, born in February 1870) moved, at least for the summer, to the Manitou Islands, near the lumber mill he still owned. Ellie and Laura went to live with Robert and Gwinney, and George found a rented room. Juliette divided her furniture between her sons, giving Arthur enough for five rooms and George the "best parlor furniture and my bed room set." Robert and Gwinney stored her remaining possessions in "an unfinished attic room."[60]

Juliette planned to spend the summer with Nellie at the Long

Island shore. From there she would decide her next steps. She had little left in Chicago. She worried most about George but felt sure that Robert would look out for him. Before she left for the East Coast, Juliette made extended visits to Chicago area relatives. For years she had been the hostess; now she was the homeless guest. In those weeks Juliette mused about whether she could "live without a settled home." She sought comfort from her faith, placing her trust in a God who has it in "his wisdom to provide us the food most suited to our needs."[61]

In July 1870 Juliette made final preparations to meet Nellie and her two oldest grandchildren at Amagansett, along the southern shore of Long Island. No more than fifty miles directly to the northwest was Middletown, where Juliette had been born and spent her early years. Her affairs were in order; she had given up her house and most of her possessions. And for the first time in years, she no longer had any court cases pending. Just before she left Chicago, William Ogden offered about $1,400 to settle his dower claim. Juliette was most thankful to get this money. She wrote to her daughter a few days before her departure saying that she had "every reason to hope" that "every weight" would be lifted from her mind.[62]

Juliette had expected George to come East with her, but in the end she traveled with the help of a longtime servant, Sarah Noonan. For all her complaints about servants over the years, Juliette was happy to have Sarah's company. They stopped in Philadelphia to consult with her publisher, J. B. Lippincott. Juliette had completed the manuscript of *Mark Logan* and wanted to finalize terms for its publication as well as to get an update on sales of *Walter Ogilby*. She was able to take page proofs of *Mark Logan* with her to correct while on her beach holiday.[63]

For over two months Juliette and Nellie stayed at Amagansett, enjoying the pleasant weather and summer pastimes. They took rooms in a boardinghouse, "a very quiet place at the seaside." Nellie and the children enjoyed "surf bathing" into September. Juliette worked on the book proofs as well as tutoring her grandchildren.

Nellie drew sketches of the beach where they spent time every day. Over the summer they were joined by other family members, including Maria Hunter and Posey Stuart.[64] It was a happy scene, far from the cold and isolation of the previous Chicago winter.

By September, only cousin Frederica (Freddie) Williams, Sarah Noonan, and one other servant remained at Amagansett with Nellie, Juliette, and the children. Nellie was pregnant with her fifth child but was not due to deliver for more than a month. She went into early labor during the first week of September, but several doses of morphine stopped her pains.[65]

In the meantime Juliette grew ill, and a local physician prescribed quinine pills to ease her symptoms. There was some mix-up, and somehow she took several morphine pills instead and became violently ill; Nellie swallowed one of the pills her mother had taken to test what they were and also got sick. Juliette became weaker and weaker, while Nellie slowly recovered. Just four days after her sixty-fourth birthday, Juliette died on September 15, 1870.[66]

Cousin Freddie and Sarah Noonan took charge of the children. They telegraphed to Willie in Savannah, Robert Kinzie in Chicago, and Juliette's cousin Henry Wolcott in New York City. Willie traveled quickly to Amagansett to be with his family. He moved Nellie to Manhattan, where a few weeks later she safely delivered her daughter Mabel. Henry Wolcott began the process of getting Juliette's remains back to Chicago. He had to persuade the board of health to release the body because Juliette's was an unexpected death. At first they refused, but Henry prevailed "through the red tape." The coroner's certificate listed the official cause as "poisoned to death."[67]

Sarah Noonan traveled with Juliette's body overnight to Chicago, to Robert and Gwinney's home. There she was greeted by "tears all round." Robert Kinzie helped George make arrangements for the funeral—a particular challenge because St. James was closed for renovation. Julian Rumsey, brother of Juliette's sister-in-law Laura Magill, stepped forward to help as "a true friend." Rumsey had "the chapel and vestibule . . . put in perfect order for Mrs. Kinzie," whom he still saw as the "mother of St. James Church."[68]

Perhaps it is fitting that Juliette, so comfortable in the small brick church that she could see from her parlor window, would be buried not from the imposing main sanctuary of the new church but from a smaller side chapel trimmed with white flowers and greens. The coffin was covered with "wreaths and crosses of the most beautiful flowers." The new pastor, Dr. Rylance, conducted a funeral service that included the choir singing "Nearer My God to Thee" and "Rock of Ages." After the service her body was interred next to her husband's in the Kinzie family plot at Graceland Cemetery.[69]

Mourning Juliette

Many people offered their condolences to Juliette's family and friends, expressing a common concern that it would be hard for her children to get on with their lives "without that dear mother's love and sympathy." Sarah Noonan was deeply saddened by the distress of Juliette's daughters-in-law, especially Ellie Kinzie, who had made her home with Juliette for almost a decade. Juliette had comforted her as a young widow and helped raise her daughter, Laura. Ellie remembered that Juliette "was a kind, sympathizing mother to me." Chicago became a difficult place to be, and Ellie found it "hard staying here without a home."[70]

George had also lost a home as well as his "dearest and most darling of friends." He wrote to Nellie that he got "so lonely sometimes I don't think I can stand it." George turned to his sister for comfort, but Nellie had five children and a large household to manage. Ellie encouraged George to leave town because without his mother Chicago "would not, could not, be home." He had lost not only his mother's love, but also her financial support. George wanted quick action on Juliette's estate, but he learned, as she had, that probate wound its way slowly.[71]

From Savannah, William Gordon organized his mother-in-law's estate. He found a Chicago real estate firm to manage the family's property. On Mark Skinner's recommendation, they hired a local lawyer to serve as probate administrator and represent their interests in court. On December 5, 1870, proof of Juliette's death and her will were entered into probate. Her heirs were identified as her three surviving children. Juliette had already given her son John's widow and granddaughter a share of her personal property. Juliette's nephew Alexander Wolcott, who had helped her after John Kinzie's death, and George posted bond for the estate.[72]

A standard inventory was ordered of Juliette's personal effects. In January 1871 Gwinney Kinzie oversaw the itemizing of all that Juliette had left in her attic, mostly furniture, carpets, and clothing. Juliette had already given her children most of her furniture and household goods in anticipation of her trip east. Among the most valuable pieces remaining were the portraits of John and Juliette done by George Peter Healy in 1856. The appraisal from the inventory totaled $520.[73]

The Michigan Street lots had been divided among her children and her granddaughter Laura on the settlement of John's estate. Each also had separate control of individual parcels in the remaining Northwood property. And all the dower claims Juliette had successfully pressed ended with her death. Juliette's estate, then, consisted only of her personal property. There was little left.

In the following months, claims were made on her estate. The final list, made March 9, 1871, totaled $4,791.66: Nellie Gordon ($290.95); James Wright ($105.00); R. A. Kinzie ($175.00); Clerk of the Superior Court ($65.75); Ann Noonan ($230.80); trustees of W. M. Newberry ($2,147.03); David Hunter ($669.15); and J. B. Lippincott ($1,107.98). Nellie's claim included costs from their summer in Amagansett as well as the cost of transporting Juliette's remains. James Wright was the undertaker. Ann Noonan was likely Sarah Noonan, and her claim appears to be for back wages and travel expenses. The claim from the Newberry estate related to money advanced for dower claims that had to be reimbursed. And both of Juliette's brothers-in-law, Robert Kinzie and David Hunter, claimed money. All were allowed by the probate court, and her personal effects were sold on August 18, 1871, for $528.40.[74]

The largest claimant to Juliette's estate was her publisher, J. B. Lippincott, for the initial printing costs of *Walter Ogilby*. Production on her second novel, *Mark Logan*, was halted because of the debt. Nellie worked with Lippincott to get the second novel published, but it would take fifteen years to accomplish.[75]

Before Juliette Kinzie's estate could be settled, the October 9, 1871, fire swept away much that remained of the Chicago Juliette had helped to build. George telegraphed Nellie two days later: "All saved lost everything city in ashes."[76] Only a very few buildings on the Near North Side remained. The Michigan Street house, as well as both the original St. James and the second St. James Church, burned to the ground. For a time the land between the Chicago River and the Water Tower was free of buildings, as it had not been since the 1830s when Juliette arrived in Chicago.

Although no one in the Kinzie family was killed, they were in the direct path of the fire as it tore through the Near North Side. George was twice "hemmed in by flames." Arthur, Carrie, and their children made it safely to Lake View, where Sarah Noonan offered them shelter. Robert and Gwinney Kinzie's house was destroyed, but all of their family survived the conflagration. Little was saved of family mementos and furnishings, including those that had been in the Michigan Street house during Juliette's lifetime. Among what remained were the Healy portraits of John and Juliette, which Nellie had shipped to Savannah just before the fire. They arrived there safely and adorned the Gordon parlor for years.[77]

The fire destroyed the open probate file regarding Juliette Kinzie's estate. The family reconstructed as best they could the documents needed to close it. Ultimately there were not enough assets in Juliette's estate to pay all the creditors in full. On September 26, 1873, the estate was "declared insolvent and ordered to distribute pro rata to creditors. In October 1873, with all receipts filed and the administrator discharged, the estate was declared "SETTLED."[78]

Juliette's children all made their way in the world thereafter. Ellie married David Hunter Kinzie. David made a career in the US Army and the couple were posted across the United States, with children born in Massachusetts, Wisconsin, and South Carolina. Both Arthur and George remained in Chicago. No longer involved with the Michigan lumber mill, Arthur took a series of jobs as a bookkeeper and clerk. At first he and his wife, Carrie, and two children lived with their uncle Robert and aunt Gwinney. Eventually he landed at the City of Chicago telegraph office. As his family grew to five children, they moved to the western suburb of Riverside. He continued to suffer the aftereffects of the war. His oldest son, Jack (John Harris), moved to Savannah, where Nellie offered to help him establish a career. Like many of his forebears, Jack took advantage of the hospitality of extended family to get a toehold in the world. In recognition of her help, Jack named his first daughter after Nellie; Eleanor Gordon Kinzie was born in Savannah in 1900.[79]

George continued to live in Chicago for a time, eking out a living in real estate and boarding at 1074 South Wabash. After his mother's estate was settled he received a civil appointment in the US Army with the help of his uncle General David Hunter. He married Mary (Molly) Blatchford, and they took postings across the West, including New Mexico, Texas, and North Dakota. The couple's first child, born in 1875, was named Juliette Augusta in honor of George's mother. Three more children were born over the next six years. George died in 1890, and his widow returned to Chicago.[80]

Nellie Kinzie had the most success of the family in a traditional sense. Her husband, "having lost everything," had to start again after the Civil War. Chicago connections helped him secure a loan that eased the rebuilding of his cotton commission business. By 1876 the couple were able to travel to Europe, and in the 1880s they made major renovations to their Savannah home. Nellie devoted herself to her husband, her children, and her community. Like her mother, "in matters of public importance Mrs. Gordon took a deep and practical interest."[81]

Juliette's Tombstone

Not until the 1880s, though, did Nellie Kinzie Gordon finally erect a memorial to her parents at their graves in Graceland Cemetery. She kept a photograph of the headstones in a gilt frame. Today the Kinzie burial plot, once prominent near the southern entrance to the cemetery, is easily overlooked. After the couple were buried there, landscape architect H. W. S. Cleveland transformed the grounds into a lovely park. Some of the city's most prominent families—including those of George Pullman, Cyrus McCormick, Marshall Field, and Potter Palmer—are buried around a small lake at the north end of the cemetery. Visitors who stop closer to the cemetery's entrance often congregate around the haunting Lorado Taft sculpture *Eternal Silence,* marking the Dexter Graves family

Fig. 21 Photograph of John's and Juliette's headstones at the Kinzie burial plot, Graceland Cemetery, Chicago. Nellie Gordon Kinzie kept this framed photograph of her parents' graves after she paid for the installation of headstones in the 1880s. Courtesy of the Georgia Historical Society, MS 318-41-455-5817.

Fig. 22 Headstones marking Juliette and John Kinzie's graves in Graceland
Cemetery, 2017. Photo by John Keating.

plot. Only a few turn directly west from that monument to consider the Kinzie graves.

The gravestones memorializing Juliette and John Kinzie have
eroded over time, as has the low stone wall Juliette had built around
the family plot. The memorial that was initially a single slab of
stone now looks like two separate markers sinking into the ground.
It is almost impossible to decipher the script, but the image of a
book remains visible on Juliette's tombstone, a fitting memorial to
the writing that was a central part of her life.

Epilogue

Erasing Juliette

For good reasons, historians have long been challenged in understanding Chicago before the 1871 fire. What we know of that earlier Chicago is circumscribed by the blaze that took hundreds of lives, razed thousands of buildings, and destroyed untold pages of writing and other artifacts. Because Chicago rose "phoenix-like" from the ashes, what came before seemed not to matter very much as that city became difficult even to imagine.[1]

This stark divide was heightened by Chicago's rapid growth, based on its rich agricultural hinterland, dense network of railroads, and early industrial production. Juliette watched as this new economy transformed her neighborhood. Before she died, she had become deeply alienated from this changing city that she barely recognized.

William Ogden, her longtime neighbor and eventual nemesis, came to feel a similar dislocation because of the fire. He also lost his beloved home and roughly one-third of his wealth in October 1871. He lamented "the loss of the beautiful City I spent the best and almost the majority of the years of my life in assisting to build."

Ogden understood that his generation had created a "very beautiful and fortunate City" that was no more. After putting his affairs
in order, Ogden abandoned Chicago for New York City.[2]

Industrial capitalism had shaped a more heterogeneous, contentious place that required formal institutions and larger government. Although the household economy declined in the face of
this capitalism, with its relentless expansion of the market, it did
not disappear but remained a centering force for neighborhoods.
Immigrants and migrants used religious and educational institutions, as well as businesses, to foster neighborhood economies
even as large corporations controlled more and more of the metropolitan economy. Household economies continued to flourish
in Chicago's neighborhoods and suburbs, where women exerted
considerable influence. In this way Juliette's vision of civic culture
can still be seen in Chicago, often described as a city of neighborhoods.[3]

Despite their resilience, neighborhoods were constantly evolving and largely out of the control of any one individual, family, or
group. Juliette experienced this change firsthand. At the end of her
life, she grieved the deaths of close family members, but also her
lost home and neighborhood. She was left without the moorings
and attachments she had steadily cultivated over the years.[4] Many
Chicagoans in subsequent generations shared her loss of place
as their neighborhoods also evolved beyond recognition. But the
idea of a neighborhood, grounded not in individuals or the market
but in families and households working together, endures to the
present.

When Jane Addams and Ellen Gates Starr founded Hull House
in 1889, they created a household and settled into the Near West
Side neighborhood. The idea of a settlement house recalled their
childhoods, when the family claim was strong. Both had grown up
in midwestern households where families worked with their neighbors to build and maintain community. Addams and Starr sought
to re-create a household like Juliette's without the patriarchy, with
the deliberate purpose of doing good on a neighborhood scale.[5]

Juliette in Chicago History

Juliette devoted considerable energy to structuring the early history of Chicago around the experiences of her family. Much of her legacy rests on continued interest in her 1856 *Wau-Bun: The "Early Day" in the North-West*. From its publication, *Wau-Bun* was highly praised for providing a "faithful and well-drawn picture of the life of those pioneers of the American wilderness." She was one of the first historians in the United States who wrote about the American west.[6]

Wau-Bun comprises several distinct parts in the course of its thirty-eight chapters. Thirty of the chapters describe Juliette's experiences in Wisconsin in the years just before and after the 1832 Black Hawk War. She draws a vivid picture of the lives of the Ho-Chunk that "sparkles with humor and with the pleasure of youth."[7] This part of the book is a highly personal and detailed memoir of a world that by 1856 had already disappeared. Her attention centered on women and families as she wrote sympathetically of the Indian world.

The *Wau-Bun* chapters on Chicago include Juliette's recollections of the settlement in 1831, but they also lay out the earliest history of the city. In two chapters she described the events of August 1812 and the Battle of Fort Dearborn (what she described as "the massacre") as seminal to Chicago history. Without question, Juliette placed the Kinzie family front and center; she wanted to be sure the accomplishments of her husband and his extended family provided the foundation for the city's history. Indeed, her writing was the base for many later histories of Chicago.

Juliette did not use sources like newspapers or government documents. History in her era reflected a world based in households, communities, and dense networks of kin and friendship ties, so she relied on family stories and the accounts of friends and acquaintances. Her topics and sources make *Wau-Bun* a work of social history.

Juliette was accepted as a historian in her day, when there was no graduate training. She gained her expertise from a number of sources. As a young woman she encountered Henry Schoolcraft, who wrote an 1821 travelogue of an expedition through the western Great Lakes region that included Chicago, and she pored over his powerful combination of sketches and written descriptions. Juliette was also influenced by her studies with Emma Willard, who wrote early histories and geographies of the United States. In addition, she read women authors who found commercial success during these years, including the fiction of the Brontë sisters and Catharine Beecher's writings on domestic economy. All offered models for her own writing.

Wau-Bun was read and discussed by historical societies both in the Midwest and on the East Coast. State public schools in Michigan and Wisconsin adopted it for their curricula. Nineteenth-century historians like A. T. Andreas relied heavily on Juliette's accounts— Andreas reprinted her 1812 map and several of the lithographs from Wau-Bun. His widely available volumes on Chicago history solidified the Kinzie historical legacy.[8]

Despite the acceptance of Wau-Bun, during Juliette's lifetime history was written primarily by men with the time, skill, and inclination to explore the past. Juliette was an exception. Local and state historical societies were founded across the country by men who wanted to preserve their communities' past. The Chicago Historical Society, which had initially included women in its gatherings, remained largely in the hands of elite men into the twentieth century.[9] Juliette's litigiousness left a trail of ill will among those elites that diminished the Kinzie family in Chicago history as well as weakening her reputation as a historian.

Instead, it was William Ogden, who spent the last years of his life in New York City, who became linked in the public mind with early Chicago. Why? In 1881 Ogden's brother-in-law Charles Butler wrote a letter to the Chicago Historical Society suggesting that Chicago was a monument "to [Ogden's] genius and his enterprise." The following year his friends Isaac Newton Arnold and J. Young

Scammon presented essays to the Historical Society on Ogden's central role in Chicago history.[10]

Juliette found her historical work outmoded by precisely the changes she first documented. Placing William Ogden, a highly successful capitalist, at the center of Chicago's early history made great sense by the early twentieth century, when American society had been fully transformed by industrialization and urbanization. The market had expanded deeply into the public sphere as more people became wage and salaried employees and purchased more and more of the goods their households used. Formal institutions and government developed to mitigate the worst excesses of the market. Women, who did not have equal standing with men in the formal public sphere, were sidelined.

The writing of history also changed. The first generation of university-trained historians challenged the work of earlier chroniclers without graduate degrees, including Juliette Kinzie. Although barriers to women's entering the academy were not insurmountable, only a few women became trained researchers. Professional male historians were skeptical of earlier local histories that did not hew to their standards or deal with government, politics, and corporations. Women seldom wrote history, and topics relating to them were seldom deemed important enough to study.[11]

Juliette's *Wau-Bun* came under skeptical scrutiny as a focus on individuals and their families was replaced with an emphasis on successful businessmen and political leaders. New graduate training in history included collecting and analyzing a range of sources in hopes of presenting as objective a view of the past as possible. Juliette's works, so deliberately shaped to highlight the role of her family, stood out. She was an easy target.

Milo Milton Quaife was the young historian, trained at the University of Missouri and the University of Chicago, who took aim at *Wau-Bun*. He wrote unequivocally "that Mrs. Kinzie had but the vaguest comprehension of the historian's calling." Quaife was among a group of historians who sought to debunk American myths; in Chicago that meant countering what he saw as Juliette's mythologizing of the crucial role in early Chicago history of her father-in-law, John Kinzie. He dismissed her work because she was not dispassionate about her subject: "Nothing would have been more abhorrent to her than the disclosure of anything unflattering to a member of her family." In 1913 Quaife wrote his own account of this early period that included a critical assessment of Juliette's work, drawing on a wide range of archival records.[12]

Juliette, dead for more than forty years, could not defend herelf. But her daughter, seventy-seven-year-old Nellie Kinzie Gordon, launched a counteroffensive. She commissioned a new edition of *Wau-Bun* as a response to Quaife's critique. A Chicago bookseller wrote to Nellie reassuringly, "I do not think that you need fear the opinion of Mr. Quaife. . . . Your books are far better known than his and will carry more weight with most of the Chicago public."[13]

Nellie worked to keep her mother's legacy alive within her own family as well, especially with her namesake Juliette (Daisy), born in 1860. Daisy did not meet her "Yankee Gammy" until after the Civil War, but Juliette cast a long shadow in her Savannah home. Her grandparents' Healy portraits had pride of place in their parlor. Daisy heard *Wau-Bun* read aloud from an early age and grew up with romantic stories of Indian country and early Chicago. She heard about her grandmother's skill in traditional household tasks— from baking and canning to sewing and nursing.[14]

In 1912, when Juliette Gordon Low founded the Girl Scouts of America in Savannah, the influence of her grandmother's life was evident. Girls were encouraged to learn traditional household arts by earning badges that rewarded mastery of skills like cooking and sewing, central to Juliette's vision of a well-trained woman: "In every century it has been woman's work to direct the household, and very largely her responsibility to maintain a happy, efficient, hospitable spirit there." Girls also focused on their broader obligations; each Scout professed an oath "to do my duty to God and my country; to help other people at all times; to obey the Girl Scout Laws." Among the ten laws that all Girl Scouts affirmed were several that focused on these obligations, including their "duty . . . to be useful and to help others."[15]

Until her death in 1917, Nellie Gordon was a champion of her daughter's efforts in founding the Girl Scouts as well as of her mother's Chicago history. No one replaced Nellie as her mother's defender, but Milo Quaife moderated his indictment over time, eventually endorsing Juliette as "Chicago's earliest author" and arguing that her work still had value as a primary source.[16] However, when Bessie Louise Pierce published the first volume of her monumental history of Chicago in 1937, she relied on Milo Quaife, with almost no references to *Wau-Bun*. Indeed, Pierce hardly mentioned Juliette Kinzie, even in telling the foundation story of St. James Episcopal Church, and she was not listed in the index. In contrast, William Ogden merited than fifty mentions in Pierce's index.[17]

In subsequent years some historians and literary critics have embraced Quaife's early harsh criticism of *Wau-Bun* as a work of fiction, not of history.[18] Against this tide, in 1971 the editors of *Notable American Women: A Biographical Dictionary* included Juliette as one of twenty-six historians listed in the volume. Nina Baym, in the introduction to the 1992 edition of *Wau-Bun*, unequivocally described Juliette's book as "a key narrative of early Illinois history." But the controversy lingers, and Juliette Kinzie's reputation has languished.[19]

My work on this era made use of *Wau-Bun*. What Juliette included in it is truthful, but she left out many people and stories that would cast a less than positive light on her family. She did not provide the documentation Quaife expected of history, but that does not mean her work was not part of the genre. History written in the first half of the nineteenth century emerged from literary culture, not from academia, and Juliette's style put her squarely within the norms of her era.[20] *Wau-Bun* reminds us that history reflects the construction of the world in which it is crafted. That Quaife did not value her perspective reflects his era of high industrialization, when the individual, the market, and formal institutions were paramount in understanding events and trends.

Perhaps Quaife did not realize he was as trapped by his own time as Juliette had been by hers. His work on early Chicago focused not on families, but on government and military records. Through these sources Quaife was able to uncover the experience of soldiers, officers, and political leaders in early Chicago. He added much to our understanding of this era, as Juliette had done before him. My work here offers another view of that past, shaped in turn by our present. All three approaches offer paths into the past, but they also are evidence of the world in which they were created. My concern with the profound inequalities based in race and gender that were generally accepted in Juliette's world is shaped by my own experience as a historian in the early twenty-first century. No doubt new questions will emerge as future historians aim to better understand Chicago's early history.

Juliette in United States History

Juliette's erasure from United States history is less personal than her erasure from the Chicago history she helped to write. As we have seen, she was a significant woman but not exceptional. She was not a leader like Abraham Lincoln or Frederick Douglass, nor was she a strident reformer like Mary Livermore or Myra Bradwell. She was generally a rule follower, not a rule breaker. Whereas exceptional people defy conventions and challenge orthodox thinking, Juliette's life offers insight into the world of more ordinary people.

She is representative of the majority of white Northerners who were not strong proponents of slavery but were willing to see it continue until the crises of the 1850s. In this she was much like Abraham Lincoln and the western Republican Party on the cusp of the Civil War. Understanding her views can help us better understand this crucial time. Historians too frequently have focused on figures who held extreme views.

Juliette's life suggests that, alongside a narrative that emphasizes individual rights, historians should consider household responsibilities to better understand the United States in the decades before the Civil War. Her life and views challenged me to reconsider several of the broad frames that have informed long years of teaching and research about America's nineteenth century. The fight for individual rights (freedoms) has been a critical organizing tool for much of the recent history of nineteenth-century America. From the 1776 Declaration of Independence, individual rights expanded beyond a limited notion of propertied men who were heads of households to the broader sense in Lincoln's 1863 Gettysburg Address, which offered "a new birth of freedom" with the end of slavery. The extension of suffrage (to all men), the individualism of the Second Great Awakening, abolition, women's rights, and the Civil War itself are parts of this powerful interpretation that have dominated thinking and teaching about American history for more than a generation. But focusing on individual rights alone cannot help us understand the complexity of this past.[21]

Tracing Juliette has caused me to rethink much that I thought I understood about nineteenth-century America. Her experiences reminded me that individualism is not the only lens for viewing the past. Juliette looked to households, not the market, as the central arbiter of the value of civic culture. She was not much concerned with individual rights: household responsibilities were at the center of her worldview. Although there is much to admire in this view, it is rightfully reviled today because it supported the enslavement of millions of people and accepted inequality for most Americans. Indeed, the profound racial and gender prejudices and stereotypes that underlay this patriarchal worldview must be confronted, both in history and in our world today.

Juliette's intense prejudices were real, but to dismiss her commitment to households simply as racist misses an opportunity to consider an alternative to our market-driven world. The problem was not with her acceptance of a household compact of shared responsibilities that stood outside the market, but with the patriarchy grounded in racism and sexism that it was coupled with.

By the end of Juliette's lifetime, the household world of shared responsibilities was losing ground to an individualism that was at the heart of capitalism. Although an end to slavery marked a significant gain for individual rights, Juliette and other women still encountered a patriarchal world, even as the market became the primary social and economic arbiter. During the height of industrial capitalism at the turn of the twentieth century, progressive reforms mitigated the worst excesses of the market through an activist government, unionism, and a strong core of formal social service institutions. Occasionally reformers like settlement house workers returned to the model of household responsibilities, but most looked to large-scale solutions to match the power of industrial capitalism.

Nearly 150 years later, Chicagoans are at another crossroads. Many of the public institutions of the industrial era have fallen to privatization as the formal market has made inroads into virtually every aspect of life, almost exactly the inverse of the small formal economy of Chicago in the 1830s and 1840s. Still, civic engagement and responsibility continue to matter in city life. While individual rights and a commitment to equality are fundamental, they should not eclipse a commitment to common obligations. Juliette's life and times challenge us to envision a world where monetization and privatization do not entirely dominate, where the end goal is not to atomize the individual in the marketplace. With an added commitment to individual rights, Juliette's focus on common responsibilities within the informal sphere offers us a possible path to a better future.

Acknowledgments

Chicago is not only a fascinating place to study, it is also a wonderful place to be an urban historian. I have benefited from many insights gleaned over the years at the urban history seminar at the Chicago History Museum. I thank my co-conveners Michael Ebner, D. Bradford Hunt, and the late Russell Lewis for their work in sustaining the group. I am also grateful to the many Newberry seminars that have offered me a place to hear new ideas and participate in historical discussions.

I benefited greatly from many conversations about Juliette Kinzie with Rima Lunin Schultz. I am grateful to Amanda Seligman for her insightful editorial comments and broad support for this project. I thank those who have commented on some or all of this book, including Joseph C. Bigott, Jane Durkin, Michael Ebner, Suellen Hoy, John Keating, Julie Martin, Lamar Murphy, Harold Platt, John Reda, Margaret Durkin Roche, Rima Lunin Schultz, Peter Shrake, Ellen Skerrett, Mary Smith, and Jon Teaford.

My thanks to North Central College students who let me try out ideas about Juliette Kinzie on them, especially Stasia Tanzer and

Katie Dickson, who spent a summer working on the project with me. I want to acknowledge the support of North Central College for several summers of research and writing, as well as the help of Dean Stephen Caliendo in arranging a reduced teaching load that made possible the timely completion of this project. I am grateful for the support and encouragement of the members of my department: William C. Barnett, Luke Franks, Brian Hoffert, Shereen Ilahi, and Bruce Janacek. I miss the advice of B. Pierre Lebeau, who before his 2017 death helped shape my thinking about Juliette Kinzie.

Chicago History Museum archivists Lesley Martin and Ellen Keith helped me track down Kinzie family materials. I thank staff at the Juliette Gordon Low Birthplace, the Girl Scouts of the USA headquarters, the Georgia Historical Society, the University of North Carolina Archives, the Newberry Library, the Archives of the Clerk of the Circuit Court of Cook County, Chicago, the New Hartford Historical Society, the Middlesex Historical Society, and the Historic Indian Agency House in Portage, Wisconsin, for helping me locate materials for this book. I am grateful to Paul Lane for his expert help with photographs and to Dennis McClendon of Chicago Cartographics for the wonderful map of Juliette Kinzie's world.

Timothy Mennel has guided this project at the University of Chicago Press, and I thank him for his advice at every stage in this process. I am grateful to Rachel Kelly Unger and Erin DeWitt for shepherding the manuscript to publication, to Alice Bennett for her careful editing, and to Lauren Salas for promotion of the project.

Most of all, I want to thank John, Jack, and Betsy for listening to me think about Juliette during countless trips, meals, swims, and walks. They make my family claim a pleasure rather than a burden.

Appendix 1

Selected Households of Juliette and John Kinzie

1817 Chicago, Illinois Territory (fig. 9)

Parents: birth family, John Kinzie (1763–1828) married 1798 Eleanor McKillip (1771–1834)

Children: Margaret McKillip Helm (divorced daughter of Eleanor and first husband, Captain Daniel McKillip, and her son Edwin Helm); John Kinzie (1803–1865); sister Ellen Marion (1805–1860); sister Maria Indiana (1807–1887); brother Robert Allan (1810–1894)

1820 Middletown, Connecticut (fig. 3)

Parents: Arthur W. Magill (1783–1855) married 1805 Frances Wolcott Homans (1786–1835)

Children: Frances Homans (daughter of Frances and first husband, Thomas Homans, b. 1805), **Juliette Magill** (1806–1870), William (1808–1835), Mary Ann (1810–1833?), Arthur (1813–1833), Henry (1815–1818?), Alexander (1817–1867), Julian (1822–1897)

1833 Portage, Michigan Territory (now Wisconsin) (fig. 4)

Parents: John and **Juliette Kinzie**

Children: Alexander Wolcott (Sandie) Kinzie (1833–1839)

John's family: widowed mother, Eleanor Kinzie; stepsister, Margaret McKillip Helm, and her son, Edwin Helm

Juliette's family: brother Julian Magill (1822–1897)

1839 Michigan Street House, Chicago (fig. 2)

Parents: John and **Juliette Kinzie**

Children: Alexander (Sandie) Wolcott Kinzie; Eleanor (Nellie) Lytle Kinzie (1835–1917); Julian Kinzie (1843); John Kinzie (1838–1862)

John's family: nephew Edwin Helm; nephew Kinzie Bates

Juliette's family: father, Arthur; brother Julian; cousin Alexander Wolcott; cousin Mary Anne Williams; cousin Elizabeth Williams (married Mark Skinner, 1841); cousin Frederica Williams; cousin Caroline Wolcott (married Joseph Balestier); cousin Henry Wolcott

1850 Michigan Street House, Chicago (fig. 2)

Parents: John and **Juliette Kinzie**

Children: Nellie Kinzie, John Kinzie, Arthur Kinzie (1841–1901); Francis (Frank) William Kinzie (1844–1850); George Kinzie (1846–1890)

1868 Lake View house (fig. 1)

Parent: widow **Juliette Kinzie**

Children: widowed daughter-in-law, Elevanah (Ellie) Janes Kinzie; granddaughter Laura Kinzie (b. 1862); Arthur Kinzie married 1867 Caroline Gilbert Wilson (grandson John Harris Kinzie, b. 1868); George Kinzie

Appendix 2

Juliette Kinzie's Published Works

Narrative of the Massacre at Chicago. Chicago: Fergus, 1844.

Narrative of the Massacre at Chicago. Chicago: Fergus, 1914.

Wau-Bun: The "Early Day" in the North-West. New York: Derby and Jackson, 1856.

Wau-Bun: The "Early Day" in the North-West. Chicago: D. B. Cooke, 1857.

Wau-Bun: The "Early Day" in the North-West. Philadelphia: J. B. Lippincott, 1873.

Wau-Bun: The Early Day in the North-West. Chicago: Rand McNally, 1901.

Wau-Bun: The "Early Day" of the North-West. Chicago: Caxton Club, 1901.

Wau-Bun: The Early Day in the Northwest. Menasha, WI: George Banta, 1930.

Wau-Bun: The "Early Day" in the North-West. Chicago: Lakeside Press, 1932.

Wau-Bun: The "Early Day" in the North-West. Urbana: University of Illinois Press, 1992.

Walter Ogilby. Philadelphia: J. B. Lippincott, 1868.

"Col. John H. Kinzie." Part of Isaac N. Arnold, "Address." In Chicago Historical Society, *Introductory Address*. Chicago: Fergus, 1877.

Mark Logan: The Bourgeois. Philadelphia: J. B. Lippincott, 1887.

Notes

Preface

1. Nina Baym, introduction to Mrs. Juliette M. Kinzie (Juliette Magill Kinzie), *Wau-Bun: The "Early Day" in the North-West* (Urbana: University of Illinois Press, 1992), xi.

2. There are two biographical essays on Kinzie: Archibald J. Byrne, "Kinzie, Juliette Augusta Magill (Sept. 11, 1806-Sept. 15, 1870)," in *Notable American Women, 1607–1950*, ed. Edward T. James, Janet Wilson James, and Paul S. Boyer (Cambridge, MA: Harvard University Press, 1971), https://loginlibproxy.noctrl .edu/logn?url=http://search.credoreference.com/content/entry/hupnaw/kinzie _juliette_augusta_magill_sept_11_1806_sept_15_1870/0, accessed August 11, 2014; and Rima Lunin Schultz, "Kinzie, Juliette Augusta Magill," in *Women Building Chicago* (Bloomington: Indiana University Press, 2001), 476. There is also a recent children's biography of Juliette Kinzie, based largely on *Wau-Bun*. See Kathe Crowly Conn, *Juliette Kinzie: Frontier Storyteller* (Madison: Wisconsin State Historical Society Press, 2015). Additionally, there is biographical material on Juliette Kinzie in biographies of her granddaughter Juliette Gordon Low, the founder of the Girl Scouts of America. See Gladys Denny Shultz and Daisy Gordon Lawrence, *Lady from Savannah: The Life of Juliette Low* (1958; New York: Girl Scouts of America, repr. 1988), esp. 22–45. (Based in family lore, the material does not always hew to the historical record.) Also see Stacy A. Cordery, *Juliette Gordon Low: The Remarkable Founder of the Girl Scouts* (New York: Penguin, 2012), 1–10.

3. C. Vann Woodward, ed., *Mary Chesnut's Civil War* (New Haven, CT: Yale University Press, 1975), contains excerpts from the diaries.

4. Juliette A. Kinzie, *Walter Ogilby* (Philadelphia: J. B. Lippincott, 1868), 10. Jane Addams described how women were subject to a "family claim" based on their devotion "to their families"; she reported that "they want to live with their parents, their brothers and sisters, and kinsfolk and will sacrifice a good deal to accomplish this." Jane Addams, "Domestic Service and the Family Claim," in *The World's Congress of Representative Women*, ed. May Wright Sewall (Chicago: Rand, McNally, 1894), 2:628. Victoria Bissell Brown notes that Jane Addams understood this focus on family responsibilities as the "family claim" on women, married or unmarried. See Brown, *The Education of Jane Addams* (Philadelphia: University of Pennsylvania Press, 2004), 110.

5. William Cronon, discussing Juliette Kinzie and her experiences in Portage, Wisconsin, suggested that even those "nearest to us" in the past remain "really unlike us." Cronon, http://www.williamcronon.net/biography/cronon -kreisler-interview-april-2013.htm. I was drawn to Juliette Kinzie because I found her life surprising. This idea of cultivating surprise was discussed by Edmund Morgan in "Cultivating Surprise," *Huntington Frontiers* (Spring/Summer 2005), which I have long assigned in my historical methods class.

6. Emma Willard, *A Plan for Improving Female Education* (Middlebury, VT: S. W. Copeland, 1819), 15.

7. Juliette Kinzie to Nellie Gordon, January 27, 1858, Juliette A. Kinzie letters in the Gordon Papers at the University of North Carolina (microform), 1858–70; microfilm accessed at Chicago History Museum (hereafter microfilm Kinzie letters, UNC).

8. She makes this point when advising her daughter as a young bride to accept her subordinate position: "You belong to him and he must make such arrangements as he sees proper for you and himself. . . . You must remember that as an individual you have ceased to exist, being only part and parcel of Mr. William Gordon[;] what is right for him is right for you." Juliette Kinzie to Nellie Kinzie Gordon, January 27, 1858, microfilm Kinzie letters, UNC.

Introduction

1. Juliette Kinzie to Nellie Gordon, May 2, 1867, Gordon Family Papers, Georgia Historical Society.

2. Juliette Magill Kinzie, *Wau-Bun: The "Early Day" in the North-West* (Urbana: University of Illinois Press, 1992), 101.

3. A contemporary observer noted that it was the "General Government of the United States" that was pursuing a "scheme of removing the whole of the Indian population westward." Charles Joseph Latrobe, cited in Bessie Louise Pierce, *As Others See Chicago: Impressions of Visitors, 1673–1933* (Chicago: University of Chicago Press, 1933), 55–56. Over Juliette's lifetime, the Kinzie and Magill families responded to the tactics of an interventionist state that created new

opportunities through public policy and direct intervention in the economy. See William J. Novak, "The Myth of the 'Weak' American State," *American Historical Review* 113 (June 2008): 754–57.

4. Mrs. Juliette A. Kinzie, *Mark Logan: The Bourgeois* (Philadelphia: J. B. Lippincott, 1887), 42–43.

5. Ellen Hartigan-O'Connor recently noted that our "familiar male-female binary hardened in the middle of the nineteenth century" after a civic culture first emerged in Chicago. See Hartigan-O'Connor, "The Personal Is Political Economy," *Journal of the Early Republic* 36 (Summer 2016): 339. See also Hartigan-O'Connor, "Gender's Value in the History of Capitalism," *Journal of the Early Republic* 36 (Winter 2016): 612–35. Nancy Hewitt found that before the Civil War "women activists emerged in a community where the segregation of work and home, public and private life, and men's and women's spheres was incomplete." See Hewitt, *Women's Activism and Social Change: Rochester, New York, 1822–1872* (Ithaca, NY: Cornell University Press, 1984), 22.

6. Stephanie Coontz, *The Social Origins of Private Life: A History of American Families, 1600–1900* (New York: Verso, 1988), 177; and Nancy F. Cott, *The Bonds of Womanhood: "Woman's Sphere" in New England, 1780–1835* (New Haven, CT: Yale University Press, 1997). See also Mary P. Ryan, *Cradle of the Middle Class: The Family in Oneida County, New York, 1790–1865* (New York: Cambridge University Press, 1981). For the experience of Catholic women religious, see Suellen Hoy, *Good Hearts: Catholic Sisters in Chicago's Past* (Urbana: University of Illinois Press, 2006), esp. chaps. 2 and 3.

7. Carol Lasser and Stacey Robertson, *Antebellum Women: Private, Public, Partisan* (Lanham, MD: Rowman and Littlefield, 2010), xviii–xix. In the twenty-first century, with attention to gender nonconformity and transgender, perhaps it is easier to explore a more fluid view and to recognize that gender roles were particular to this time and place. I thank Ellen Hartigan-O'Connor for the insight on the changes from the twentieth century to the twenty-first. Jeanne Boydston notes that we must always remember that gender, like so many other "categories of historical analysis," always reflects a "very local and particular character." See Boydston, "Gender as a Question of Historical Analysis," *Gender and History* 20 (November 2008): 559. More broadly, John Demos argues that we cannot know the past "by any route save that which leads back from our own experience." See Demos, *Past, Present and Personal: The Family and Life Course in American History* (New York: Oxford University Press, 1981), xi.

8. Rima Lunin Schultz, "The Businessman's Role in Western Settlement: The Entrepreneurial Frontier, Chicago, 1833–1872" (PhD diss., Boston University, 1984), vi. Julie Roy Jeffrey notes that much work was done in "informal groupings like church sewing circles" that "usually left no written evidence of their involvement at all." See Jeffrey, *The Great Silent Army of Abolitionism: Ordinary Women in the Antislavery Movement* (Chapel Hill: University of North Carolina Press, 1998), 4.

9. Sam Bass Warner Jr., as cited in *The Private City: Philadelphia in Three Periods of Growth* (Philadelphia: University of Pennsylvania Press, 1968), 3–4, described this as "privatism"—a rejection of public-oriented civic responsibility. Notably, Warner did not include women directly in his story. Nor did Robin Einhorn when she applied this perspective to her exploration of Chicago during the decades before and during the Civil War, where she found a "segmented system" of government in which property holders preferred to pay for services through special assessments instead of general funding. See Einhorn, *Property Rules: Political Economy in Chicago, 1833–1872* (Chicago: University of Chicago Press, 1991), 16–17. More recently, Philip J. Ethington suggests a "republican liberalism" that envisioned a more unitary notion of public good than would come later in the nineteenth century. See Ethington, *The Public City: The Political Construction of Urban Life in San Francisco, 1850–1900* (New York: Cambridge University Press, 1994), 8.

10. Although Juliette Kinzie grew up in and around the Beecher family in Connecticut, as a staunch Episcopalian she was generally critical of Lyman Beecher and his daughters. Still, she embodied Catharine Beecher's philosophy. Quotation as cited in Kathleen McCarthy, *Noblesse Oblige: Charity and Cultural Philanthropy in Chicago, 1849–1929* (Chicago: University of Chicago Press, 1982), 17.

11. Coontz, *Social Origins of Private Life*, 176. See Rima Lunin Schultz, *The Church and the City: A Social History of 150 Years at St. James, Chicago* (Chicago: Cathedral of St. James, 1986), 25–26, for Juliette's role in the development of that congregation. Maureen Flanagan has suggested that describing these women as "prominent middle class" is "the best way to designate the status of a group of people not all of whom could be classified as upper class in terms of wealth and property but whose position in Chicago's social structure was surely prominent." See Flanagan, *Seeing with Their Hearts: Chicago Women and the Vision of the Good City, 1871–1933* (Princeton, NJ: Princeton University Press, 2002), 228n52. Flanagan builds on the earlier work of Frederic Cople Jaher, *The Urban Establishment: Upper Strata in Boston, New York, Charleston, Chicago, and Los Angeles* (Urbana: University of Illinois Press, 1982); and Stuart Blumin, *The Emergence of the Middle Class: Social Experience in the American City* (New York: Cambridge University Press, 1989).

12. Bessie Louise Pierce, *A History of Chicago*, vol. 1, *1673–1848* (Chicago: University of Chicago Press, 1937), 187. Pierce titled one of her chapters "The Fabric of Society." Daniel Boorstin described William B. Ogden as the prototype of the urban booster and businessman and as Chicago's "representative man." See Boorstin, *The Americans: The National Experience* (New York: Vintage, 1967), 117. For more recent historians who focus almost exclusively on men, see Donald Miller, *City of the Century: The Epic of Chicago and the Making of America* (New York: Simon and Schuster, 1996); and Dominic A. Pacyga, *Chicago: A Biography* (Chicago: University of Chicago Press, 2009). I also followed this narrative in my

dissertation and in my first book, Ann Durkin Keating, *Building Chicago: Suburban Developers and the Creation of a Divided Metropolis* (Columbus: Ohio State University Press, 1988), 34.

13. See Rudi Batzell, "The Labor of Social Reproduction: Household Work and Gendered Power in the History of Capitalism, 1870–1930," *Journal of the Gilded Age and Progressive Era* 15 (2016): 311.

14. Anne F. Hyde, *Empires, Nations, and Families: A New History of the North American West, 1800–1860* (Lincoln: University of Nebraska Press, 2011), offers a recent history of the antebellum west with a focus on women and families.

15. Philip J. Ethington suggested that the republican liberalism of the 1850s, with its unitary vision of an American public, was "blown up by industrialization and the end of slavery with the Civil War." See Ethington, *Public City*, 8. But he does not argue for women in the earlier unitary notion of public sphere—he sees "severely" gendered division between public and private spheres (39).

Chapter One

1. Mrs. Juliette M. Kinzie (Juliette Magill Kinzie), *Wau-Bun: The "Early Day" in the North-West* (Urbana: University of Illinois Press, 1992), 5. Born in 1790 in Connecticut, Wolcott graduated from Yale in 1809 and trained as a medical doctor. During the War of 1812, he served as a surgeon's mate and then a surgeon in the US Army. After the war, he practiced medicine in Vincennes, Indiana. Chicago Medical Society, *History of Medicine and Surgery, and Physicians and Surgeons of Chicago* (Chicago: Biographical Publishing, 1922), 22–23.

2. Alexander Wolcott Jr., Chicago, to Juliette Magill, Middletown, November 6, 1820, Alexander Wolcott Jr. Papers, Chicago History Museum. The Wolcotts and Magills were not alone in using letters to maintain family ties as the US government extended postal service across the westernmost regions of the country. See Richard R. John, *Spreading the News: The American Postal System from Franklin to Morse* (Cambridge, MA: Harvard University Press, 1995), 158–59. The federal government's extensions contrasted with the limited postal service in Great Britain and France. In the 1820s, postage was based on both the distance the letter needed to travel and the number of sheets. It could cost as much as a dollar for a letter to travel from the East Coast into the west.

3. Henry R. Schoolcraft, *Narrative Journal of Travels through the Northwestern Regions of the United States Extending from Detroit through the Great Chain of American Lakes to the Sources of the Mississippi River in the Year 1820* (Albany, NY: E. and E. Hosford, 1821), 383.

4. Alexander Wolcott, Chicago, to Colonel John McNeil, Green Bay, November 17, 1824, Wolcott Papers, Chicago History Museum. Kinzie had unsuccessfully lobbied to be Indian agent before Wolcott was appointed. The Kinzie family had been at Chicago since 1804 except for an interruption of four years because of the War of 1812. See Ann Durkin Keating, *Rising Up from Indian Country: The*

Battle of Fort Dearborn and the Birth of Chicago (Chicago: University of Chicago Press, 2012).

5. Alexander Wolcott, Chicago, to Frances Magill, August 10, 1822, Alexander Wolcott Jr. Papers, Chicago History Museum; Alexander Wolcott Jr., Chicago, to Arthur Magill, November 6, 1820, Alexander Wolcott Jr. Papers, Chicago History Museum.

6. The factory system was eliminated nationally in 1822, and there was not always a US Army company posted at Chicago, so Wolcott often managed on his own.

7. Wolcott as quoted in Alexander Wolcott Jr., Chicago, to Arthur Magill, November 6, 1820, Alexander Wolcott Jr. Papers, Chicago History Museum. Nina Baym, introduction to Kinzie, *Wau-Bun* (1992), ix.

8. Wolcott as quoted in Alexander Wolcott Jr., Chicago, to Arthur Magill, November 6, 1820, Alexander Wolcott Jr. Papers, Chicago History Museum.

9. Schoolcraft, *Narrative Journal*, 384–86. In 1823 a second western expedition traveled through Chicago. Again, one of the travelers, William H. Keating, published an account that helped fuel interest in the region. Keating, *Narrative of an Expedition to the Source of St. Peter's River, Lake Winnepeck, Lake of the Woods, &c. &c.* (Philadelphia: H. C. Carey, 1824).

10. In the meantime the Potawatomi could continue to live on the lands, "at the same time . . . drawing annuities for them." Schoolcraft, *Narrative Journal*, 125–26.

11. Quotation from Juliette A. Kinzie, *Walter Ogilby* (Philadelphia: J. B. Lippincott, 1868), 476. On her cousins, see Juliette Kinzie, Chicago, to Nellie Gordon, Savannah, March 1858, Juliette A. Kinzie letters in the Gordon Papers at University of North Carolina [microform], 1858–70. Microfilm accessed at Chicago History Museum (hereafter microfilm Kinzie letters, UNC). Juliette's mother, Frances, married Thomas Homans and gave birth to a daughter, also named Frances; after being widowed, Frances Homans married Arthur W. Magill. Juliette's grandmother, Frances Burbank of Agawam, Massachusetts, was married to Alexander Wolcott in 1785. She died, and her husband married Lucy Waldo on June 7, 1807. See Eleanor Kinzie Gordon, "A Note" to Mrs. John H. Kinzie, *Wau-Bun: The Early Day in the North-West* (Chicago: Rand McNally, 1901), 395.

12. Kinzie, *Walter Ogilby*, 128.

13. Quotations from Kinzie, *Walter Ogilby*, 83–84. Juliette's daughter wrote that her mother went to boarding school in New Haven at fifteen. See Gordon, note to *Wau-Bun*, 395. Nancy F. Cott, *The Bonds of Womanhood: "Woman's Sphere" in New England, 1780–1835* (New Haven, CT: Yale University Press, 1977), esp. 101–14.

14. Captain Arthur Magill and his brother Charles are said to have come from Belfast. His brother William died in March 1791 in Port au Prince, Haiti. Arthur's older sisters Esther, Mary, and Martha all married sons of Captain John

Williams of Bermuda (who died in 1803 in Middletown). Typewritten notes, Arthur Magill Papers, Middlesex Historical Society, Middletown, Connecticut. Juliette would later write about a black servant, a "stout black woman" who "was giving directions, in no gentle voice, to a little, withered man of her own color." Kinzie, *Walter Ogilby*, 48.

15. Alexander Wolcott, Richmond, to Juliette Magill, Middletown, February 22, 1822, Alexander Wolcott Jr. Papers, Chicago History Museum. See also Richard R. John, "The State Is Back In: What Now?" *Journal of the Early Republic* 38 (Spring 2018): 105–18; and Gordon S. Wood, *Empire of Liberty: A History of the Early Republic, 1789–1815* (New York: Oxford University Press, 2009), 642–46. Peter Hall described Middletown in these years as "a place in fundamental transition" undergoing events that were "enormous, uncontrollable, and incomprehensible" to those living through them. See Hall, *Middletown: Streets, Commerce and People, 1650–1981* (Middletown, CT: Wesleyan University Sesquicentennial Papers, 1981), 7, 15.

16. For instance, Connecticut governor Oliver Wolcott (a cousin of Juliette's grandfather) had been a Federalist in the 1790s but shifted his support to President Jefferson. See Sean Wilentz, *The Rise of American Democracy: Jefferson to Lincoln* (New York: Norton, 2005), 184.

17. He was also a friend of President James Madison, who nominated him in 1811 to the US Supreme Court, although his nomination was rejected by the Senate. Alexander Wolcott graduated from Yale in 1778, practiced law in Hartford County, and was collector of customs in the district of Middletown until his death in 1828. "Book of Yale Graduates," Middlesex Historical Society, Middletown, Connecticut. Daniel Walker Howe, *What Hath God Wrought: The Transformation of America, 1815–1848* (New York: Oxford University Press, 2007), 165.

18. Kinzie, *Walter Ogilby*, 215; Wilentz, *Rise of American Democracy*, 183.

19. Wilentz, *Rise of American Democracy*, 204; Hall, *Middletown*, 15.

20. To ensure that he fulfilled his duties faithfully, Magill enlisted three Republican allies as his bondsmen. See Jane Kamensky, *The Exchange Artist: A Tale of High-Flying Speculation and America's First Banking Collapse* (New York: Penguin, 2008), 137, for description of a cashier's duties.

21. Charles Sellers, *The Market Revolution* (New York: Oxford University Press, 1991), 137; Howe, *What Hath God Wrought*, 143–45; Wilentz, *Rise of American Democracy*, 206–7.

22. Hall, *Middletown*, 14; *Boston Daily Advertiser*, November 7, 1820, and December 16, 1820. Magill deeded Middletown property to his bondsmen. Second quotation as given in March 2, 1821, letter of Arthur Magill to Nathan Starr from New Haven Jail, Magill Papers, Middlesex Historical Society.

23. Mary Ann Wolcott, Middletown, to Arthur Magill, New Haven, February 18, 1821, Wolcott Papers, Chicago History Museum. The will of Alexander Wolcott, made July 27, 1825, and probated June 30, 1828, leaves specific sums to children Henry, Alexander, and Mary Ann but separately mentions daughter

Frances, whose money is left in trust for her to be distributed annually. Frances Magill would use this money to buy land in LaSalle County, Illinois. Magill Papers, Middlesex Historical Society, Middletown, Connecticut. More broadly, see Scott Reynolds Nelson, *A Nation of Deadbeats: An Uncommon History of America's Financial Disasters* (New York: Vintage, 2012).

24. Alexander Wolcott Jr., Chicago, to Arthur Magill, Middletown, November 6, 1820, Alexander Wolcott Jr. Papers, Chicago History Museum.

25. Kinzie, *Walter Ogilby*, 77–78, 97.

26. Alexander Wolcott, Richmond, to Juliette Magill, Middletown, February 1822, and Mary Ann Wolcott to Frances Magill, September 20, 1822, Alexander Wolcott Jr. Papers, Chicago History Museum. Mason graduated from West Point in 1820 and was then stationed at Fort Dearborn. Alexander Wolcott to Frances Magill, August 10, 1822, Alexander Wolcott Jr. Papers, Chicago History Museum.

27. Juliette's brother William accompanied Alexander Wolcott back to Chicago. Alexander Wolcott, Chicago, to his sister Frances Magill, Middletown, August 10, 1822, Alexander Wolcott Jr. Papers, Chicago History Museum.

28. Ibid.

29. Alexander Wolcott Jr., Chicago, to Mrs. Frances Magill, Middletown, June 20, 1821, Alexander Wolcott Jr. Papers, Chicago History Museum. See also Hall, *Middletown*, 17.

30. Kinzie, *Walter Ogilby*, 363. Alexander Wolcott to Frances Magill, August 10, 1822, Alexander Wolcott Jr. Papers, Chicago History Museum.

31. West Point would remain an important place for Juliette for the rest of her life. Quotation from Alexander Wolcott, Chicago, to Frances Magill, January 18, 1823, Alexander Wolcott Jr. Papers, Chicago History Museum.

32. Juliette's half-sister Frances had visited Washington, DC, while her brother William accompanied Alexander Wolcott to Chicago. Elizabeth Cass, daughter of Michigan territorial governor Lewis Cass, and Catherine Sibley, daughter of Judge Solomon Sibley, both attended Willard's school during these years. Mary J. Mason Fairbanks, *Emma Willard and Her Pupils, or Fifty Years of Troy Female Seminary, 1822–1872* (New York: Mrs. Russell Sage, 1898).

33. Juliette A. Kinzie, *Mark Logan: The Bourgeois* (Philadelphia: J. B. Lippincott, 1887), 32.

34. Emma Willard, *A Plan for Improving Female Education* (Middlebury, VT: S. W. Copeland, 1819), 3; Joan D. Hedrick, *Harriet Beecher Stowe: A Life* (New York: Oxford University Press, 1994), 61, 65–66.

35. Willard, *Plan for Improving Female Education*, 15.

36. Ibid., 15. See also Cott, *Bonds of Womanhood*, 79.

37. George Younglove Cutler, law student in 1820, as quoted in Cott, *Bonds of Womanhood*, 79. See also Linda Kerber, *Women of the Republic: Intellect and Ideology in Revolutionary America* (Raleigh: University of North Carolina Press, 1997), 77–78.

38. Robert Winthrop, Massachusetts Historical Society, to Juliette Kinzie, Chicago, December 12, 1857; Juliette A. Kinzie Papers, Chicago History Museum. See also Walter Muir and Lawrence W. Kennedy, *Boston: A Topographical History* (Cambridge, MA: Belknap, 2000).

39. Juliette Kinzie, Chicago, to Nellie Gordon, Savannah, February 19, 1864, Gordon Family Papers, Georgia Historical Society.

40. Alexander Wolcott to Frances Magill, April 24, 1829, Wolcott Papers, Chicago History Museum; George H, Smith, "Rambling Tale of a Rambling Town" (privately published for New Hartford Central School, 1955), New Hartford Historical Society; Janice Reilly, "St. Stephen's Episcopal Church," unpublished manuscript, New Hartford Historical Society, New Hartford, New York. On canal towns, see especially Mary P. Ryan, *Cradle of the Middle Class: The Family in Oneida County, New York, 1790–1865* (New York: Cambridge University Press, 1981); and Paul Johnson, *A Shopkeeper's Millennium: Society and Revivals in Rochester, New York, 1815–1837* (Boston: Hill and Wang, 2004).

41. Kinzie, *Walter Ogilby*, 45. Brief to the Superior Court to be held at Middletown, in and for the County of Middlesex, as a court of equity, on the 4th Tuesday of February, A.D. 1829, Magill Papers, Middlesex County Historical Society, Middletown, Connecticut.

42. Alexander Wolcott to Frances Magill, August 10, 1822, Alexander Wolcott Jr. Papers, Chicago History Museum.

43. A description like "fat and hearty" was an indication of a pregnancy in a family that seldom acknowledged the condition directly. For example, see Mary Ann Wolcott, Middletown, September 20, 1822, to Frances Magill, Fishkill, Alexander Wolcott Jr. Papers, Chicago History Museum. See also Alexander Wolcott, Chicago, to Frances Magill, New Hartford, April 24, 1829, Alexander Wolcott Jr. Papers, Chicago History Museum.

44. Alexander Wolcott to Frances Magill, August 10, 1822, Alexander Wolcott Jr. Papers, Chicago History Museum.

45. Alexander Wolcott to Frances Magill, April 24, 1829, Alexander Wolcott Jr. Papers, Chicago History Museum.

46. John's uncle, Thomas Forsyth, was the US Indian agent just to the south at Rock Island. See Peter Shrake, *The Silver Man: The Life and Times of Indian Agent John Kinzie* (Madison: Wisconsin Historical Society, 2016), 27–37; and Margaret Beattie Bogue, "As She Knew Them: Juliette Kinzie and the Ho-Chunk, 1830–1833," *Wisconsin Magazine of History* 85 (December 2001): 23. For more on Lewis Cass's long career, see Willard Carl Klunder, *Lewis Cass and the Politics of Moderation* (Kent, OH: Kent State University Press, 1996).

47. Quotation from Isaac N. Arnold, "Address," in Chicago Historical Society, *Introductory Address* (Chicago: Fergus, 1877), 10–11. See also Herman J. Viola, *Thomas L. McKenney, Architect of America's Early Indian Policy: 1816–1830* (Chicago: Sage Books, 1974), 155–56, 174–76; Klunder, *Lewis Cass*, 53–55; Peter Shrake, "Chasing an Elusive War: The Illinois Militia and the Winnebago Upris-

ing of 1827," *Journal of Illinois History* 12 (Spring 2009): 27–52; and Kinzie, *Mark Logan*, 5.

48. Kinzie, *Mark Logan*, 39.

49. As quoted in Shrake, *Silver Man*, 58. See also *Boston Recorder*, November 28, 1828, 187 (NewsBank, American Antiquarian Society); and Viola, *Thomas L. McKenney*, 147.

50. *Boston Traveler*, November 4, 1828 (NewsBank, American Antiquarian Society); *Boston Commercial Gazette*, November 6, 1828 (NewsBank, American Antiquarian Society); *Boston Recorder*, November 28, 1828 (NewsBank, American Antiquarian Society); and Viola, *Thomas L. McKenney*, 123.

51. Kinzie, *Wau-Bun* (1992), 48–49.

52. *Boston Recorder*, January 8, 1829 (NewsBank, American Antiquarian Society); and Viola, *Thomas L. McKenney*, 98–99.

53. In contrast, Thomas McKenney, superintendent of the Indian Bureau since 1818, lost his job in 1830, in large part because of his political opposition to Jackson. *National Intelligencer*, September 1, 1830 (NewsBank, American Antiquarian Society). For more on Cass as Jackson's secretary of war, see Klunder, *Lewis Cass*, 59–95.

Chapter Two

1. Eleanor Gordon wrote that her parents met in Boston. Eleanor Kinzie Gordon, "A Note" to Mrs. John H. Kinzie, *Wau-Bun: The Early Day in the North-West* (Chicago: Rand McNally, 1901), 395.

2. To see reproductions of the paintings, go to https://www.mfa.org/collections/object/the-tea-party-31744. See also Walter Muir Whitehead, *Boston: A Topographical History* (Cambridge, MA: Harvard University Press, 1959).

3. Juliette A. Kinzie, *Wau-Bun: The "Early Day" in the North-West* (Urbana: University of Illinois Press, 1992), 4. Alexander Wolcott, Chicago, to Frances Magill, New Hartford, April 24, 1829, Alexander Wolcott Jr. Papers, Chicago History Museum. As Tamara G. Miller notes, the westward movement into Ohio was a family affair: "Recognizing their dependence upon men, both legally and economically, the women of Washington County sought to strengthen ties with kin in order to provide themselves with an alternative source of material and emotional support." As quoted in Lucy Eldersveld Murphy and Wendy Hamand Venet, *Midwestern Women: Work, Community, and Leadership at the Crossroads* (Bloomington: Indiana University Press, 1997), 130. See also Susan E. Gray, *The Yankee West: Community Life on the Michigan Frontier* (Chapel Hill: University of North Carolina Press, 1996).

4. Mrs. John H. Kinzie, *Narrative of the Massacre at Chicago* (Chicago: Fergus Printing, 1914), 11, 13. A biographical sketch of John Kinzie written by Juliette was published as part of Isaac N. Arnold, *Address*, in Chicago Historical Society, *Introductory Address* (Chicago: Fergus, 1877), 22–28. Peter Shrake, John Kinzie's

biographer, noted similarly that "much that we know about John Kinzie comes from the writings of his wife, Juliette Magill Kinzie." See Shrake, *The Silver Man: The Life and Times of Indian Agent John Kinzie* (Madison: Wisconsin Historical Society, 2016), 2.

5. Ann Durkin Keating, *Rising Up from Indian Country: The Battle of Fort Dearborn and the Birth of Chicago* (Chicago: University of Chicago Press, 2012), 10.

6. Juliette Kinzie as quoted in Arnold, *Address*, 22.

7. Ibid., 25.

8. Ibid., 10.

9. Ibid., 25.

10. Ibid., 10. See also Keating, *Rising Up from Indian Country*, 142–50; and John Kinzie, Chicago, to John Harris Kinzie, Mackinac, August 9, 1821, John Kinzie Papers, Chicago History Museum.

11. Juliette Kinzie as quoted in Arnold, *Address*, 27. Juliette Kinzie to Nellie Gordon, February 22, 1866, Juliette A. Kinzie letters in Gordon Papers at University of North Carolina [microform], 1858–70. Microfilm accessed at Chicago History Museum (hereafter microfilm Kinzie letters, UNC).

12. Kinzie, *Wau-Bun* (1992), 50; Shrake, *Silver Man*, 77; Margaret Beattie Bogue, "As She Knew Them: Juliette Kinzie and the Ho-Chunk, 1830–1833," *Wisconsin Magazine of History* 85 (December 2001): 45–57. The box is on display at the Indian Agency House at Portage.

13. John H. Kinzie to David Hunter, September 24, 1834, Gordon Family Papers, Georgia Historical Society.

14. Ibid.; Kinzie, *Wau-Bun* (1992), 61.

15. John Kinzie (father), Chicago, to John Kinzie (son), Mackinac, August 9, 1821, John Kinzie Papers, Chicago History Museum.

16. Initially Juliette did not write to her daughter about this, at John's request, "fearing that it might worry you—but I need your sympathy and you may hear from other sources eventually." Juliette Kinzie to Nellie Gordon, August 29, 1860, microfilm Kinzie letters, UNC.

17. Kinzie, *Wau-Bun* (1992), 5.

18. Juliette A. Kinzie, *Mark Logan: The Bourgeois* (Philadelphia: J. B. Lippincott, 1887), 15, 3–4.

19. Quotation as in Kinzie, *Wau-Bun* (1992), 13.

20. Kinzie, *Wau-Bun* (1992), 45–46. Davis was sent to Fort Winnebago in April 1829 (after graduating from West Point the previous year), where he assisted Major David E. Twiggs in building the fort. See P. L. Scanlan, "The Military Record of Jefferson Davis in Wisconsin," *Wisconsin Magazine of History* 24 (December 1940): 175–76.

21. Kinzie, *Wau-Bun* (1992), 181.

22. John H. Kinzie, Fort Winnebago, to George R. Porter, Detroit, October 1, 1832, copy, Wisconsin Historical Society (original in the National Archives). See also Frances Magill, Pikestown, Kentucky, to Juliette Kinzie, Fort Winnebago,

February 3, 1833, Juliette Kinzie Papers, Chicago History Museum, and Gladys Dennis Schultz and Daisy Gordon Lawrence, *Lady from Savannah: The Life of Juliette Low* (1958; repr., New York: Girl Scouts of America, 1988), 39. The house stands today in Portage as a museum operated since 1932 by the National Society of Colonial Dames in the State of Wisconsin. Among the Kinzie items are pieces of china donated to the museum by her descendants. One pattern was blue and white with scenes mainly from New York. The other, a white china patterned in browns and yellows, shows frontier scenes—log houses and outposts.

23. Kinzie, *Wau-Bun* (1992), 51, 60. On the US Army and slavery in the Northwest Territory, see Lea Vander Velde, *Mrs. Dred Scott: A Life on Slavery's Frontier* (New York: Oxford University Press, 2007), 21–84. For more on slavery in the western Great Lakes region during these years, see Christopher P. Lehman, *Slavery in the Upper Mississippi Valley, 1787–1865* (Jefferson, NC: McFarland, 2011), 62–79.

24. Kinzie, *Wau-Bun* (1992), 161–62.

25. Ibid., 62, 68, 161.

26. Ibid., 11–12.

27. Kinzie, *Mark Logan*, 33; Kinzie, *Wau-Bun* (1992), 21; Shrake, *Silver Man*, 100–101.

28. Another subagent worked with Indians along the Rock River to the south. The principal agency for the Ho-Chunk was at Prairie du Chien. Shrake, *Silver Man*, 70–71. On the agent's work, see ibid., 3.

29. Kinzie, *Wau-Bun* (1992), 149–50.

30. Shrake, *Silver Man*, 27.

31. Nancy Oestreich Lurie, "The Winnebago Indians: A Study in Cultural Change" (PhD diss., Northwestern University, June 1952), 77, 102. See also Paul Radin, *The Winnebago Tribe* (Lincoln: University of Nebraska Press, 1970). For more on métis, see Susan Sleeper-Smith, *Indian Women and French Men: Rethinking Cultural Encounter in the Western Great Lakes* (Amherst: University of Massachusetts Press, 2001); and Sophie White, *Wild Frenchmen and Frenchified Indians: Material Culture and Race in Colonial Louisiana* (Philadelphia: University of Pennsylvania Press, 2012). For a broad view of Indian country during the fur trade era, see Richard White, *The Middle Ground: Indians, Empires, and Republics in the Great Lakes Region, 1650–1815* (New York: Cambridge University Press, 1991).

32. Kinzie, *Wau-Bun* (1992), 186–87.

33. Ibid., 57, 63. For more on maple sugaring practices, see Susan Wade, "Indigenous Women and Maple Sugar in the Upper Midwest, 1760 to 1848" (MA thesis, University of Wisconsin–Milwaukee, 2011).

34. Kinzie, *Wau-Bun* (1992), 193–94, also 48–49.

35. Kinzie, *Mark Logan*, 73–75; Kinzie, *Wau-Bun* (1992), 183.

36. Kinzie, *Wau-Bun* (1992), 64.

37. Harriet Martineau, as quoted in Bessie Louis Pierce, *As Others See Chi-*

cago: Impressions of Visitors, 1673–1933 (Chicago: University of Chicago Press, 1933), 83–84.

38. Kinzie, *Mark Logan*, 42–43. Bogue argues that "during their thirty-three months at Fort Winnebago, Juliette and John Kinzie clearly had come to feel very critical of the way the United States government handled Indian affairs, and yet they agreed with the general principle of land cessions and removal to minimize contact with white culture, which they perceived to be a degrading influence on the Ho-Chunk. Bogue, "As She Knew Them," esp. 22.

39. Kinzie, *Wau-Bun* (1992), 57; Kinzie, *Mark Logan*, 40–41.

40. Bessie Louise Pierce, *History of Chicago*, vol. 1, *1673–1848* (Chicago: University of Chicago Press, 1937), 46.

41. Carl R. Roden, "The Beaubien Claim," *Journal of the Illinois State Historical Society* 32 (1949): 150.

42. Harold M. Mayer and Richard C. Wade, *Chicago: Growth of a Metropolis* (Chicago: University of Chicago Press, 1969), 14–15.

43. Eleanor was said to reply, "Take my advice, my boy, or you will live one day to regret it," as quoted in Kinzie, *Wau-Bun* (1992), 141.

44. Ibid., 138.

45. Ibid., 139.

46. Ibid., 61.

47. Ibid., 139.

48. Jacqueline Peterson, "Goodbye, Madore Beaubien: The Americanization of Early Chicago Society," *Chicago History* (Summer 1980): 98.

49. Kinzie, *Wau-Bun* (1992), 140–41.

50. Ibid., 149–50.

51. Ibid., 157, 159.

52. The garrison stationed at Chicago was reassigned to Fort Howard in the spring of 1831 when Fort Dearborn closed down; see Kinzie, *Wau-Bun* (1992), 208. Edward A. Miller Jr., *Lincoln's Abolitionist General: The Biography of David Hunter* (Columbia: University of South Carolina Press, 1997), 10, dates the Hunter marriage several years later.

53. Arthur Magill, Green Bay, to Juliette Kinzie, Fort Winnebago, March 3, 1833, Alexander Wolcott Jr. Papers, Chicago History Museum. See also "Julian Magill Dies Suddenly," *Chicago Daily Tribune*, June 21, 1899.

54. Kinzie, *Wau-Bun* (1992), 215. For more on John Kinzie, see Shrake, *Silver Man*, 89–94; and the Thomas Forsyth account in the appendix of Kinzie, *Wau-Bun*. For a broader discussion on the Black Hawk War, see John W. Hall, *Uncommon Defense: Indian Allies in the Black Hawk War* (Cambridge, MA: Harvard University Press, 2009); Kerry A. Trask, *Black Hawk: The Battle for the Heart of America* (New York: Henry Holt, 2006); Donald Jackson, *Black Hawk: An Autobiography* (Urbana: University of Illinois Press, 1990); and David Walker Howe, *What Hath God Wrought: The Transformation of America, 1815–1848* (New York: Oxford University Press, 2007), 419–23.

55. Shrake, *Silver Man*, 9–11.

56. Kinzie, *Wau-Bun* (1992), 223.

57. Ibid., 231–32. See also Shrake, *Silver Man*, 92–93.

58. Kinzie, *Wau-Bun* (1992), 240; Shrake, *Silver Man*, 92–93.

59. Kinzie, *Wau-Bun* (1992), 242.

60. Ibid., 243. Charles E. Rosenberg, *The Cholera Years: The United States in 1832, 1849, and 1866* (1962; repr., Chicago: University of Chicago Press, 1987), 3. See also William K. Beatty, "When Cholera Scourged Chicago," *Chicago History* 11 (Spring 1982): 2–13.

61. Kinzie, *Wau-Bun* (1992), 259.

62. Ibid., 255.

63. Many Ho-Chunk traveled across the Mississippi for their winter hunt but returned to Wisconsin during the planting season because they did not "deem it safe to remain there [the trans-Mississippi west] during the summer." John H. Kinzie, Fort Winnebago Sub-Agency, to George R. Porter, Detroit Michigan, October 1, 1832, copy, Wisconsin Historical Society (original in the National Archives). See Shrake, *Silver Man*, 96–100, for discussion of other agency houses in the region and their significance.

Chapter Three

1. Michigan territorial governor George Bryan Porter, Detroit, to secretary of war, August 3, 1833, Gordon Family Papers, Georgia Historical Society.

2. John H. Kinzie, Fort Winnebago, to George R. Porter, Detroit, October 1, 1832, copy, Wisconsin Historical Society (original in the National Archives).

3. Juliette Kinzie, Chicago, to Nellie Kinzie Gordon, January 16, 1858, Juliette A. Kinzie letters in the Gordon Papers at University of North Carolina [microform], 1858–70. Microfilm accessed at Chicago History Museum (hereafter microfilm Kinzie letters, UNC). Years later Juliette dedicated *Wau-Bun* to Lewis Cass (who was US secretary of state in 1856 when the book was published). For more on Cass and his early politics, see *Lewis Cass and the Politics of Moderation* (Kent, OH: Kent State University Press, 1996), 42–45. On Forsyth, see Juliette A. Kinzie, *Wau-Bun: The "Early Day" in the North-West* (Urbana: University of Illinois Press, 1992), 263–66.

4. Kinzie, *Wau-Bun* (1992), 261; Arthur Magill, Pikesville, Kentucky, to Juliette Kinzie, Fort Winnebago, January 4, 1833, Alexander Wolcott Jr. Papers, Chicago History Museum.

5. Kinzie, *Wau-Bun* (1992), 261, 157.

6. Ibid., 261. See Michael P. Conzen, "The Historical and Geographical Development of the Illinois and Michigan Canal National Heritage Corridor," in *The Illinois and Michigan Canal National Heritage Corridor: A Guide to Its History and Sources*, ed. Michael P. Conzen and Kay J. Carr (DeKalb: Northern Illinois University Press, 1988), 9–10. Donald Miller notes that Chicago was born "not of the forces of the private market, as some historians claim, but of state planners."

Miller, *City of the Century: The Epic of Chicago and the Making of America* (New York: Simon and Schuster, 1996), 59.

7. Scott as quoted in Ulrich Danckers and Jane Meredith, *Early Chicago* (River Forest, IL: Early Chicago, 1999), 37. Arthur Bronson's father organized the New York Life Insurance and Trust Company with John Jacob Astor and Rufus King. Charles Butler made his first fortune helping tenant farmers in upstate New York obtain land. See John Denis Haeger, *The Investment Frontier: New York Businessmen and the Economic Development of the Old Northwest* (Albany: State University of New York Press, 1981), 268–69.

8. Alice Haliburton was the stepsister of John Kinzie Sr. Her daughter was married to the son of New York senator Rufus King. See 1881 Charles Butler account, Arthur Bronson Papers, Chicago History Museum. See also Jack Harpster, *The Railroad Tycoon Who Built Chicago: A Biography of William B. Ogden* (Carbondale: Southern Illinois University Press, 2009), 41–42.

9. They commissioned George W. Snow to survey the property. Snow in turn hired Joshua Hathaway Jr. See Kinzie, *Wau-Bun* (1992), 255.

10. Juliette A. Kinzie, *Mark Logan: The Bourgeois* (Philadelphia: J. B. Lippincott, 1887), 42.

11. The dwelling stood on what would soon become the southwest corner of Wolcott (State) and North Water Streets. In 1833 this land was controlled by his brother-in-law Lieutenant David Hunter, who was looking for speculators willing to purchase lots. Kinzie, *Wau-Bun* (1992), 262. See also Rima Lunin Schultz, "The Businessmen's Role in Western Settlement: The Entrepreneurial Frontier, Chicago, 1833–1872" (PhD diss., Boston University, 1984), 3; and Carl Abbott, *Boosters and Businessmen: Popular Economic Thought and Urban Growth in the Antebellum Middle West* (Westport, CT: Greenwood, 1981).

12. Women like Juliette Kinzie would anchor homes and help establish "institutions of religion and education." Charles Butler, "Chicago in 1833 in the Eyes of an Investor," as quoted in Bessie Louise Pierce, *As Others See Chicago* (Chicago: University of Chicago Press, 1933), 48. John H. Kinzie, Detroit, to Arthur Bronson, New York, May 24, 1834, and August 13, 1833, Arthur Bronson Papers, Chicago History Museum; Haeger, *Investment Frontier*, 63.

13. The Kinzie family claims related to trade goods and personal property lost during the August 15, 1812, battle at Chicago. For years the federal government had put off the claims, which were finally resolved in the 1833 treaty. Governor Porter continued to rely on John's knowledge and contacts in his new post as Indian subagent based in Detroit. See Michigan territorial governor George Bryan Porter, Detroit, to secretary of war, August 3, 1833, Gordon Family Papers, Georgia Historical Society.

14. On April 9, 1834, Juliette left Detroit with her mother and brother (one-year-old Sandie was also likely part of the group) on the steamship *Oliver Newberry*, headed across the lakes to Buffalo, then went on to New York City. Juliette Kinzie to Nellie Kinzie Gordon, March 25, 1866, microfilm Kinzie letters, UNC.

15. Robert A. Holland, *Chicago in Maps, 1612–2002* (New York: Rizzoli, 2005), 62. See also Michael P. Conzen and Diane Dillon, eds., *Mapping Manifest Destiny: Chicago and the American West* (Chicago: University of Chicago Press, 2008).

16. John H. Kinzie, Detroit, to Arthur Bronson, New York, May 24, 1834, Arthur Bronson Papers, Chicago History Museum; John H. Kinzie to David Hunter, September 24, 1834, Gordon Family Papers, Georgia Historical Society; Arthur Bronson to John H. Kinzie, May 2, 1834, Arthur Bronson Papers, Chicago History Museum. See also *Chicago Democrat*, June 18, 1834.

17. John H. Kinzie to David Hunter, September 24, 1834, Gordon Family Papers, Georgia Historical Society. John advertised the warehouse and store for rent as "situated in the handsomest part of Chicago and by far the best finished rooms in this place." Advertisement in *Chicago Democrat*, April 14, 1834, and October 8, 1834. John H. Kinzie, Chicago, to Arthur Bronson, New York City, May 24, 1834, and June 18, 1834, Arthur Bronson Papers, Chicago History Museum.

18. For instance, see John H. Kinzie to Arthur Bronson, December 17, 1838, Arthur Bronson Papers, Chicago History Museum, for a letter signed by John H. Kinzie but written in Juliette's hand.

19. From a legal standpoint, wives played a clear role when real estate was bought and sold. See Marylynn Salmon, *Women and the Law of Property in Early America* (Chapel Hill: University of North Carolina Press, 1986), 16–18. For a discussion of one woman's struggle with dower rights, see Margaret A. Oppenheimer, *The Remarkable Rise of Eliza Jumel: A Story of Marriage and Money in the Early Republic* (Chicago: Chicago Review Press, 2016), 220–28.

20. John H. Kinzie to Arthur Bronson, May 24, 1834, Bronson Papers, Chicago History Museum. See also the agreement between John Harris Kinzie, Juliette Kinzie, and Arthur Bronson, February 14, 1835, Arthur Bronson Papers, Chicago History Museum, and Charles Butler as discussed in Pierce, *As Others See Chicago*, 53. That several key investors at Chicago remained unmarried certainly suggests that wives were seen as an encumbrance in the volatile world of Chicago real estate speculation.

21. Jacqueline Peterson, "Goodbye, Madore Beaubien: The Americanization of Early Chicago Society," *Chicago History* 9 (Summer 1980): 100–101; and Kinzie, *Wau-Bun* (1992), 158.

22. Joseph Balestier, 1840 remarks to the Chicago Lyceum, as quoted in Peterson, "Goodbye, Madore Beaubien," 111.

23. Peterson, "Goodbye, Madore Beaubien," 98–111.

24. Juliette Kinzie to Nellie Gordon, September 25, 1860, microfilm Kinzie letters, UNC.

25. Of the adult white residents in 1837, 45 percent were men: 1,800 adult men and 845 adult women. See Bessie Louise Pierce, *History of Chicago*, vol. 1, *1673–1848* (Chicago: University of Chicago Press, 1937), 171–75.

26. Ibid., 1:187.

27. Kinzie, *Wau-Bun* (1992), 100; and John H. Kinzie, Chicago, to Arthur Bronson, New York City, June 18, 1834, Arthur Bronson Papers, Chicago History Museum. Bronson, in fact, owned the land Cobweb Castle stood on, and he accommodated John Kinzie's request. See also Gladys Denny Shultz and Daisy Gordon Lawrence, *Lady from Savannah: The Life of Juliette Low* (1958; New York: repr., Girl Scouts of America, 1988), 42.

28. John M. Van Osdel, "History of Chicago Architecture — Reminiscences of John M. Van Osdel," *Inland Architect* 1 (April 1883): 36, and 2 (March 1883): 17 (parts 2 and 3 of a five-part series).

29. John H. Kinzie, Detroit, to Arthur Bronson, New York, May 24, 1834, Arthur Bronson Papers, Chicago History Museum. See also Nellie Kinzie Gordon, Unpublished Reminiscences, Gordon Family Papers, Georgia Historical Society.

30. Kinzie, *Wau-Bun* (1992), 50. Nellie fondly remembered her bedroom on the east side of the house, with a "third story window facing east over the piazza." Nellie Kinzie Gordon, Unpublished Reminiscences, Gordon Family Papers, Georgia Historical Society; and John H. Kinzie to David Hunter, September 24, 1834, Gordon Family Papers, Georgia Historical Society.

31. Schultz and Lawrence, *Lady from Savannah*, 44–45.

32. Harpster, *Railroad Tycoon*, 70.

33. Nellie Kinzie Gordon, Unpublished Reminiscences, Gordon Family Papers, Georgia Historical Society.

34. Ibid.

35. Ibid.; and Kinzie, *Wau-Bun* (1992), 166.

36. Juliette Kinzie to Nellie Gordon, September 2, 1860, microfilm Kinzie letters, UNC.

37. Juliette Kinzie to Nellie Gordon, February 1, 1859, Gordon Family Papers, Georgia Historical Society.

38. Juliette A. Kinzie, *Walter Ogilby* (Philadelphia: J. B. Lippincott, 1868), 48.

39. For instance, Nellie remembered that Austin was "an old negro deaf as a post who had belonged to my Uncle Hunter and made his home with us." Nellie Kinzie Gordon, Unpublished Reminiscences, Gordon Family Papers, Georgia Historical Society.

40. Juliette Kinzie to Nellie Gordon, December 15, 1858, microfilm Kinzie letters, UNC; Juliette Kinzie to Arthur Kinzie, January 18, 1863, microfilm Kinzie letters, UNC. For more on immigrant servants, see Bessie Louise Pierce, *History of Chicago*, vol. 2, *1848–1871* (Chicago: University of Chicago Press, 1940), 152–54.

41. Juliette Kinzie to Nellie Gordon, July 11, 1860, microfilm Kinzie letters, UNC.

42. Nellie Kinzie Gordon, Unpublished Reminiscences, Gordon Family Papers, Georgia Historical Society, Savannah; and John H. Kinzie to Arthur Bronson, October 30, 1839, Arthur Bronson Papers, Chicago History Museum.

43. Even after this horrific accident, Frank remained mischievous. Nellie Kinzie Gordon, Unpublished Reminiscences, Gordon Family Papers, Georgia Historical Society.

44. Along with Juliette, Frances was a founding member of St. James Episcopal Church in 1835. Arthur Magill, Pikesville, Kentucky, to Juliette Kinzie, Fort Winnebago, January 4, 1833, Alexander Wolcott Jr. Papers, Chicago History Museum; and Frances Magill, Pikestown, Kentucky, to Juliette Kinzie, Fort Winnebago, February 3, 1833, Alexander Wolcott Jr. Papers, Chicago History Museum. In 1839 the *Fergus Chicago City Directory* (Chicago: Fergus, 1839) lists Arthur Magill and two sons but gives no residence. Arthur is listed as a clerk in John Kinzie's office. Juliette's half-sister Frances and her husband, Hiram Higby, moved to LaSalle County from New Hartford, New York. For more on the Higbys, see George H, Smith, "Rambling Tale of a Rambling Town" (privately published for New Hartford Central School, 1955), esp. 52–53. The Higbys raised six children on their farm. Frances died in 1854.

45. By 1843 the three were no longer living with the Kinzies but lived in a house just a block east on Michigan Street (between Pine and Rush). See 1843 *Fergus Chicago City Directory* (Chicago: Fergus, 1843).

46. Milo Quaife, *Chicago and the Old Northwest* (Urbana: University of Illinois Press, 2001), xxvii.

47. Alexander lived with Juliette and John or nearby with his parents into the 1840s, when he moved to Ottawa. Within a few years, he had opened a dry goods store at Ottawa, had married, and was doing some farming. In his final years, Arthur Magill (born in 1758) moved to Ottawa to live with Alexander until his death in 1855. Colonel John H. Kinzie in Isaac N. Arnold, "Address," in Chicago Historical Society, *Introductory Address* (Chicago: Fergus, 1877), 27.

48. Nellie Kinzie Gordon, Unpublished Reminiscences, Gordon Family Papers, Georgia Historical Society. Over the course of his career, Alexander Wolcott "waded every marsh in our [Cook] county." He would serve as the Cook County surveyor as well as the first Chicago city surveyor. John Wentworth reminiscences, as cited in Mabel McIlvaine, *Reminiscences of Early Chicago* (Chicago: Lakeside Press, 1912), 136–37. Henry Wolcott stayed in Chicago until 1846, when he went back east. Joseph and Caroline Balestier returned to New York City in 1842. One of Juliette's favorite family connections came when Carrie's daughter married Rudyard Kipling. Nellie Kinzie Gordon, Unpublished Reminiscences, Gordon Family Papers, Georgia Historical Society.

49. Martha Magill married Samuel Williams in 1811 in Middletown. Martha was one of three sisters of Juliette's father. All three married Williams brothers. The three brothers had been born in Bermuda (they were known as the Bermuda devils). Juliette's grandfather Arthur Magill had been a ship captain out of Middletown with connections to Bermuda. Samuel Williams settled in Middletown and became the postmaster. Skinner was a successful lawyer and a prominent business leader in Chicago. Lizzie and Mark Skinner would have

three daughters. Nellie Kinzie Gordon, Unpublished Reminiscences, Gordon Family Papers, Georgia Historical Society.

50. Mary Ann Hubbard, *Family Memories* (Chicago, 1912), 56.

51. After her first husband's death in 1839, Elizabeth married another Middletown man, Thomas Dyer, in 1844. In 1848 Dyer bought the Lake House hotel from the estate of Arthur Bronson for about $6,000. See Memorandum, July 27, 1848, Arthur Bronson Papers, Chicago History Museum. Elizabeth had several sisters who lived in New York as well as a brother who also came to Chicago. Her niece Louise DeKoven Bowen would become a prominent Progressive reformer later in the century. Nellie Kinzie Gordon, Unpublished Reminiscences, Gordon Family Papers, Georgia Historical Society. See also Pierce, *History of Chicago*, 1:115.

52. Nellie Kinzie Gordon, Unpublished Reminiscences, Gordon Family Papers, Georgia Historical Society.

53. Ibid. One of Nellie's fondest memories of childhood was accompanying her father on a long trip to Minnesota and Mackinac.

54. Ibid. The dancing distinguished the Kinzies by denomination, since Presbyterians did not allow dancing.

55. See Schultz, "The Businessmen's Role in Western Settlement," for more on the Rumsey/Dole/Turner families and their business ties. On the Kinzie family, see Nellie Kinzie Gordon, Unpublished Reminiscences, Gordon Family Collection (318), box 13, folder 131, Georgia Historical Society. For a broader view see Naomi Lamoreaux, *Insider Lending: Banks, Personal Connections, and Economic Development in Industrial New England*, (New York: Cambridge University Press, 1996), 35.

56. Mrs. Partington, an American Mrs. Malaprop, was found in a B. P. Shillaber novel of the time. Nellie Kinzie Gordon, Unpublished Reminiscences, Gordon Family Papers, Georgia Historical Society. See also Shultz and Lawrence, *Lady from Savannah*, 49.

57. Juliette Kinzie to Nellie Gordon, January 12, 1858, and October 2, 1860, microfilm Kinzie letters, UNC. See also Richard L. Bushman, *The Refinement of America: Persons, Houses, Cities* (New York: Vintage Books, 1992), 280–82.

58. Eleanor Kinzie Gordon, "A Note" to Mrs. John H. Kinzie, *Wau-Bun: The Early Day in the North-West* (Chicago: Rand McNally, 1901), 398.

59. Fredrika Bremer, 1849, as quoted in Pierce, *As Others See Chicago*, 128.

60. Perry Duis, "Foreword to 2004 Edition," in Bessie Louise Pierce, *As Others See Chicago: Impressions of Visitors, 1673–1933* (Chicago: University of Chicago Press, 2004), xxii. On Harriet Martineau, see 83–84.

61. Mrs. John H. Kinzie, advertisement and preface, *Narrative of the Massacre at Chicago*, 2nd ed. (Chicago: Fergus, 1914), unpaginated.

62. On writing all day, see Juliette Kinzie to Nellie Gordon, July 7, 1860, microfilm Kinzie letters, UNC. On the comfort of writing, see Juliette Kinzie to Nellie Gordon, April 24, 1860, microfilm Kinzie letters, UNC.

63. Juliette Kinzie to Nellie Gordon, December 25, 1857, microfilm Kinzie letters, UNC. Nellie Kinzie Gordon, Unpublished Reminiscences, Gordon Family Collection (318), box 13, folder 131, Georgia Historical Society. See also Shultz and Lawrence, *Lady from Savannah*, 49.

64. Robert Fergus, annotation to advertisement that served as front matter in 1914 edition of the *Narrative*. Writing was an acceptable profession for a middle-class woman like Juliette, and she joined a small group of women who were part of the print revolution. See Carol Lasser and Stacey Robertson, *Antebellum Women: Private, Public, Partisan* (Lanham, MD: Rowman and Littlefield, 2010), 20.

65. Mrs. John H. Kinzie, *Narrative of the Massacre at Chicago* (Chicago: Fergus, 1914), 28–29. Although one historian has credited Eleanor with the "prescient realization" that future generations would be interested in her experiences, it could also be that it was Juliette, "her talented daughter in law," who understood their value. See Milton Milo Quaife, "Historical Introduction," in Mrs. John H. Kinzie, *Wau-Bun: The "Early Day" in the North-West* (Chicago: Lakeside Press, 1932), l.

66. Kinzie, *Narrative*, 13, 37–39.

67. Ibid., 43.

Chapter Four

1. Gladys Dennis Schultz and Daisy Gordon Lawrence, *Lady from Savannah: The Life of Juliette Low* (1958; repr., New York: Girl Scouts of America, 1988), 48.

2. As Rima Lunin Schultz notes, "The human infrastructure created out of kinship and credit ties that emanated from New York and New England . . . transformed the frontier." Schultz, "The Businessmen's Role in Western Settlement: The Entrepreneurial Frontier, Chicago, 1833–1872" (PhD diss., Boston University, 1984), vi. See also Schultz, "'What's Love Got to Do with It?' Divorce and Bankruptcy in Mid-Nineteenth Century Chicago," 26 (unpublished essay).

3. Charles Butler as quoted in Bessie Louis Pierce, *As Others See Chicago* (Chicago: University of Chicago Press, 1933), 48. Philip J. Ethington describes the republican liberalism that Juliette Kinzie and others embraced. Ethington, *The Public City: The Political Construction of Urban Life in San Francisco, 1850–1900* (New York: Cambridge University Press, 1994), esp. 8–12. On New England public civic culture, see Peter Dobkin Hall, *The Organization of American Culture, 1700–1900: New York Institutions, Elites, and the Origins of American Nationality* (New York: New York University Press, 1982), 33–35.

4. Kathleen McCarthy, *Noblesse Oblige: Charity and Cultural Philanthropy in Chicago, 1849–1929* (Chicago: University of Chicago Press, 1982), ix. This is an era when city government begins to move away from privatism, as described in Sam Bass Warner Jr., *The Private City: Philadelphia in Three Periods of Growth* (Philadelphia: University of Pennsylvania Press, 1968), to more government responsi-

bility for the common good, as seen in Jon Teaford, *The Municipal Revolution in America* (Chicago: University of Chicago Press, 1975).

5. Six churches were listed in the 1839 *Fergus Directory of the City of Chicago* (Chicago: Fergus, 1839). Rima Lunin Schultz has written the definitive history of St. James Episcopal Church. See Schultz, *The Church and the City: A Social History of 150 Years at St. James, Chicago* (Chicago: Cathedral of St. James, 1986), 22–25.

6. Harriet Martineau as quoted in Pierce, *As Others See Chicago*, 85. Nellie Kinzie Gordon, Unpublished Reminiscences, Gordon Family Papers, Georgia Historical Society. Isaac Hallam reports in 1835, 1837, and 1841, Diocesan Convention Minutes, Richard R. Seidel Archives of the Episcopal Diocese of Chicago. For more background on St. James within the Chicago diocese, see also Rima Lunin Schultz, "The Making of an American Church: A Study of Leadership, 1834–1945," manuscript, 1988, Seidel Archives.

7. Schultz, *Church and the City*, 26; Mary Ann Hubbard, *Family Memories* (Chicago, 1912), 62. In fact, in 1858, when there was fire in the church building, Juliette could recount the whole scene to her daughter from her windows. See Juliette Kinzie to Nellie Gordon, February 1, 1858, Juliette A. Kinzie letters in the Gordon Papers at University of North Carolina [microform], 1858–1870. Microfilm accessed at Chicago History Museum (hereafter microfilm Kinzie letters, UNC). Nellie Kinzie Gordon, Unpublished Reminiscences, Gordon Family Papers, Georgia Historical Society.

8. Schultz, *Church and the City*, 20, 25.

9. Hubbard, *Family Memories*, 62. Nellie Kinzie Gordon, Unpublished Reminiscences, Gordon Family Papers, Georgia Historical Society.

10. Schultz, *Church and the City*, 29.

11. James Silk Buckingham as quoted in Pierce, *As Others See Chicago*, 88.

12. McCarthy, *Noblesse Oblige*, 6–7. See Julie Roy Jeffrey, *The Great Silent Army of Abolitionism: Ordinary Women in the Antislavery Movement* (Chapel Hill: University of North Carolina Press, 1998), 72.

13. Account from John Dean Caton, as quoted in A. T. Andreas, *History of Chicago* (Chicago: Lakeside Press, 1884), 461. See also McCarthy, *Noblesse Oblige*, 7.

14. Bessie Louise Pierce, *History of Chicago*, vol. 1, *1673–1848* (Chicago: University of Chicago Press, 1937), 270.

15. Andreas, *History of Chicago*, 132; Pierce, *History of Chicago*, 1:274–75.

16. The original investors in the hotel were Gurdon S. Hubbard, David S. Hunter, Dr. W. B. Egan, Major James B. Campbell, and John Kinzie. It appears that Kinzie took over Hunter's portion of the investment during the 1837 Panic, and probably Campbell's as well. See Andreas, *History of Chicago*, 634. Description of the Sauganash Hotel from Charles Joseph Latrobe as cited in Pierce, *As Others See Chicago*, 60. Quotation on the need for better hotel from John H. Kinzie, Chicago, to Arthur Bronson, New York City, June 18, 1834, Arthur

Bronson Papers, Chicago History Museum. See also Juliette Kinzie, *Wau-Bun: The "Early Day" in the North-West* (Urbana: University of Illinois Press, 1992), 101. The Exchange Coffee House built in 1811 in Boston was one of the very first hotels in the United States. It was near the townhouse of Juliette Kinzie's grandmother, so she may have visited it (it burned in 1817). See Jane Kamensky, *The Exchange Artist: A Tale of High-Flying Speculation and America's First Banking Collapse* (London: Penguin Random House, 2008), 178.

17. Description of Lake House, December 30, 1843, Arthur Bronson Papers, Chicago History Museum. For discussion on women in similar public places in New York, see Cindy R. Lobel, *Urban Appetites: Food and Culture in Nineteenth-Century New York* (Chicago: University of Chicago Press, 2014), 125–30.

18. James Silk Buckingham as quoted in Pierce, *As Others See Chicago*, 87–88.

19. See September 26, 1842, description of furniture in the Lake House, Arthur Bronson Papers, Chicago History Museum.

20. Fredrika Bremer as quoted in Pierce, *As Others See Chicago*, 125.

21. For more on town and early city government, see Ann Durkin Keating, *Building Chicago: Suburban Developers and the Creation of a Divided Metropolis* (Urbana: University of Illinois Press, 2002), 36–38.

22. Juliette Kinzie to Nellie Gordon, August 27, 1866, microfilm Kinzie letters, UNC. See also Jack Harpster, *The Railroad Tycoon Who Built Chicago: A Biography of William B. Ogden* (Carbondale: Southern Illinois University Press, 2009), 74.

23. Harriet Martineau as quoted in Pierce, *As Others See Chicago*, 84.

24. John H. Kinzie to Arthur Bronson, December 18, 1838, Arthur Bronson Papers, Chicago History Museum. There is a penciled note that the letter was written in the hand of Juliette Kinzie. See also Arthur Bronson to US secretary of the treasury Ewing, July 24, 1841, and May 24, 1842, Arthur Bronson Papers, Chicago History Museum. In 1838 John tried to collect over $5,000 from the federal government for Indian claims. He would be partially successful but could not avoid defaulting on the Bronson loan. See John H. Kinzie, Chicago, to Arthur Bronson, New York, October 30, 1839, Arthur Bronson Papers, Chicago History Museum.

25. "Constitutionality of Valuation and Stop Laws," *New York Spectator*, October 1841.

26. For another Chicagoan who was unable to pay back loans to Arthur Bronson during these years, see Craig Buettinger, "The Rise and Fall of Hiram Pearson: Mobility on the Urban Frontier," *Chicago History* 9 (Summer 1980): 114–16.

27. Arthur Bronson, Chicago, to US secretary of the treasury Ewing, July 24, 1841; David Hunter, Washington, DC, to John H. Kinzie, Chicago, November 23, 1841; and Arthur Bronson to US secretary of the treasury Farrar, January 24, 1842, Arthur Bronson Papers, Chicago History Museum.

28. On the completion of the Illinois and Michigan Canal in 1848, Kinzie was

appointed collector of tolls, a post he held until the Civil War. John Kinzie did not appear in credit reports, as one of his colleagues did, with "too many irons in the fire ever to meet his engagements." John S. Wright report, Dunn and Bradstreet Credit Reports, Illinois, vol. 27, 1849–81, Chicago, Baker Library, Harvard University Business School.

29. Schultz, "Businessmen's Role in Western Settlement," appendix 10. See also Edward J. Balleisen, *Navigating Failure: Bankruptcy and Commercial Society in Antebellum America* (Chapel Hill: University of North Carolina Press, 2001).

30. Juliette Kinzie to Nellie Gordon, March 30, 1858, and May 25, 1858, microfilm Kinzie letters, UNC.

31. Clare L. McCausland, *Children of Circumstance: A History of the First 125 Years (1849–1974) of Chicago Child Care Society* (Chicago: Chicago Child Care Society, 1976), 2.

32. On the pig, see Andreas, *History of Chicago*, 483. On Juliette, see Nellie Kinzie, Chicago, to Addie Butterfield, Washington, DC, November 28, 1849, Gordon Family Papers, Georgia Historical Society.

33. Eleanor Kinzie Gordon, "A Note" to Mrs. John H. Kinzie, *Wau-Bun: The Early Day in the North-West* (Chicago: Rand McNally, 1901), 401; Carol Lasser and Stacey Robertson, *Antebellum Women: Private, Public, Partisan* (Lanham, MD: Rowman and Littlefield, 2010), xviii–xix, 27–28, 36.

34. Juliette Kinzie to Nellie Gordon, March 17, 1858, microfilm Kinzie letters, UNC.

35. Nellie Kinzie Gordon, Unpublished Reminiscences, Gordon Family Papers, Georgia Historical Society; Charles E. Rosenberg, *The Cholera Years: The United States in 1832, 1849, and 1866* (1962; repr., Chicago: University of Chicago Press, 1987), 3; William K. Beatty, "When Cholera Scourged Chicago," *Chicago History* 11 (Spring 1982): 2–13; Nancy Tomes, *The Gospel of Germs: Men, Women and the Microbe in American Life* (Cambridge, MA: Harvard University Press, 1998), 26.

36. Gordon, "Note," in Kinzie, *Wau-Bun* (1901), 401.

37. Ibid.

38. Suellen Hoy, *Good Hearts: Catholic Sisters in Chicago's Past* (Urbana: University of Illinois, 2006), 37–40.

39. McCausland, *Children of Circumstance*, 6–10, 12, 35; Mamie Ruth Davis, "A History of Policies and Methods of Social Work in the Chicago Orphan Asylum" (MA thesis, University of Chicago, 1927), 6; Mrs. Charles Gilbert Wheeler, *Annals of the Chicago Orphan Asylum from 1849 to 1892* (Chicago: Board of the Chicago Orphan Asylum, 1892), 16.

40. Davis, "History of Policies and Methods of Social Work," 7; Wheeler, *Annals of the Chicago Orphan Asylum*, 15, 21.

41. McCausland, *Children of Circumstance*, 17, 32–33; Wheeler, *Annals of the Chicago Orphan Asylum*, 21. See also Davis, "History of Policies and Methods of Social Work"; Kenneth Cmiel, *A Home of Another Kind: One Chicago Orphan-*

age and the Tangle of Child Welfare (Chicago: University of Chicago Press, 1992), chap. 1; and Nellie Kinzie Gordon, Unpublished Reminiscences, Gordon Family Papers, Georgia Historical Society.

42. McCausland, *Children of Circumstance*, 15.

43. Andreas, *History of Chicago*, 483.

44. Quotations from "New England Festival," *Chicago Daily Tribune*, December 22, 1857; and Bessie Louise Pierce, *History of Chicago*, vol. 2, *1848–1871* (Chicago: University of Chicago Press, 1940), 10.

45. Pierce, *History of Chicago*, 2:472.

46. *Chicago Press and Tribune*, January 20, 1860. Historian Helen L. Horowitz opined that groups like the Chicago Historical Society were "intended primarily for the direct satisfaction of *the men* [my emphasis] who initiated and sustained them." See Horowitz, *Culture and the City: Cultural Philanthropy in Chicago from the 1880s to 1917* (Chicago: University of Chicago Press, 1986), 34–35.

47. Juliette Kinzie to Nellie Gordon, November 30, 1859, microfilm Kinzie letters, UNC; Pierce, *History of Chicago*, 2:400. See entry on Kate Doggett in Rima Lunin Schultz and Adele Hast, eds., *Women Building Chicago: 1790–1990* (Bloomington: Indiana University Press, 2001), for her role in the Chicago Academy of Sciences during these decades.

48. Mrs. John H. Kinzie, *Wau-Bun, The "Early-Day" in the North-West* (Chicago: Lakeside Press, 1932), lix. The public success of *Wau-Bun* must have pleased Juliette (and encouraged her to continue writing), but it does not appear that she made much in royalties on the work. Juliette Kinzie to Nellie Gordon, March 30, 1858, microfilm Kinzie letters, UNC.

49. Kinzie, *Wau-Bun* (1932), lix–lx.

50. Juliette joined a small group of women historians in the first half of the nineteenth century. See Kathryn Kish Sklar, "American Female Historians in Context, 1770–1930," *Feminist Studies* 3 (Autumn 1975): 175.

51. Kinzie, *Wau-Bun* (1992), 103.

52. Ibid., 102.

53. Ibid., 100.

54. Ibid., 138.

55. Juliette Kinzie to Nellie Gordon, December 2, 1858, microfilm Kinzie letters, UNC.

56. *Chicago Tribune*, May 7, 1856.

57. *New York Herald*, May 25, 1856; Robert Winthrop, Boston, to Juliette Kinzie, Chicago, December 12, 1857, Juliette Kinzie Papers, Chicago History Museum; Juliette Kinzie to Nellie Gordon, January 12, 1858, microfilm Kinzie letters, UNC.

58. Juliette Kinzie to Nellie Gordon, September 25, 1860, microfilm Kinzie letters, UNC. Although the book was never published in England, Juliette did have preliminary discussions with firms in London and Edinburgh about a

British edition of *Wau-Bun*. Juliette Kinzie to Nellie Gordon, November 1, 1860, microfilm Kinzie letters, UNC.

59. After the exhibition at the Mechanic's Institute, Hesler opened a studio and gallery in Chicago. See classified display advertisement for "Hesler's Daguerreotype, Photography and Fine Art Gallery," *Chicago Tribune*, February 11, 1856; and Ellen Manchester, "Alexander Hesler: Chicago Photographer," *Image* 16 (March 1973): 7–8.

60. Alexander Hesler took some of the earliest (if not the earliest) extant photographs of the city of Chicago.

61. He advertised regularly in the *Chicago Tribune* after 1856 and received occasional notices in the press about his work.

62. Ogden offered him "the hospitality of his house." See George P. A. Healy, *Reminiscences of a Portrait Painter* (Chicago: McClurg, 1894), 58–59.

63. Ibid., 67.

Chapter Five

1. Juliette Kinzie to Nellie Gordon, June 27, 1860, Juliette A. Kinzie letters in the Gordon Papers at University of North Carolina [microform], 1858–70. Microfilm accessed at Chicago History Museum (hereafter microfilm Kinzie letters, UNC).

2. William Cronon, *Nature's Metropolis: Chicago and the Great West* (New York: Norton, 1991), 111–13.

3. Jack Harpster, *The Railroad Tycoon Who Built Chicago: A Biography of William B. Ogden* (Carbondale: Southern Illinois University Press, 2000), 108–14.

4. In 1850 the Lake House became the first hospital in Chicago, the Illinois General Hospital of the Lakes, established to care for the growing number of immigrants in the area, especially during the cholera epidemic. Two years later the Sisters of Mercy took it over and renamed it Mercy Hospital. See Wallace Best, "Mercy Hospital," in *The Encyclopedia of Chicago*, ed. James Grossman, Ann Durkin Keating, and Janice Reiff (Chicago: University of Chicago Press, 2004), 522. See also Harold M. Mayer and Richard C. Wade, *Chicago: Growth of a Metropolis* (Chicago: University of Chicago Press, 1969), 31.

5. Homer Hoyt, *One Hundred Years of Land Values in Chicago* (Chicago: University of Chicago Press, 1933), 474, 483, 487. See Bessie Louise Pierce, *A History of Chicago*, vol. 2, *1848–1871* (Chicago: University of Chicago Press, 1940), esp. 150–51.

6. Edward L. Peckham, as quoted in Bessie Louise Pierce, *As Others See Chicago: Impressions of Visitors, 1673–1933* (Chicago: University of Chicago Press, 1933), 168.

7. Robin Einhorn, "Lager Beer Riot," in Grossman, Keating, and Reiff, *Encyclopedia of Chicago*, 451–52.

8. Peckham, as quoted in Pierce, *As Others See Chicago*, 168.

9. For more on the Sands and other cases involved in settling lakeshore real estate issues, see Joseph D. Kearney and Thomas W. Merrill, "Contested Shore: Property Rights in Reclaimed Land and the Battle for Streeterville," *Northwestern University Law Review* 107 (2015), accessed at https://scholarlycommons.law .northwestern.edu/nulr/vol107/iss3/1.

10. Other improvements followed, including gas lighting in 1850 and more adequate pavement. Omnibuses (public carriages to carry Chicagoans around the city on regular streets) were introduced in 1850. By 1859 horse railways that ran on tracks down major streets (such as State Street), along with early commuter use of railroads, made it possible for people to live and work farther from the city center, which was rapidly becoming denser and more expensive.

11. Juliette Kinzie, Chicago, to Nellie Kinzie Gordon, Savannah, May 25, 1858, Easter 1858, microfilm Kinzie letters, UNC. They were listed as boarders at the Lake House in the *1855–56 City Directory*. Juliette's brother Julian raised "his house after sewers and water pipes" had been laid along his street. Juliette Kinzie to Nellie Gordon, July 27, 1858, microfilm Kinzie letters, UNC.

12. Juliette Kinzie to Nellie Gordon, February 11, 1860, microfilm Kinzie letters, UNC.

13. Juliette Kinzie to Nellie Gordon, February 16, 1860, microfilm Kinzie letters, UNC.

14. Juliette Kinzie to Nellie Gordon, January 19, 1859, March 14, 1860, microfilm Kinzie letters, UNC.

15. Juliette Kinzie to Nellie Gordon, July 17, 1858, June 22, 1858, and June 11, 1858, microfilm Kinzie letters, UNC.

16. Juliette Kinzie to Nellie Gordon, October 5, 1860, Gordon Family Papers, Georgia Historical Society. See also Juliette Kinzie to Nellie Gordon, September 1, 1865, and December 11, 1866, microfilm Kinzie letters, UNC.

17. Juliette Kinzie to Nellie Gordon, May 10, 1861, and February 1, 1858, microfilm Kinzie letters, UNC.

18. Juliette Kinzie to Nellie Gordon, July 29, 1861, and March 30, 1861, microfilm Kinzie letters, UNC.

19. Juliette Kinzie to Nellie Gordon, July 9, 1858, and April 3, 1859, microfilm Kinzie letters, UNC.

20. Juliette Kinzie to Nellie Gordon, September 2, 1860, November 30, 1859, June 13, 1860, and December 7, 1859, microfilm Kinzie letters, UNC.

21. Nellie Kinzie Gordon, Unpublished Reminiscences, Gordon Family Papers, Georgia Historical Society.

22. Both did "very well." Rev. Robert Clarkson, Chicago, to Nellie Kinzie, New York City, May 26, 1853, Gordon Family Papers, University of North Carolina Archives. Juliette and John did not give their full support to the Illinois diocese's efforts to establish an Episcopal institution (Jubilee College) at Peoria under Bishop Philander Chase. Instead, they supported the Wisconsin diocese for doctrinal and personal reasons, so they sent their sons to Racine College. See

Rima Lunin Schultz, *The Church and the City: A Social History of 150 Years at St. James, Chicago* (Chicago: Cathedral of St. James, 1986), 148.

23. Juliette Kinzie to Nellie Gordon, November 22, 1859, microfilm Kinzie letters, UNC; *History of Middlesex County, Connecticut* (New York: Beers, 1884), 96.

24. Juliette Kinzie to Nellie Gordon, May 27, 1858, microfilm Kinzie letters, UNC. See also Juliette Kinzie to Nellie Gordon, April 12, 1858, Gordon Family Collection, Georgia Historical Society; Juliette Kinzie to Nellie Gordon, January 16, 1858, microfilm Kinzie letters, UNC.

25. Juliette Kinzie to Nellie Gordon, November 8, 1860, May 27, 1858, and September 12, 1860, microfilm Kinzie letters, UNC.

26. Juliette Kinzie to Nellie Gordon, February 11, 1860, June 11, 1858, June 18, 1858, July 8, 1858, and July 12, 1858, microfilm Kinzie letters, UNC; John B. Jentz and Richard Schneirov, *Chicago in the Age of Capital: Class, Politics, and Democracy during the Civil War and Reconstruction* (Urbana: University of Illinois Press, 2012), 45–46; John B. Jentz, "Bread and Labor: Chicago's German Bakers Organize," *Chicago History* 12 (Summer 1983): 24–35.

27. Juliette Kinzie to Nellie Gordon, February 1, 1861, microfilm Kinzie letters, UNC.

28. Juliette Kinzie to Nellie Gordon, April 23, 1859, and November 4, 1859, microfilm Kinzie letters, UNC.

29. Juliette Kinzie to Nellie Gordon, April 4, 1860, November 22, 1859, and February 11, 1860, microfilm Kinzie letters, UNC.

30. Juliette Kinzie to Nellie Gordon, March 14, 1861, microfilm, Chicago History Museum. See also Juliette Kinzie to Nellie Gordon, June 22, 1858, and June 27, 1860, microfilm Kinzie letters, UNC.

31. David Goldfield, *America Aflame: How the Civil War Created a Nation* (New York: Bloomsbury, 2011), 129, 134.

32. Rev. Clarkson to J. D. Kerfoot, June 12, 1849, Cathedral of St. James Archives, as quoted in Schultz, *Church and the City*, 47, 18. Richard L. Bushman, *The Refinement of America: Persons, Houses, Cities* (New York: Vintage Books, 1992), 313.

33. Juliette A. Kinzie, *Walter Ogilby* (Philadelphia: J. B. Lippincott, 1868), 35.

34. Ibid., 97. On the emergence of the middle class, see Stuart Blumin, *The Emergence of the Middle Class: Social Experience in the American City* (New York: Cambridge University Press, 1989), 115.

35. William S. and Jane Johnston lived just around the corner at Rush and Illinois Streets. See Juliette Kinzie to Nellie Gordon, July 17, 1858, microfilm Kinzie letters, UNC. Juliette never mentioned her new neighbors in letters to her daughter Nellie.

36. Harpster, *Railroad Tycoon*, 70. See also Juliette Kinzie to Nellie Gordon, February 1, 1858, June 26, 1858, and December 13, 1859, microfilm Kinzie letters, UNC.

37. Juliette Kinzie to Nellie Gordon, February 6, 1860, microfilm Kinzie

letters, UNC (on McCormick), and April 18, 1858 (on the bishop), microfilm Kinzie letters, UNC,

38. Juliette Kinzie to Nellie Gordon, April 8, 1858, microfilm Kinzie letters, UNC. She made an excursion to the Mississippi River and more often went to Wisconsin. In 1849 Juliette and her daughter went to New York City and Washington, DC, but this was easily eclipsed by her wealthy neighbors. See Gladys Denny Schultz and Daisy Gordon Lawrence, *Lady from Savannah: The Life of Juliette Low* (1958; repr., New York: Girl Scouts of America, 1988), 45.

39. Juliette Kinzie to Nellie Gordon, April 2, 1859, microfilm Kinzie letters, UNC.

40. Juliette Kinzie to Nellie Gordon, April 8, 1859, April 12, 1859, and April 25, 1859, microfilm Kinzie letters, UNC.

41. Juliette Kinzie to Nellie Gordon, April 12, 1859, and April 25, 1859, microfilm Kinzie letters, UNC.

42. Juliette Kinzie to Nellie Gordon, January 25, 1860, microfilm Kinzie letters, UNC.

43. Juliette Kinzie to Nellie Gordon, December 5, 1860, February 1, 1860, and November 14, 1860, microfilm Kinzie letters, UNC; see also *The Only Complete Report of the Burch Divorce Case Containing a Comprehensive History of the Case—the Preliminary Movements, the "Confession" of Mrs. Burch, Opening Speeches of Counsel, the Deposition of Parties Implicated, and All the Testimony in Full, Together with the Letters Offered in Evidence but Ruled Out by the Court. Specially Reported by the Law Reporter of the "New York Daily Times"* (New York: M. DeWitt, 1860).

44. Juliette Kinzie to Nellie Gordon, November 14, 1860, and December 13, 1860, microfilm Kinzie letters, UNC.

45. Juliette Kinzie to Nellie Gordon, April 18, 1860, microfilm Kinzie letters, UNC; Rev. Clarkson, Chicago, to Nellie Kinzie, New York City, May 26, 1853, Gordon Family Papers, University of North Carolina Archives.

46. As Rima Lunin Schultz has noted, Holy Name offered "the St. James vestry . . . a model to whet their appetite." See Schultz, *Church and the City*, 51–53.

47. Juliette Kinzie to Nellie Gordon, November 30, 1859, microfilm Kinzie letters, UNC.

48. Ibid. They often attended services twice on Sunday as well as on Wednesdays and Fridays. During Lent, services were held every day, and Juliette and her husband attended regularly.

49. Juliette Kinzie to Nellie Gordon, January 22, 1860, and February 1860, microfilm Kinzie letters, UNC.

50. Juliette Kinzie to Nellie Gordon, January 6, 1860, and January 22, 1860, microfilm Kinzie letters, UNC.

51. Juliette Kinzie to Nellie Gordon, October 9, 1860, microfilm Kinzie letters, UNC.

52. Juliette Kinzie to Nellie Gordon, September 19, 1860, microfilm Kinzie letters, UNC.

53. Juliette Kinzie to Nellie Gordon, May 21, 1860, microfilm Kinzie letters, UNC.

54. Juliette Kinzie to Nellie Gordon, January 27, 1858, microfilm Kinzie letters, UNC. When Dyer did not like her novel, Juliette consoled herself that her friend liked *Torchlight*, a popular novel that Juliette disliked. Juliette Kinzie to Nellie Gordon, July 17, 1858, microfilm Kinzie letters, UNC.

55. Kinzie, *Walter Ogilby*, 34. Karl Marx used similar language, the "*annihilation of space by time*," when describing the contradictions of capitalism in 1857. See Karl Marx, *Grundrisse* (London: Penguin, 1973), 538–39.

56. Kinzie, *Walter Ogilby*, 52.

57. Ibid., 215.

58. Ibid., 126.

59. Ibid., 128–29, 112, 53.

Chapter Six

1. See Robin Einhorn, *Property Rules: Political Economy in Chicago, 1833–1872* (Chicago: University of Chicago Press, 1991), for changes in city government; and Philip J. Ethington, *The Public City: The Political Construction of Urban Life in San Francisco, 1850–1900* (New York: Cambridge University Press, 1994). John B. Jentz and Richard Schneirov, *Chicago in the Age of Capital: Class, Politics, and Democracy during the Civil War and Reconstruction* (Urbana: University of Illinois Press, 2012), explores this era as well.

2. Nellie Kinzie Gordon, Unpublished Reminiscences, Gordon Family Papers, Georgia Historical Society.

3. Martha J. Lamb, "A Neglected Corner of the Metropolis: Historic Homes in Lafayette Place," *Magazine of American History with Notes and Queries* 16 (July 1886): 23. See also Juliette A. Kinzie, *Walter Ogilby* (Philadelphia: J. B. Lippincott, 1868), 32.

4. She enjoyed very much her cousin Caroline Balestier's collection of paintings. Another cousin, a professor of mathematics at Columbia, had her come regularly to spend Saturday to Monday. Nellie Kinzie Gordon, Unpublished Reminiscences, Gordon Family Papers, Georgia Historical Society. See also Rev. Clarkson, Chicago, to Nellie Kinzie, New York City, May 26, 1853, Gordon Family Papers, University of North Carolina Archives.

5. Nellie Kinzie Gordon, Unpublished Reminiscences, Gordon Family Papers, Georgia Historical Society.

6. William Gordon to Nellie Kinzie, April 18, 1857, Gordon Family Papers, University of North Carolina Archives. Nellie resisted her mother's efforts as a matchmaker. Nellie Kinzie Gordon, Unpublished Reminiscences, Gordon Family Papers, Georgia Historical Society.

7. Nellie Kinzie to William Gordon, November 12, 1855, Gordon Family

Papers, Georgia Historical Society. Nellie Kinzie to Eliza Gordon, September 15, 1855; John Kinzie to William Gordon, December 7, 1855; William Gordon to Nellie Kinzie April 29, 1856; and William Gordon to John Kinzie, April 30, 1856, all Gordon Family Papers, University of North Carolina Archives.

8. William Gordon, New York City, to Nellie Kinzie, Chicago, June 10, 1856, and November 10, 1856, Gordon Family Papers, University of North Carolina Archives. For an assessment of Illinois antislavery politics, Abraham Lincoln, and Stephen A. Douglas, see Graham A. Peck, *Making an Antislavery Nation: Lincoln, Douglas, and the Battle over Freedom* (Urbana: University of Illinois Press, 2017).

9. Willie Gordon, Savannah, to Nellie Kinzie, Chicago, October 9, 1856, Gordon Family Papers, University of North Carolina Archives. For more on Douglas and Lincoln in Chicago, See Bessie Louise Pierce, *A History of Chicago*, vol. 2, *1848–1871* (Chicago: University of Chicago Press, 1940), 213–14.

10. Nellie Kinzie to William Gordon, November 12, 1855, Gordon Family Papers, Georgia Historical Society.

11. William Gordon to Nellie Kinzie, February 24, 1857, Gordon Family Papers, University of North Carolina Archives; Nellie Kinzie to William Gordon, April 11, 1857, Gordon Family Papers, University of North Carolina Archives. At one point Mrs. Gordon refused to change her travel plans to make a wedding possible. Nellie Kinzie to William Gordon, May 16, 1855, Gordon Family Papers, Georgia Historical Society.

12. William Gordon to Nellie Kinzie, August 20, 1857 (Manchester), October 11, 1857 (NYC), October 22, 1857 (NYC), Gordon Family Papers, University of North Carolina Archives.

13. Juliette Kinzie to Nellie Gordon, December 25, 1857, Juliette A. Kinzie letters in the Gordon Papers at University of North Carolina [microform], 1858–70. Microfilm accessed at Chicago History Museum (hereafter microfilm Kinzie letters, UNC). William Gordon to Nellie Kinzie, December 12, 1857, Gordon Family Papers, University of North Carolina Archives.

14. Willie Gordon to Nellie Kinzie, June 16, 1856, Gordon Family Papers, University of North Carolina Archives.

15. Juliette Kinzie to Nellie Gordon, March 1, 1858, March 30, 1858, and May 25, 1858, microfilm Kinzie letters, UNC.

16. Linda Kerber, *No Constitutional Right to Be a Lady: Women and the Obligations of Citizenship* (New York: Hill and Wang, 1998), xxi, xxiii. Carol Lasser and Stacey Robertson note that "with experience from these interventions and organizations they generated, some northern women began to contemplate not only companionate co-work in reform but also co-equality that suggested their standing in the civil society and in the political process." See Lasser and Robertson, *Antebellum Women: Private, Public, Partisan* (Lanham, MD: Rowman and Littlefield, 2010), 27–28. See also Mary Beth Norton, *Liberty's Daughters: The Revolutionary Experience of American Women, 1750–1800* (Ithaca, NY: Cornell University Press, 1996), 40–41.

17. Juliette Kinzie to Nellie Gordon, August 9, 1858, and Easter 1858, microfilm Kinzie letters, UNC.

18. Quotation from Nancy F. Cott, *The Bonds of Womanhood: "Woman's Sphere" in New England, 1780–1835* (1977; repr., New Haven, CT: Yale University Press, 1997), 77–78. See also Linda Kerber, *Women of the Republic: Intellect and Ideology in Revolutionary America* (Raleigh: University of North Carolina Press, 1997), 77–78.

19. Juliette Kinzie to Nellie Gordon, January 27, 1858, March 1, 1858, March 17, 1858, and Easter 1858, microfilm Kinzie letters, UNC.

20. William Gordon to Nellie Kinzie, April 18, 1856, and April 29, 1856, Gordon Family Papers, University of North Carolina Archives. On their engagement, William wrote to Nellie that "you told me once you longed to belong to someone." Now she belonged to him. William Gordon to John Kinzie, April 30, 1856, Gordon Family Papers, folder 69, Southern History Collections, University of North Carolina Archives. See also Juliette Kinzie to Nellie Gordon, March 17, 1858, microfilm Kinzie letters, UNC.

21. Juliette Kinzie to Nellie Gordon, January 27, 1858, microfilm Kinzie letters, UNC.

22. Thavolia Glymph, *Out of the House of Bondage: The Transformation of the Plantation Household* (New York: Cambridge University Press, 2008), 4.

23. Juliette Kinzie to Nellie Gordon, January 19, 1859, and January 16, 1858, microfilm Kinzie letters, UNC.

24. Juliette Kinzie to Nellie Gordon, May 10, 1861, microfilm Kinzie letters, UNC.

25. Juliette Kinzie to Nellie Gordon, March 27, 1860, microfilm Kinzie letters, UNC. See also Kerber, *Women of the Republic*, 77–78.

26. Juliette Kinzie to Nellie Gordon, June 11, 1858, microfilm Kinzie letters, UNC.

27. Juliette Kinzie to Nellie Gordon, April 12, 1858, Gordon Family Papers, Georgia Historical Society.

28. Juliette Kinzie to Nellie Gordon, December 2, 1858 (seeds and recipes), and March 17, 1858 (muffin recipe), microfilm Kinzie letters, UNC.

29. Juliette Kinzie to Nellie Gordon, August 29, 1860, microfilm Kinzie letters, UNC.

30. Juliette Kinzie to Nellie Gordon, June 8, 1860, and July 2, 1860, microfilm Kinzie letters, UNC.

31. Juliette Kinzie to Nellie Gordon, August 29, 1860, and September 2, 1860, microfilm Kinzie letters, UNC.

32. Juliette Kinzie to Nellie Kinzie Gordon, November 23, 1860, microfilm Kinzie letters, UNC.

33. Juliette Kinzie to Nellie Gordon, November 20, 1860, microfilm Kinzie letters, UNC.

34. Juliette Kinzie to Nellie Gordon, May 29, 1860, microfilm Kinzie letters,

UNC. Lincoln is often presented as being afraid of women, but Juliette did not find him either timid or awkward. On Abraham Lincoln, see William Lee Miller, *Lincoln's Virtues: An Ethical Biography* (New York: Vintage, 2002), 55. For more on Mary Lincoln and her relationship with her husband and politics, see Jean H. Baker, *Mary Todd Lincoln: A Biography* (New York: Norton, 1987); and Catherine Clinton, *Mrs. Lincoln: A Life* (New York: HarperCollins, 2009). On Mary Lincoln's widowhood, see Daniel Mark Epstein, *The Lincolns: Portrait of a Marriage* (New York: Ballantine, 2009); and Jason Emerson, *The Madness of Mary Lincoln* (Carbondale: Southern Illinois University Press, 2007).

35. Philip Ethington explores these issues in pre–Civil War San Francisco in Ethington, *Public City*, 8, 12. Ethington describes the era from after the Revolution into the 1850s as a time of "republican liberalism" that will be blown up by industrialization and the end of slavery with the Civil War.

36. Juliette Kinzie to Nellie Kinzie Gordon, November 23, 1860, microfilm Kinzie letters, UNC.

37. Lincoln's views as presented in the 1858 Lincoln-Douglas debates are revealing. I have been particularly influenced by the work of historians including David Donald, Eric Foner, Michael Holt, Gabor Boritt, James McPherson, James Oakes, and Harold Holzer.

38. David Goldfield, in *America Aflame: How the Civil War Created a Nation* (New York: Bloomsbury, 2011), 73, notes: "The parlor of mid-nineteenth-century homes functioned as a gathering place for family, friends and ideas."

39. Juliette Kinzie to Nellie Gordon, April 29, 1861, microfilm Kinzie letters, UNC. Since abolitionism was a minor part of even Northern sentiment going into the Civil War, Juliette's views offer a sense of the mainstream acceptance of hierarchy, with slavery a part of the whole. This contrasted with the view of Southern women like Mary Chesnut, who equated Harriet Beecher Stowe's attitudes with those of all Northern women. See LeeAnn Whites, "The Civil War as a Crisis in Gender," in *Divided Houses: Gender and the Civil War*, ed. Catherine Clinton and Nina Silber (New York: Oxford University Press, 1992), 5.

40. Juliette Kinzie to Nellie Gordon, December 1, 1860, microfilm Kinzie letters, UNC.

41. Juliette Kinzie to Nellie Gordon, May 21, 1861, microfilm Kinzie letters, UNC. See Stacey M. Robertson, *Betsy Mix Cowles: Champion of Equality* (Boulder, CO: Westview Press, 2014), 90; Julie Roy Jeffrey, *The Great Silent Army of Abolitionism: Ordinary Women in the Antislavery Movement* (Chapel Hill: University of North Carolina Press, 1999); and Stacey M. Robertson, *Hearts Beating for Liberty: Women Abolitionists in the Old Northwest* (Chapel Hill: University of North Carolina Press, 2010).

42. Juliette Kinzie to Nellie Gordon, January 18, 1861, and May 10, 1861, microfilm Kinzie letters, UNC.

43. Juliette Kinzie to Nellie Gordon, December 1, 1860, and May 10, 1861, microfilm Kinzie letters, UNC.

44. Theodore J. Karamanski, *Rally 'Round the Flag: Chicago and the Civil War* (Lanham, MD: Rowman and Littlefield, 2006), 26–32.

45. Juliette Kinzie to Nellie Gordon, May 14, 1860, microfilm Kinzie letters, UNC.

46. Ibid.

47. Ibid.

48. Juliette Kinzie to Nellie Gordon, May 21, 1860, microfilm Kinzie letters, UNC. In fact Mary Livermore, as the only female newspaper correspondent, was the only woman on the platform.

49. Ibid.

50. Juliette Kinzie to Nellie Gordon, November 2, 1860, microfilm Kinzie letters, UNC.

51. Juliette Kinzie to Nellie Gordon, November 28, 1860, microfilm Kinzie letters, UNC.

52. Juliette Kinzie to Nellie Gordon, November 9, 1860, microfilm Kinzie letters, UNC.

53. Juliette Kinzie to Nellie Gordon, December 1, 1860, and November 14, 1860, microfilm Kinzie letters, UNC. Nicole Etcheson suggests, "The process of defining the Midwest began when Northern and Southern migrants began to identify themselves more as Westerners than as Southerners and Northerners. . . . The firing on Fort Sumter, however, would cause a resurgence of divisions." As quoted in Ginette Aley and J. L. Anderson, eds., *Union Heartland: The Midwestern Homefront during the Civil War* (Carbondale: Southern Illinois University Press, 2013), 5.

54. Juliette Kinzie to Nellie Gordon, January 21, 1861, microfilm Kinzie letters, UNC.

55. Jacqueline Jones, *Saving Savannah: The City and the Civil War* (New York: Knopf, 2008), 151.

56. Even Nellie's Episcopal pastor preached in favor of secession. Nellie felt betrayed by her religion. See Nellie Kinzie Gordon, Unpublished Reminiscences, Gordon Family Papers, Georgia Historical Society. Juliette raised the specter of a "servant insurrection" to encourage her daughter to come North. Juliette Kinzie to Nellie Gordon, December 5, 1860, and December 10, 1860, microfilm Kinzie letters, UNC.

57. Juliette Kinzie to Nellie Gordon, February 7, 1861, microfilm Kinzie letters, UNC.

58. Juliette Kinzie to Nellie Gordon, January 18 1861, microfilm Kinzie letters, UNC.

59. Juliette Kinzie to Nellie Gordon, April 21, 1861, microfilm Kinzie letters, UNC.

60. Juliette Kinzie to Nellie Gordon, February 7, 1861, and February 11, 1861, microfilm Kinzie letters, UNC.

Chapter Seven

1. Exploring the role of women in the Civil War has transformed our understanding of the conflict. See Stephanie McCurry, *Confederate Reckoning: Power and Politics in the Civil War South* (Cambridge, MA: Harvard University Press, 2010). See also Catherine Clinton and Nina Silber, eds., *Divided Houses: Gender and the Civil War* (New York: Oxford University Press, 1992); Drew Gilpin Faust, *Mothers of Invention: Women in the Slaveholding South in the American Civil War* (Chapel Hill: University of North Carolina Press, 1996); and Elizabeth D. Leonard, *Yankee Women: Gender Battles in the Civil War* (New York: Norton, 1994).

2. Abraham Lincoln Papers at the Library of Congress, ser. 1, General Correspondence, 1833–1916, March 1861, First Inaugural, Final Draft. Daniel Mark Epstein, *The Lincolns: Portrait of a Marriage* (New York: Ballantine, 2008).

3. Carolyn J. Stefanco, "Poor Loving Prisoners of War: Nellie Kinzie Gordon and the Dilemma of Northern-Born Women in the Confederate South," in *Enemies of the Country: New Perspectives on Unionists in the Civil War South*, ed. John C. Inscoe and Robert C. Kenzer (Athens: University of Georgia Press, 2001), 155.

4. Abraham Lincoln Papers at the Library of Congress, ser. 1, General Correspondence, 1833–1916, March 4, 1865, Second Inaugural. There is a rich literature on Lincoln's evolving views on slavery, including works by Eric Foner, James McPherson, and James Oakes.

5. Jack Harpster, *The Railroad Tycoon Who Built Chicago: A Biography of William B. Ogden* (Carbondale: Southern Illinois University Press, 2000), 184. See also Isaac N. Arnold and J. Young Scammon, *William B. Ogden, and Early Days in Chicago* (Chicago: Fergus, 1882), 30.

6. Juliette Kinzie to Nellie Gordon, November 7, 1863, Juliette A. Kinzie letters in the Gordon Papers at University of North Carolina [microform], 1858–1870. Microfilm accessed at Chicago History Museum (hereafter microfilm Kinzie letters, UNC); Juliette Kinzie to Nellie Gordon, May 10, 1861, microfilm Kinzie letters, UNC.

7. LeeAnn Whites makes this connection between the Industrial Revolution, slavery, and the changing family dynamic, albeit only in the South. I suggest it applies more generally. See Whites, "The Civil War as a Crisis in Gender," in *Divided Houses: Gender and the Civil War*, ed. Catherine Clinton and Nina Silber (New York: Oxford University Press, 1992), 6, 9.

8. Juliette Kinzie to Nellie Gordon, February 21, 1861, and September 12, 1860, microfilm Kinzie letters, UNC. Captain David Hunter accompanied President Lincoln east before the inauguration in his personal detail. Juliette Kinzie to Nellie Gordon, February 28, 1861, microfilm Kinzie letters, UNC. On the divisions within Chicago during the Civil War, see Theodore J. Karamanski, *Rally*

'*Round the Flag: Chicago and the Civil War* (Lanham, MD: Rowman and Littlefield, 2006), 185–89, 208–14.

9. Juliette Kinzie to Nellie Gordon, March 5 and March 8, 1861, microfilm Kinzie letters, UNC; Arthur Kinzie to Nellie Gordon, March 28, 1861, microfilm Kinzie letters, UNC.

10. Juliette Kinzie to Nellie Gordon, March 28, 1861, also April 21, 1861, and April 29, 1861, microfilm Kinzie letters, UNC.

11. Juliette Kinzie to Nellie Gordon, February 11, 1861, microfilm Kinzie letters, UNC.

12. Juliette Kinzie to Nellie Gordon, March 28, 1861, microfilm Kinzie letters, UNC. LeeAnn Whites makes it clear that this was a broader problem, one of "relational loyalty" in conflict with political or sectional loyalty. LeeAnn Whites and Alecia P. Long, *Occupied Women: Gender, Military Occupation, and the American Civil War* (Baton Rouge: Louisiana State University Press, 2009), 2–3.

13. Juliette Kinzie to Nellie Gordon, June 11, 1861, and January 28, 1863, microfilm Kinzie letters, UNC.

14. Juliette Kinzie to Nellie Gordon, July 30, 1863, also July 1, 1861, and July 19, 1861, microfilm Kinzie letters, UNC.

15. Mary D. Robertson portrays Nellie as unwavering in her support: she describes Nellie as a "northern rebel." See Robertson, ed., "Northern Rebel: The Journal of Nellie Kinzie Gordon, Savannah, 1862," *Georgia Historical Quarterly* 70 (Fall 1986): 477–517. George Arthur Gordon, Nellie's youngest son, similarly portrays his mother's loyalty to the South in his posthumous sketch of her life, "Eleanor Kinzie Gordon: A Sketch," *Georgia Historical Quarterly* 1 (September 1917): 186. Carolyn J. Stefanco argues that Nellie's views of the Confederacy were more complex and changed over the war, but she does not allow Juliette a similar latitude to be complex and changing. See Stefanco, "Poor Loving Prisoners of War," 148, 152–53.

16. Juliette Kinzie to Nellie Gordon, April 21, 1861, microfilm Kinzie letters, UNC. See also Theodore J. Karamanski and Eileen M. McMahon, eds., *Civil War Chicago: Eyewitness to History* (Athens: Ohio University Press, 2014); and Randall Miller, "The Great National Struggle in the Heart of the Union," in *Union Heartland: The Midwestern Homefront during the Civil War*, ed. Ginette Aley and J. L. Anderson (Carbondale: Southern Illinois University Press, 2013), 5.

17. Juliette Kinzie to Nellie Gordon, April 21, 1861, microfilm Kinzie letters, UNC.

18. Abraham Lincoln from *W. S. Johnson vs. William Jones* (1860) as cited in Isaac N. Arnold, "Address," in Chicago Historical Society, *Introductory Address* (Chicago: Fergus, 1877), 29; Juliette Kinzie to Nellie Gordon, July 19, 1861, microfilm Kinzie letters, UNC. On David Hunter's promotions, see Edward A. Miller Jr., *Lincoln's Abolitionist General: The Biography of David Hunter* (Columbia: University of South Carolina Press, 1997), 57, 70–71.

19. Harpster, *Railroad Tycoon*, 157–62, 183.

20. These groups were in place and mobilized, not new on the scene. This contrasts with Maureen A. Flanagan's view that "organizing sanitary fairs during the war undoubtedly contributed to Chicago women's learning how to organize." Flanagan, *Seeing with Their Hearts: Chicago Women and the Vision of the Good City, 1871–1933* (Princeton, NJ: Princeton University Press, 2002), 228n56.

21. Juliette Kinzie to Nellie Gordon, April 21, 1861, microfilm Kinzie letters, UNC.

22. David T. Courtright, *Dark Paradise: A History of Opiate Addiction in America* (Cambridge, MA: Harvard University Press, 2001), 35. See also H. Wayne Morgan, *Drugs in America: A Social History, 1800–1980* (Syracuse, NY: Syracuse University Press, 1981).

23. Juliette Kinzie to Nellie Gordon, July 7, 1861, microfilm Kinzie letters, UNC.

24. Juliette Kinzie to Nellie Gordon, July 19, 1861, and July 24, 1861, microfilm Kinzie letters, UNC.

25. Juliette Kinzie to Nellie Gordon, November 21, 1861, microfilm Kinzie letters, UNC.

26. Stefanco, "Poor Loving Prisoners of War," 149.

27. Juliette Kinzie to Nellie Gordon, July 15, 1861, microfilm Kinzie letters, UNC.

28. Juliette Kinzie to Nellie Gordon, April 29, 1861, April 26, 1861, and May 29, 1861, microfilm Kinzie letters, UNC.

29. See Kathryn Burke, "Letter Writing in America: Civil War," Postal Museum, Smithsonian, https://postalmuseum.si.edu/letterwriting/lw04.html.

30. Juliette Kinzie to Nellie Gordon, March 28, 1861, June 5, 1861, July 19, 1861, March 31, 1862, December 21, 1862, and December 7, 1861 (on flags of truce), microfilm Kinzie letters, UNC.

31. Juliette Kinzie to Nellie Gordon, July 15, 1861, June 11, 1861, June 17, 1861, December 2, 1862, October 30, 1863, October 31, 1863, and April 3, 1863, microfilm Kinzie letters, UNC. For various methods see Juliette Kinzie to Nellie Gordon, May 10, 1861, March 31, 1862, April 19, 1863, June 22, 1863, and October 2, 1863, microfilm Kinzie letters, UNC.

32. Juliette Kinzie to Nellie Gordon, December 7, 1864, Gordon Family Papers, Georgia Historical Society.

33. Juliette Kinzie to Nellie Gordon, July 15, 1863, microfilm Kinzie letters, UNC, was sent via a friend in London. Juliette Kinzie to Nellie Gordon, November 7, 1863, microfilm Kinzie letters, UNC, was sent via Halifax. See also Juliette Kinzie to Nellie Gordon, December 2, 1862, December 21, 1862, November 7, 1863, and December 15, 1863, microfilm Kinzie letters, UNC.

34. Juliette Kinzie to Nellie Gordon, October 22, 1863, microfilm Kinzie letters, UNC, and Juliette Kinzie to Nellie Gordon, October 12, 1864, Gordon Family Papers, Georgia Historical Society.

35. Juliette Kinzie to Nellie Gordon, December 15, 1863, and December 2, 1862, microfilm Kinzie letters, UNC.

36. Juliette Kinzie to Nellie Gordon, July 19, 1861, microfilm Kinzie letters, UNC. Carolyn Stefanco notes that Nellie "exchanged as many letters with her mother, who lived in Chicago, as she did with her husband." See Stefanco, "Poor Loving Prisoners of War," 148–49.

37. Juliette Kinzie to Nellie Gordon, April 3, 1864, and April 21, 1861, microfilm Kinzie letters, UNC.

38. Juliette wrote that she would "do the same" and keep a journal. If that journal still exists, it is not in a major archive. Juliette Kinzie to Nellie Gordon, March 28, 1861, microfilm Kinzie letters, UNC.

39. Juliette Kinzie to Nellie Gordon, April 19, 1863, and January 12, 1863, microfilm Kinzie letters, UNC.

40. Juliette Kinzie to Nellie Gordon, January 15, 1861, microfilm Kinzie letters, UNC.

41. Juliette Kinzie to Nellie Gordon, April 3, 1864, February 25, 1863, March 12, 1863, January 1, 1864, and April 3, 1864, microfilm Kinzie letters, UNC; Stefanco, "Poor Loving Prisoners of War," 159.

42. In a postscript she added greetings from her husband. Juliette A. Kinzie to Abraham Lincoln, Monday, November 16, 1863, Abraham Lincoln Papers at the Library of Congress, ser. 1, General Correspondence, 1833–1916. General John Turner agreed to send another trunk to Savannah under a flag of truce. See Juliette Kinzie to Nellie Gordon, April 3, 1864, microfilm Kinzie letters, UNC.

43. Juliette Kinzie to Nellie Gordon, July 30, 1863, and August 23, 1864, microfilm Kinzie letters, UNC.

44. Juliette Kinzie to Nellie Gordon, April 13, 1863, microfilm Kinzie letters, UNC. Juliette could not help wishing her son-in-law acted more like Posey's husband, who had "sense enough not to entirely alienate her affections by tyrannically keeping her away from the friends she so dearly loves."

45. Stefanco, "Poor Loving Prisoners of War," 148–49, argues that "some Northern-born women were held to higher standards of loyalty than white women from the South." Juliette Kinzie to Nellie Gordon, March 12, 1863, microfilm Kinzie letters, UNC.

46. Robertson, "Northern Rebel," 500. President Lincoln issued the preliminary Emancipation Proclamation in September 1862. He rebuked General Hunter, who in May 1862, while heading Union operations in South Carolina, Georgia, and Florida, declared enslaved people in his department "forever free." Miller, Lincoln's Abolitionist General, 99, 105. See also Juliette A. Kinzie to Abraham Lincoln, June 16, 1864, Abraham Lincoln Papers at the Library of Congress, ser. 1, General Correspondence, 1833–1916.

47. Juliette Kinzie to Nellie Gordon, March 18, 1862, microfilm Kinzie letters, UNC. Nellie perhaps remained more a Northerner than a Southern mis-

tress. See Catherine Clinton, *The Plantation Mistress: Woman's World in the Old South* (New York: Pantheon, 1982), 8–9.

48. Nellie Gordon Journal, May 10, 1862, in Robertson, "Northern Rebel," 500. Also Juliette Kinzie to Nellie Gordon, October 20, 1862, microfilm Kinzie letters, UNC.

49. Arthur Kinzie, Hilton Head, to his sister Nellie, Savannah, February 15, 1863, Gordon Family Papers, Georgia Historical Society; Juliette Kinzie to Nellie Gordon, March 3, 1863, microfilm Kinzie letters, UNC.

50. Juliette understood that Nellie would come to Chicago only if Willie Gordon died. See Juliette Kinzie to Nellie Gordon, February 25, 1863, microfilm Kinzie letters, UNC.

51. Juliette Kinzie to Nellie Gordon, April 14, 1862, microfilm Kinzie letters, UNC.

52. Juliette Kinzie to Nellie Gordon, January 11, 1863, microfilm Kinzie letters, UNC. See also James M. Merrill, "Cairo, Illinois: Strategic Civil War River Port," *Journal of the Illinois State Historical Society* 76 (Winter 1983): 242–56.

53. Robertson, "Northern Rebel," 505–8.

54. Juliette Kinzie to Nellie Gordon, May 25, 1864, microfilm Kinzie letters, UNC.

55. William O. Bryant, *Cahaba Prison and the "Sultana" Disaster* (Tuscaloosa: University of Alabama Press, 1990), 2. For more on this episode see also Arthur Kinzie's typescript reminiscence "A Prisoner of War," Gordon Family Papers, Georgia Historical Society.

56. Juliette Kinzie to Nellie Gordon, September 15, 1864, microfilm Kinzie letters, UNC. See also *The War of the Rebellion: A Compilation of the Official Records of the Union and Confederate History*, ser. 2 (Washington, DC: Government Printing Office, 1899), 7:715; and Juliette Kinzie to Ellie Kinzie, September 5, 1864, Gordon Family Papers, Georgia Historical Society.

57. Arthur and George were not released immediately; the two opposing generals hashed out a wider prisoner exchange that ultimately included sending prison supplies South. See *War of the Rebellion*, 7:715.

58. Peter Shrake, *The Silver Man: The Life and Times of Indian Agent John Kinzie* (Madison: University of Wisconsin Press, 2016), 122. Shrake cites a letter, Eleanor Kinzie Gordon to Jefferson Davis, September 1, 1864, Museum of the Confederacy, and Jefferson Davis, "Indian Policy of the United States," *North American Review* 143 (November 1886): 444.

59. Juliette Kinzie, Chicago, to Nellie Gordon, Savannah, October 7, 1864, Gordon Family Papers, Georgia Historical Society. See also Juliette Kinzie to Nellie Gordon, September 15, 1864, microfilm Kinzie letters, UNC, and Robertson, "Northern Rebel," 513.

60. Juliette Kinzie to Nellie Gordon, October 6, 1864, microfilm Kinzie letters, UNC, and Juliette Kinzie to Nellie Gordon, October 12, 1864, Gordon Family Papers, Georgia Historical Society.

61. Juliette Kinzie to Nellie Gordon, September 15, 1864, and October 12, 1864, Gordon Family Papers, Georgia Historical Society.

62. Juliette Kinzie to Nellie Gordon, December 26, 1864, microfilm Kinzie letters, UNC.

63. Nellie Kinzie, manuscript account, December 21, 1864, Gordon Family Papers, Georgia Historical Society.

64. Ibid.

65. Jacqueline Jones, *Saving Savannah: The City and the Civil War* (New York: Knopf, 2008), 244.

66. William Gordon to Nellie Gordon, March 15, 1865, microfilm Kinzie letters, UNC.

67. Juliette Kinzie to Nellie Gordon, May 12, 1865 microfilm Kinzie letters, UNC.

68. John H. Kinzie to Abraham Lincoln, March 7, 1865, Abraham Lincoln Papers at the Library of Congress, ser. 1, General Correspondence.

69. Juliette Kinzie to Nellie Gordon, May 28, 1865, microfilm Kinzie letters, UNC, and Jones, *Saving Savannah*, 244.

70. Juliette Kinzie to Arthur Kinzie, January 28, 1863, and February 25, 1863, microfilm Kinzie letters, UNC. See also Juliette Kinzie to Nellie Gordon, August 28, 1863, microfilm Kinzie letters, UNC.

71. Juliette Kinzie to Nellie Gordon, August 22, 1863, microfilm Kinzie letters, UNC. Also Juliette Kinzie to Nellie Gordon, October 28, 1860, Gordon Family Collection, Georgia Historical Society.

72. Juliette Kinzie to Nellie Gordon, December 15, 1863, microfilm Kinzie letters, UNC.

73. Juliette Kinzie to Nellie Gordon, August 10, 1865, microfilm Kinzie letters, UNC. General Hunter sent his brother-in-law's accounts to the Department of the Army for further review. See Juliette Kinzie to Nellie Gordon, April 9, 1866, microfilm Kinzie letters, UNC.

74. Juliette Kinzie to Nellie Gordon, May 12, 1865, microfilm Kinzie letters, UNC. For a time these symptoms kept him from "his duty as paymaster in the army." See "Obituary: Major John H. Kinzie," *Chicago Tribune*, June 23, 1865, 1. See also Juliette Kinzie to Nellie Gordon, May 28, 1865, microfilm Kinzie letters, UNC.

75. Juliette Kinzie to Nellie Gordon, September 28, 1865, microfilm Kinzie letters, UNC; "Obituary: Major John H. Kinzie," 1.

76. Juliette Kinzie to Nellie Gordon, April 23, 1866, and November 6, 1865, microfilm Kinzie letters, UNC.

77. Chicago Property, Gordon Family Papers, Georgia Historical Society. See also Nellie Gordon to Mrs. Gordon (her mother-in-law), July 26, 1865, and Nellie Gordon to Elise (one of her sisters-in-law), July 26, 1865, microfilm Kinzie letters, UNC.

Chapter Eight

1. Juliette Kinzie to Nellie Gordon, June 21, 1868, Gordon Family Papers, Georgia Historical Society.

2. Juliette Kinzie to Nellie Gordon, January 12, 1866, Juliette A. Kinzie letters in the Gordon Family Papers at University of North Carolina [microform], 1858–1870. Microfilm accessed at Chicago History Museum (hereafter microfilm Kinzie letters, UNC).

3. "Personal: Mrs. John H. Kinzie," *New York Times*, September 23, 1870. Juliette Kinzie to Nellie Gordon, August 10, 1865, and August 24, 1865, microfilm Kinzie letters, UNC.

4. Frederick Douglass in Chicago, speech on "behalf of the rights of colored American citizens." *Chicago Tribune*, February 26, 1864. See also John B. Jentz and Richard Schneirov, *Chicago in the Age of Capital: Class, Politics, and Democracy during the Civil War and Reconstruction* (Urbana: University of Illinois Press, 2012), 101–4.

5. "The Women: Progress of the Female Suffrage Movement in Chicago," *Chicago Tribune*, February 13, 1869.

6. Ibid.; Lana Ruegamer, "Mary Livermore," in *Women Building Chicago: 1790–1990*, ed. Rima Lunin Schultz and Adele Hast (Bloomington: Indiana University Press, 2001); Jane M. Friedman, *America's First Woman Lawyer: The Biography of Myra Bradwell* (New York: Prometheus Books, 1993), 19, 196–201.

7. Juliette Kinzie to Nellie Gordon, October 8, 1865, and October 15, 1865, microfilm Kinzie letters, UNC.

8. Juliette Kinzie to Nellie Gordon, May 30, 1868, Gordon Family Papers, Georgia Historical Society. Although Linda Kerber does not take up probate in detail, she places it within a broader context of women and citizenship over the course of American history. See Kerber, *No Constitutional Right to Be a Lady: Women and the Obligations of Citizenship* (New York: Hill and Wang, 1998), esp. 17–19, for a discussion on widowhood. See also Victoria Bynum, "Reshaping the Bonds of Womanhood: Divorce in Reconstruction North Carolina," in *Divided Houses: Gender and the Civil War*, ed. Catherine Clinton and Nina Silber (New York: Oxford University Press, 1992), 321; Caroline K. Goddard, "Law, Women's Rights, and the Organization of the Legal Profession in the Gilded Age: Myra Bradwell's *Chicago Legal News*, 1865–1890" (PhD diss., University of Chicago, 2001); and Friedman, *America's First Woman Lawyer*.

9. The specifics of the probate of John's estate are not clear. The records of the probate court were destroyed during the Great Chicago Fire of 1871. Juliette's appointment as administrator indicates that no will was submitted. The heirs were Juliette's three living children and the granddaughter of her son John, who was killed in the war. See Juliette Kinzie to Nellie Gordon, August 27, 1865, microfilm Kinzie letters, UNC. On the probate process in Illinois, see Daniel W. Stowell, "Femes UnCovert: Women's Encounters with the Law," in *In Tender Consideration: Women, Families, and the Law in Abraham Lincoln's*

Illinois, ed. Daniel W. Stowell (Chicago: University of Illinois Press, 2002), 17–45.

10. Docket 1–1 (Estate of Andrew Adams), Archives of the Clerk of the Circuit Court of Cook County, Chicago, provides an example of an inventory that was also found in other probate cases in that first probate box after the 1871 fire. The docket also includes receipts from a newspaper for running a notice about the debts of the deceased six times. Another example is Docket 3–3 (Estate of Charles T. Adams), Archives of the Clerk of the Circuit Court of Cook County, Chicago.

11. Elizabeth Blackmar, "Inheriting Property and Debt: From Family Security to Corporate Accumulation," in *Capitalism Takes Command: The Social Transformation of Nineteenth-Century America*, ed. Michael Zakim and Gary J. Kornblith (Chicago: University of Chicago Press, 2012), 97. See also Elaine Lewinnek, "I Consider It Un-American Not to Have a Mortgage: Immigrant Homeownership in Chicago," in *Debt: Ethics, the Environment, and the Economy*, ed. Peter Y. Paik and Merry Wiesner-Hanks (Bloomington: Indiana University Press, 2013), 26–38; and Lendol Calder, *Financing the American Dream: A Cultural History of Consumer Credit* (Princeton, NJ: Princeton University Press, 2001).

12. Juliette Kinzie to Nellie Gordon, October 1, 1865, microfilm Kinzie letters, UNC, and Edward A. Miller Jr., *Lincoln's Abolitionist General: The Biography of David Hunter* (Columbia: University of South Carolina Press, 1997), 249–52.

13. Juliette Kinzie to Nellie Gordon, August 22, 1865, and September 1, 1865, microfilm Kinzie letters, UNC.

14. Juliette Kinzie to Nellie Gordon, August 27, 1865, microfilm Kinzie letters, UNC.

15. Juliette Kinzie to Nellie Gordon, January 16, 1866, microfilm Kinzie letters, UNC.

16. Juliette Kinzie to Nellie Gordon, July 20, 1866, microfilm Kinzie letters, UNC.

17. Juliette Kinzie to Nellie Gordon, August 10, 1865, microfilm Kinzie letters, UNC. In 1878 the estate of William B. Ogden had to pay the US Army $20,000. See "The City," *Chicago Daily Tribune*, February 9, 1878; and "A Paymaster's Defalcation," *New York Times*, February 9, 1878.

18. Ellen Hartigan-O'Connor, "Gender's Value in the History of Capitalism," *Journal of the Early Republic* 36 (Winter 2016): 623.

19. Rima Lunin Schultz, "Kate Newell Doggett," in *Women Building Chicago, 1790–1990*, ed. Rima Lunin Schultz and Adele Hast (Bloomington: Indiana University Press, 2001), 224–29.

20. On Mary Lincoln's widowhood, see Daniel Mark Epstein, *The Lincolns: Portrait of a Marriage* (New York: Ballantine, 2009); and Jason Emerson, *The Madness of Mary Lincoln* (Carbondale: Southern Illinois University Press, 2007).

21. Juliette Kinzie to Nellie Gordon, August 27, 1865, microfilm Kinzie letters, UNC.

22. Juliette Kinzie to Nellie Gordon, September 6, 1865, October 29, 1865, and March 17, 1866, microfilm Kinzie letters, UNC.

23. Juliette Kinzie to Nellie Gordon, March 22, 1866, microfilm Kinzie letters, UNC. See also "The Kinzie Homestead," *Chicago Tribune*, March 22, 1866.

24. Juliette Kinzie to Nellie Gordon, March 21, 1868; also January 20, 1869, Gordon Family Papers, Georgia Historical Society.

25. Juliette Kinzie to Nellie Gordon, April 10, 1868, July 22, 1868, and July 7, 1869, Gordon Family Papers, Georgia Historical Society.

26. Juliette Kinzie to Nellie Gordon, August 27, 1866, microfilm Kinzie letters, UNC. Juliette also recounted stories of William Ogden's giving hush money to a young woman abused by one of his partners. See Juliette Kinzie to Nellie Gordon, December 2, 1867, microfilm Kinzie letters, UNC. Jack Harpster, in his largely complimentary account of Ogden's life, does recount the hush money Ogden paid to another woman after an alleged affair. See Harpster, *The Railroad Tycoon Who Built Chicago: A Biography of William B. Ogden* (Carbondale: Southern Illinois University Press, 2000), 225–26.

27. Juliette Kinzie to Nellie Gordon, August 22, 1865, and September 1, 1865, microfilm Kinzie letters, UNC.

28. Kerber, *No Constitutional Right to Be a Lady*, 17.

29. In 1872 Illinois repealed its version of that law and passed a statute requiring only the husband's signature on the deed conveyances. See Friedman, *America's First Woman Lawyer*, 201.

30. Juliette Kinzie to Nellie Gordon, October 5, 1865, also October 8, 1865, and October 10, 1865, microfilm Kinzie letters, UNC.

31. For one successful case, see "The Kinzie Dower Case," *Chicago Tribune*, November 17, 1866. Juliette Kinzie to Nellie Gordon, September 28, 1865, microfilm Kinzie letters, UNC. In one action she sued all the owners of property in the original canal subdivision. In another she took on the claimants to the sandbar east of Kinzie's Addition, including the Bard Trust, the Robbins, the Canal and Dock Company, and Tim Wright. See also Juliette Kinzie to Nellie Gordon, October 5, 1865, October 19, 1865, November 1, 1865, February 1, 1867, and March 4, 1867, microfilm Kinzie letters, UNC.

32. Juliette Kinzie to Nellie Gordon, October 29, 1865, October 27, 1865, November 1, 1865, and November 13, 1865, microfilm Kinzie letters, UNC.

33. Isaac N. Arnold and J. Young Scammon, *William B. Ogden; and Early Days in Chicago* (Chicago: Fergus, 1882), 50, 44, for information about Kinzie's Addition.

34. Harpster, *Railroad Tycoon*, 224. The sandbar case was officially *Johnson v. Jones and Marsh*. Ibid., 159–61.

35. Juliette Kinzie to Nellie Gordon, January 20, 1867, also September 10, 1867, microfilm Kinzie letters, UNC.

36. Juliette Kinzie to Nellie Gordon, August 24, 1865, microfilm Kinzie letters, UNC. See also Joan G. Shroeter, "Julia Butler Newberry and Mary Todd

Lincoln: Two 'Merry' Widows," *Journal of the Illinois State Historical Society* 95 (Autumn 2002): 270; Harpster, *Railroad Tycoon*, 225.

37. Harpster, *Railroad Tycoon*, 225. See also Juliette Kinzie to Nellie Gordon, February 14, 1866, microfilm Kinzie letters, UNC; and Juliette Kinzie, Chicago, to George Kinzie, Savannah, February 19, 1868, Gordon Family Papers, Georgia Historical Society.

38. Juliette Kinzie to Nellie Gordon, December 4, 1869, Gordon Family Papers, Georgia Historical Society.

39. Juliette Kinzie to Nellie Gordon, April 1, 1868, Gordon Family Papers, Georgia Historical Society.

40. Juliette Kinzie to Nellie Gordon, September 10, 1866, microfilm Kinzie letters, UNC.

41. Juliette Kinzie to Nellie Gordon, February 26, 1868, Gordon Family Papers, Georgia Historical Society.

42. Juliette Kinzie to Nellie Gordon, August 18, 1866, and August 24, 1865, microfilm Kinzie letters, UNC.

43. The couple was married by the pastor at St. James Episcopal Church, and the event was noted in newspapers. See "Married," *Chicago Tribune*, May 24, 1867, 4. Also Juliette Kinzie to Nellie Gordon, February 6, 1867, microfilm Kinzie letters, UNC. See also Juliette Kinzie to Nellie Gordon, June 5, 1866, and June 6, 1867, Gordon Family Papers, Georgia Historical Society; and Juliette Kinzie to Nellie Gordon, February 6, 1867, December 21, 1867, January 1, 1866, and August 24, 1865, microfilm Kinzie letters, UNC.

44. Juliette Kinzie to Nellie Gordon, May 28, 1870, also August 12, 1868, Gordon Family Papers, Georgia Historical Society.

45. Juliette Kinzie to Nellie Gordon, June 11, 1868, Gordon Family Papers, Georgia Historical Society. See also Juliette Kinzie to Nellie Gordon, June 5, 1866, and February 6, 1867, microfilm Kinzie letters, UNC; and Juliette Kinzie to George Kinzie, February 19, 1868, and March 1, 1868, Gordon Family Papers, Georgia Historical Society.

46. George Kinzie to William Gordon, June 23, 1869, Gordon Family Papers, Georgia Historical Society; Baird and Bradley to William Gordon, August 19, 1870, Gordon Family Papers, Georgia Historical Society.

47. See Juliette Kinzie to Nellie Gordon, February 6, 1867 (for George quotation), and October 1, 1865 (for Juliette), microfilm Kinzie letters, UNC.

48. Eleanor Kinzie Gordon, "A Note" to Mrs. John H. Kinzie, *Wau-Bun: The Early Day in the North-West* (Chicago: Rand McNally, 1901), 406. See also Juliette Kinzie to Nellie Gordon, February 10, 1870, Gordon Family Papers, Georgia Historical Society.

49. Quotation on the neighborhood from "The Lake House," *Chicago Tribune*, June 2, 1872, 4. For Juliette's descriptions, see Juliette Kinzie to Nellie Gordon, August 22, 1865, October 10, 1865, and November 6, 1865, microfilm Kinzie letters, UNC.

50. On the fire, see Juliette Kinzie to Nellie Gordon, February 1, 1867; on cholera, see Juliette Kinzie to Nellie Gordon, August 27, 1866; on Unitarians, see Juliette Kinzie to Nellie Gordon, May 15, 186[6], all microfilm Kinzie letters, UNC.

51. Juliette Kinzie to Nellie Gordon, June 11, 1868, Gordon Family Papers, Georgia Historical Society; Juliette Kinzie to Nellie Gordon, August 22, 1865, and August 23, 1864, microfilm Kinzie letters, UNC.

52. Juliette Kinzie to Nellie Gordon, March 20, 1868, and May 2, 1867, Gordon Family Papers, Georgia Historical Society.

53. Juliette Kinzie to Nellie Gordon, April 20, 1868, April 29, 1868, May 4, 1868, and June 11, 1868, Gordon Family Papers, Georgia Historical Society.

54. Juliette Kinzie to Miss Nellie Gordon [her granddaughter], March 28, 1868, Gordon Family Papers, Georgia Historical Society. Also Juliette Kinzie to Nellie Gordon, April 29, 1868, and May 12, 1868, Gordon Family Papers, Georgia Historical Society.

55. Juliette Kinzie to Nellie Gordon, August 12, 1868; also December 18, 1868, Gordon Family Papers, Georgia Historical Society.

56. Juliette Kinzie to Nellie Gordon, June 21, 1868, and March 28, 1868, Gordon Family Papers, Georgia Historical Society.

57. Juliette Kinzie to Nellie Gordon, March 3, 1866, microfilm Kinzie letters, UNC. Clarkson was appointed the Episcopal bishop of Nebraska. See Juliette Kinzie to Nellie Gordon, October 29, 1865, microfilm Kinzie letters, UNC.

58. Juliette Kinzie to Nellie Gordon, April 29, 1868, Gordon Family Papers, Georgia Historical Society.

59. Juliette Kinzie to Nellie Gordon, August 25, 1869; also August 12, 1868, Gordon Family Papers, Georgia Historical Society.

60. Juliette Kinzie to Nellie Gordon, November 4, 1869, Gordon Family Papers, Georgia Historical Society.

61. Juliette Kinzie to Nellie Gordon, May 1, 1870; also May 15, 1870, Gordon Family Papers, Georgia Historical Society.

62. Juliette Kinzie to Nellie Gordon, July 8, 1870, Gordon Family Papers, Georgia Historical Society.

63. Juliette Kinzie to Nellie Gordon, July 3, 1870, microfilm Kinzie letters, UNC.

64. Nellie Gordon [Juliette's granddaughter] to William Gordon, September 5, 1870, Gordon Family Papers, University of North Carolina Archives.

65. Nellie Gordon to William Gordon, September 8, 1870, Gordon Family Papers, University of North Carolina Archives.

66. Gladys Denny Schultz and Daisy Gordon Lawrence, *Lady from Savannah: The Life of Juliette Low* (1958; repr., New York: Girl Scouts of America, 1988), 109. In this family version, Willie is with the family, but letters of the time confirm that he was not.

67. H. H. Wolcott to Nellie Gordon, September 20, 1870, Gordon Family

Papers, Georgia Historical Society. See also "Personal," *New York Times*, September 23, 1870, 2; and Ellie Kinzie to Nellie Gordon, September 20, 1870, Gordon Family Papers, Georgia Historical Society.

68. Ellie Kinzie to Nellie Gordon, September 20, 1870, Gordon Family Papers, Georgia Historical Society, and Sarah Noonan to Ellen [Willie's sister], September 1870, Gordon Family Papers, Georgia Historical Society.

69. Sarah Noonan to Ellen [Willie's sister], September, 1870, Gordon Family Papers, Georgia Historical Society. Also Ellie Kinzie to Nellie Gordon, September 26, 1870, Gordon Family Papers, Georgia Historical Society.

70. Ellie Kinzie to Nellie Gordon, September 20, 1870, and September 26, 1870, Gordon Family Papers, Georgia Historical Society.

71. George Kinzie to Nellie Gordon, September 29, 1870, Gordon Family Papers, Georgia Historical Society; and Ellie Kinzie to Nellie Gordon, September 26, 1870, Gordon Family Papers, Georgia Historical Society.

72. Anson Sperry (attorney) to Nellie Gordon, December 3, 1870, and December 5, 1870, Gordon Family Papers, University of North Carolina Archives. The full probate record for Juliette Kinzie was destroyed in the October 1871 fire. All that survives is the probate docket with cursory information. Probate Docket, Juliette A. Kinzie, died September 14, 1870, first probate box after the 1871 Chicago fire, #15-0688, Archives of the Clerk of the Circuit Court of Cook County, Chicago.

73. Anson Sperry (attorney) to Nellie Gordon, January 31, 1871 Gordon Family Papers, University of North Carolina Archives.

74. Probate Docket, Juliette A. Kinzie and Anson Sperry (attorney) to Nellie Gordon, December 29, 1870, Gordon Family Papers, University of North Carolina Archives.

75. J. R. Lippincott and Co., Philadelphia, to Mrs. Nellie Kinzie Gordon, Savannah, September 20, 1870, Gordon Family Papers, Georgia Historical Society. Upon her death Juliette was also at work on another manuscript, "The Guardian." See George Kinzie to Nellie Gordon, September 29, 1870, Gordon Family Papers, Georgia Historical Society.

76. Telegram from George Kinzie to Nellie Gordon, October 11, 1871, Gordon Family Papers, Georgia Historical Society.

77. George Kinzie to William and Nellie Gordon, October 21, 1871, Gordon Family Papers, Georgia Historical Society.

78. Probate Docket, Juliette A. Kinzie.

79. In the 1885 *Lakeside Annual Directory of the City of Chicago* (Chicago: Lakeside Press, 1885), Arthur M. Kinzie is listed as a bookkeeper at Paulina and Blue Island, living in Riverside. In 1892 Arthur is identified as "paymaster" at the same South Paulina Street address and still living in Riverside. See *Lakeside Annual Directory of the City of Chicago* (Chicago: Lakeside Press, 1892). See also Arthur Kinzie to Nellie Gordon, April 15, 1897, Gordon Family Papers, Georgia Historical Society.

80. "George H. Kinzie, real estate, bds. 1074 Wabash," *Edwards General and Business Directory of the City of Chicago* (Chicago, 1873); Mary Kinzie, widow of George, *Lakeside Annual Directory of the City of Chicago* (Chicago: Lakeside Press, 1892).

81. George Arthur Gordon, "Eleanor Kinzie Gordon: A Sketch," *Georgia Historical Review* 1 (September 1917): 189–91. Schultz and Lawrence, *Lady from Savannah*, 102–3, suggests that the rebuilding was funded by the sale of Nellie's Chicago property.

Epilogue

1. There are of course, important works available, including the first two volumes of Bessie Louise Pierce's *History of Chicago* (Chicago: University of Chicago Press, 1937 and 1940); Rima Lunin Schultz, "The Businessmen's Role in Western Settlement: The Entrepreneurial Frontier, Chicago, 1833–1872" (PhD diss., Boston University, 1984); Robin Einhorn, *Property Rules: Political Economy in Chicago, 1833–1872* (Chicago: University of Chicago Press, 1991); Theodore J. Karamanski, *Rally 'Round the Flag: Chicago and the Civil War* (Lanham, MD: Roman and Littlefield, 2006); and John B. Jentz and Richard Schneirov, *Chicago in the Age of Capital: Class, Politics, and Democracy during the Civil War and Reconstruction* (Urbana: University of Illinois Press, 2012).

2. Ogden as quoted in Jack Harpster, *The Railroad Tycoon Who Built Chicago: A Biography of William B. Ogden* (Carbondale: Southern Illinois University Press, 2000), 242.

3. Dominic A. Pacyga and Ellen Skerrett use the phrase in their title. See Pacyga and Skerrett *Chicago, City of Neighborhoods: Histories and Tours* (Chicago: Loyola University Press, 1986). Joseph C. Bigott, in his work on Polish Catholic workers in Chicago, found that alongside the corporate capitalism of industrial America, a strong strain of local capitalism, often supported by ethnic buyers, fueled economic growth. See Bigott, *From Cottage to Bungalow: Houses and the Working Class in Metropolitan Chicago, 1869–1929* (Chicago: University of Chicago Press, 2001), 7–12. See also Elizabeth Blackmar, "Inheriting Property and Debt: From Family Security to Corporate Accumulation," in *Capitalism Takes Command: The Social Transformation of Nineteenth-Century America*, ed. Michael Zakim and Gary J. Kornblith (Chicago: University of Chicago Press, 2012), 95.

4. Peter Marris, *Loss and Change*, 2nd ed. (London: Routledge and Keegan Paul, 1986), esp. vii and 44. See also Marris, *The Politics of Uncertainty: Attachment in Private and Public Life* (London: Routledge, 1996). I thank Mary Smith for connecting me with this literature.

5. Victoria Bissell Brown, *The Education of Jane Addams* (Philadelphia: University of Pennsylvania Press, 2004), 110.

6. *New York Herald*, May 25, 1856. *Wau-Bun*, published in 1856, preceded most of the work of Francis Parkman, who along with George Bancroft, was one of the "giants of nineteenth-century American historical writing." Like Juliette

Kinzie, Parkman wrote about the west and Indian life. See Peter Charles Hoffer, *Past Imperfect* (New York: Public Affairs, 2004), 21.

7. For more information on Juliette, see Louise Phelps Kellogg, introduction to Mrs. John H. Kinzie, *Wau-Bun: The Early Day in the Northwest* (Menasha, WI: George Banta, 1930), xx; and Nina Baym, introduction to Juliette M. Kinzie, *Wau-Bun, The "Early Day" in the North-West* (Urbana: University of Illinois Press, 1992), xix. Also see Rima Lunin Schultz, "Juliette Kinzie," in *Women Building Chicago*, ed. Rima Lunin Schultz and Adele Hast (Bloomington: Indiana University Press, 2001), 472–76; and Constance R. Buckley, "Searching for Fort Dearborn: Perceptions, Commemoration, and Celebration of the Urban Collective Memory" (PhD diss., Loyola University, Chicago, 2005), esp. 72–79.

8. A. T. Andreas, *History of Chicago* (Chicago: Lakeside Press, 1884), unpaginated preface. Andreas mentions the writings of Juliette Kinzie as providing "invaluable aid."

9. The Chicago Historical Society did enroll its first two "lady members" in 1870. See Paul M. Angle, *The Chicago Historical Society, 1856–1956: An Unconventional History* (Chicago: Rand McNally, 1956), 59. For more on the generation of historians that Juliette was a part of, see Hoffer, *Past Imperfect*, 18–19.

10. Charles Butler to Chicago Historical Society, December 17, 1881, as quoted in Bessie Louise Pierce, *As Others See Chicago: Impressions of Visitors, 1673–1933* (Chicago: University of Chicago Press, 1933), 53; Isaac N. Arnold and J. Young Scammon, *William B. Ogden; and Early Days in Chicago* (Chicago: Fergus, 1882).

11. Kathryn Kish Sklar includes Juliette Kinzie among the cohort of women historians writing in the first half of the nineteenth century in "American Female Historians in Context, 1770–1930," *Feminist Studies* 3 (Autumn 1975): 177. Rima Lunin Schultz described in detail both her works of history, the 1844 pamphlet and the 1856 *Wau-Bun*; see "Juliette Kinzie," in Schultz and Hast, *Women Building Chicago*. William Cronon devotes considerable attention to *Wau-Bun*'s value to the history of Wisconsin in Cronon, "Why the Past Matters," *Wisconsin Magazine of History* 84 (Autumn 2000): 2–13. See Hoffer, *Past Imperfect*, 39–43, for more on the generation of professional historians who emerged in the twentieth century.

12. Milo Milton Quaife, "Historical Introduction" to Mrs. John H. Kinzie, *Wau-Bun: The "Early Day" in the North-West* (Chicago: Lakeside Press, 1932), lii. Quaife went so far as to suggest that Juliette Kinzie presented her father-in-law as "the Captain John Smith of Chicago history" (liv). See Perry Duis, introduction to Milo Milton Quaife, *Chicago and the Old Northwest, 1673–1871* (Urbana: University of Illinois Press, 2001), vii–xviii, for more on the publication of Quaife's book and his interactions with the Chicago Historical Society. Nellie Kinzie Gordon successfully kept the Chicago Historical Society from publishing Quaife's *Chicago and the Old Northwest*, but it was then published in 1913 by the University of Chicago Press.

13. James McNally, Chicago, to Mrs. Gordon, London, August 15, 1913, and November 12, 1913; O. McClurg to Mrs. Gordon, November 26, 1913. McClurg wrote of the "dark and maladroit Quaife"; box 7, folder 74, Gordon Family Papers, Georgia Historical Society. As the reviews of Quaife's book came in, Nellie worried about the effect it would have on the Kinzie legacy in Chicago. She corresponded with several historians, who were all critical of the book. One suggested that regarding the Kinzie family Quaife's "view was prejudiced and his statements unwarranted." Nellie wrote to the anonymous reviewer of *Chicago and the Old Northwest* in the *Nation*, December 25, 1913, thanking him for being "critical of Quaife's methods of writing history." J. Seymour Currey, Evanston Historical Society, to Mrs. Gordon, March 18, 1914, and Mrs. Gordon to the *Nation*, March 23, 1914, box 7, folder 74, Gordon Family Papers, Georgia Historical Society. Nellie sent copies of *Wau-Bun* to everyone from the incoming US president (historian Woodrow Wilson) to Rudyard Kipling (married to one of her cousins) to the heads of historical societies across the Midwest and to each of the Chicago newspapers for review. She arranged for McClurg's bookstore in Chicago to take fifty additional copies of *Wau-Bun* for sale (by offering the bookstore more of the profit). The owner guaranteed Nellie that he would do all he could "to push the sale of them." O. McClurg, Chicago, to Mrs. Gordon, London, November 26, 1913, and book distribution list, undated, box 7, folder 74, Gordon Family Papers, Georgia Historical Society.

14. Nellie Kinzie Gordon, Unpublished Reminiscences, Gordon Family Papers, Georgia Historical Society.

15. *Girl Scout Handbook* (New York: Girl Scouts of America, 1920), frontispiece, 14.

16. Milo Milton Quaife, Detroit Public Library, to Frank Farnsworth Starr, Middletown, August 14, 1931, Magill Family Papers, Middlesex Historical Society, Middletown, Connecticut. When Quaife had the opportunity to write a new introduction for *Wau-Bun*, to be published as the Christmas gift offering of the Lakeside Press at Christmas 1932 (in anticipation of the opening of the 1933 Century of Progress Exposition), he took the opportunity to directly address his concerns with *Wau-Bun*. Quaife, Introduction to Mrs. John H. Kinzie, *Wau-Bun* (Chicago: Lakeside Press, 1932), xxiii and liii. Perry Duis does not agree. He wrote in his 2001 introduction to *Chicago and the Old Northwest* that Quaife places *Wau-Bun* "in the realm of fiction" (xiv).

17. Bessie Louise Pierce, *History of Chicago*, vol. 1, *1673–1848* (Chicago: University of Chicago Press, 1937). *Wau-Bun* is not used once in the chapters titled "The Passing of the Indian" and "The Speculative Era."

18. Timothy Spears, "Literary Careers," in *Encyclopedia of Chicago*, ed. James R. Grossman, Ann Durkin Keating, and Janice Reiff (Chicago: University of Chicago Press, 2004), 482, has gone so far as to suggest that *Wau-Bun* was "perhaps the city's first novel." See also Bill Savage, "Fiction," in *Encyclopedia of Chicago*, 291: "Aspects of fictional technique appear even in the earliest auto-

biographical and historical narratives about Chicago, such as Juliette Kinzie's *Wau-Bun: The "Early Day" in the North-West*, and historians now agree that many of Chicago's founding narratives are more interesting as fiction than accurate as history." Countering this, Bernice E. Gallagher includes *Mark Logan* and *Walter Ogilby*, but not *Wau-Bun*, in her analysis of Juliette Kinzie's novels. See Gallagher, *Illinois Women Novelists in the Nineteenth Century: An Analysis and Annotated Bibliography* (Urbana: University of Illinois Press, 1994), 138–43,

19. Nina Baym, introduction to *Wau-Bun* (1992), ix. Also, the "Classified List of Selected Biographies," in *Notable American Women, a Biographical Dictionary*, 3 vols., ed. Edward James, Janet James, and Paul Boyer (Cambridge, MA: Harvard University Press, 1971), includes Juliette under the category "Historians."

20. Sklar, "American Female Historians in Context," 176, noted that nineteenth-century women historians "began their careers with a literary rather than an historical work. Most continued throughout their careers to publish fiction, poetry, travel, and translations as well as history."

21. I was exposed to this trope early in my graduate studies by material ranging from John Hope Franklin's *From Slavery to Freedom*, 9th ed. (New York: McGraw-Hill, 2010), to the work of Eric Foner, including the textbook *Give Me Liberty! An American History* (New York: Norton, 2011) and *The Fiery Trial: Abraham Lincoln and American Slavery* (New York: Norton, 2011), to that of James McPherson, as in *Battle Cry of Freedom: The Civil War Era* (New York: Oxford University Press, 1988).

Index

women (*continued*)
interest in Westward migration among, 33, 228n3; lack of political rights of, x–xi, 6, 138–41, 144, 147, 152, 249n20, 251n48; property rights of, 61, 66, 176, 234nn19–20; public acknowledgment of writing by, 75; traditional familial roles and responsibilities of, x–xi, 9, 25–26, 138, 140–41, 145, 176–77, 210–12, 220nn4–5; Willard's views on, 24–26

women's rights movement, 127–28, 132, 140–41, 158, 211, 248n16; in Chicago, 176; property rights proposals of, 176, 184, 260n29

Wright, James, 197

Wright, Tim, 260n31